WINGED VICTOR

'Winged Victor'
VICTOR M. YEATES

WINGED VICTOR

A biography of

V. M. YEATES

Author of *Winged Victory*

WITH A FOREWORD BY GUY YEATES

Gordon F. Atkin

SPRINGWATER BOOKS
2004

The cover is from a watercolour painting by Les Carter depicting Victor Yeates flying Sopwith Camel D6585 in May 1918

ISBN 0-9546881-0-4

First published in Great Britain 2004 by

SPRINGWATER BOOKS
12 Springwater Avenue
Ramsbottom, Bury BL0 9RH

Origination: C&CI Design Team, Leicester

Printed in England by Warwick Printing Company Limited, Leamington Spa

CONTENTS

ILLUSTRATIONS

FOREWORD

by

Guy Yeates

To find the facts about Victor Yeates' life and then to relate them to events in his book, *Winged Victory*, must have taken an immense amount of research, and Gordon Atkin has been dedicated in his pursuit of the correspondence between the protagonist, Tom Cundall, and the writer of this autobiographical fiction.

Both Gordon Atkin and Hugh Cecil were present at the consecration of the memorial stone on Victor's grave in Hastings Cemetery at the time of his centenary, when I had to admit that their knowledge of my father's life was far better than mine. Now, thanks to *Winged Victor*, and Cecil's two books, *Flower of Battle* and F*acing Armageddon,* I am much the wiser.

It is difficult, especially almost 70 years later, for a son who was only 12 at the time of his father's death, to do him justice. What I have now learned illuminates for me the personal memories of the man who, towards the end of his life was, it seemed, either away in hospital or sanatorium or secluded in the back room writing his book. Thus my adult knowledge of Victor was harvested almost exclusively from *Winged Victory*. In the striking opening paragraphs we are shown a young man intellectually tough, with a challenging attitude to received truths, never pompous, an iconoclast who, with sardonic humour, castigated 'brass hats', the 'patriotic' press and profiteers who stayed at home and piled up wealth. How much he hated the waste and hypocrisy of war becomes clear as the book progresses. I would have loved my children and grandchildren to have known and respected Victor, but, although nothing could replace him, they can now, thanks to *Winged Victor*, discover how his experiences in the bloody slaughter, fatuously described by grave politicians as 'the war to end wars', shaped and developed the life of a sensitive young man who later declaimed the poetry of Shakespeare and Shelley to his much-loved wife as she battled with an inadequate kitchen in the top floors of a shared house in Blackheath to produce meals for the family.

His legacy to me extended to a love of music. In the late 1920s the BBC used to broadcast on Sundays the canon of Bach cantatas and for Victor these were absolutely unmissable. To me, aged seven or eight, they were very missable indeed and I complained about having them on. His reply was, very reasonably as usual, 'Well, if you don't like it, go out until it's over.' And so I did, Sunday after Sunday, until it suddenly came to me that this was now silly because I really liked the music. So I stayed in and have never lost love for all Bach's music; and Mozart's, another of his gods. That was a very precious gift from father to son.

Such was the fate of war heroes after 1918; the promised jobs and homes failed to materialise and many, like Victor, had their health undermined. Such continues to be the fate of servicemen – and women – sent off by the politicians of whatever stripe to fight and die abroad. I believe that this book will help further to change minds about the glory of war.

PREFACE

Some thirty years ago, whilst searching for a book to read on holiday, I picked up a copy of the 1961 edition of *Winged Victory,* being attracted to it by its dust jacket. Having served in the RAF on a fighter squadron during my National Service, I was interested in aviation and I thought it would be a good read. I wasn't wrong. Once I began to read the novel, I was reluctant to put it down and it made such an impression on me that I felt I must do all I could to find out more about its author. Tragically, Victor Yeates had died just six months after his book was published which made the reading of it even more poignant. Not only is *Winged Victory* a thrilling and authentic account of life on a fighter squadron in the Great War, but it also stands by itself as a magnificent piece of writing. Had he lived longer, there is little doubt that his literary skills would have developed even further and he would have enjoyed recognition from a far wider readership.

Through the publisher, Jonathan Cape, I contacted his widow, Norah Yeates, and I spent an enjoyable couple of hours with her over afternoon tea in her apartment in London, when we talked about her late husband's book. She was naturally very proud of Victor's novel and it gave her great pleasure to see it finally receiving the recognition it deserved in the 1960s when it was reprinted.

Unfortunately pressure of work and family commitments prevented me from devoting much time to further research and it is only during the last few years that I have been able to collect and organise the information which has culminated in this book, the writing of which proved to be both rewarding and enjoyable.

I should state that my aim has been to incorporate, within a biographical format, a detailed examination of the factual aspects of *Winged Victory* and I have also provided, I hope, an insight into how the book came to be written and how it developed from the original suggestion of the author Henry Williamson, to its publication some fourteen months later in June 1934.

Winged Victor could not have been written without the assistance of Victor's three surviving children, Joy Vowles, Guy Yeates and Roz Cullinan and I would like to express my grateful thanks for their hospitality and for allowing me to invade their privacy. They generously gave me access to family papers and provided me with photographs which appear in the book. I am also indebted to Guy for kindly agreeing to write the Foreword and for giving me permission to quote from his father's *Winged Victory*.

There have been many other people who have assisted me over the years and I must thank John Belshaw who helped me during the early days, and Tony Grange Bennett. Stuart Leslie has been most helpful in providing many of the aviation photographs, and the staff at the Harry Ransom Humanities Research Center at the University of Texas at Austin assisted in supplying copies of the manuscript of both *Winged Victory* and *Family Life*, the novel Victor was writing when he died, and gave me permission to quote from these papers. I am also grateful to the Headmaster of Colfe's School and to Peter Heinecke, the Librarian, for help in tracing Victor's records in the School magazine and for permission to quote the poem 'Tourists'.

I also wish to thank Anne Williamson and the Trustees of the Henry Williamson Literary Estate for permission to include quotations from his books and for providing his photograph. I am particularly indebted to Colin and Barbara Huston for their design and typesetting, and also for enhancing the many illustrations; to my friend Les Carter who produced the watercolour painting for the cover, and also to my son, Jonathan, for his suggestions and advice.

Lastly, but not least, I would like to thank my wife, Gwen, for her support over the years and for allowing me to spend many solitary hours closeted away in my study.

GORDON F. ATKIN
April 2004

CHAPTER ONE

THE EARLY YEARS

Augustus Yeates was thirty-nine years old, a bachelor, and a clerk at the Blackheath branch of Lloyds Bank in London, when he married Lavinia Eleanor Maslin, fourteen years his junior, at the Register Office in Lambeth on 8 March 1890. They had known each other for some time and already had a two-year old daughter, Lavinia Augusta Maslin Yeates, known as Augusta, born at 37 Alival Road, Battersea on 13 June 1887.[1] She was named Lavinia and Maslin after her mother and Augusta after her father. Augustus, who was tall and thin in stature, had been a commercial traveller when his daughter was born but soon afterwards he had joined Lloyds Bank as a clerk and later became a cashier. Although always known as Augustus, his parents had named him Luther Augustus (Luther after his own father who was an accountant) but he dropped the name of Luther as soon as he could.

Some seven years later, when the family were living at 12 Ildersley Grove, West Dulwich, Lavinia became pregnant again and a son Victor Maslin was born at home on 30 September 1897; he was baptised shortly afterwards on 21 November at their local Church of All Saints in Dulwich.

It seems that Lavinia soon became the dominant person in the household. She was highly strung and gained a reputation for being difficult and emotional at times. This may have been partly due to a feeling of frustration over nascent ambitions stifled by having her first child at the comparatively early age of twenty two, marrying two years later, and then having a second child after an interval of ten years. Family commitments would inevitably have been her main preoccupation.

Victor based the character of Mrs Felce in *Family Life*, his unfinished work which he was writing when he died, on that of his mother who, it has been suggested, talked of a past career as an opera singer although this may well have been an illusion.[2] Mrs Felce who also had a good voice, declares to her son and his fiancée:

> 'It's years since I last sang. Before I was married I used to have a wonderful voice, and if I had kept it up there's no knowing what I mightn't have done .... But how could I keep it up after I was married? Father never understood music, or cared tuppence about it, and he only used to laugh at me or tell me my business was to look after him. The greatest genius couldn't have kept it up married to a man with absolutely no musical feeling in him, who sneered at anything above eating and drinking. I tried for a little while, but in the end I vowed I would never sing a note again, and I never have.'
>
> Mr Felce was so used to this story of his killing his wife's talent that he had nothing to say about it. Repetition was, indeed, making him believe it.[3]

Augustus was somewhat remote and aloof from his children and his energies were centred on holding down his job at the bank and keeping the atmosphere at home as calm as possible. It was thought by some that he had married beneath himself. There was talk of his wife having been in service (she may in fact have been his housekeeper before they married) and of Irish descent although there is no evidence of this: she was born in Highworth, Wiltshire.

Shortly after their daughter left school and started work her boyfriend Tom Stokes, whom she was later to marry, emigrated to the United States. Once he had settled, he wrote and asked her to join him in San Francisco. Augusta agreed, pleased to escape the stress of uncomfortable home life, and left the family home when she was eighteen, returning to England only once during the remainder of her life – she died in the USA in 1977.

From the age of eight, therefore, Victor became the only child at home and received all the attention. Being employed as a cashier by one of the London Clearing Banks, Augustus with his wife possessed middle-class ideals although his salary would have been modest.

When Victor was two years old, the family moved to Hurstleigh, Ravensbourne Road in Bromley and as they wanted to give their son a sound education and had ambitions for him to attend a good grammar school, they sent Victor to a local private Preparatory School, St Andrews in South Hill Park, Cumberland Road, Bromley, as soon as he attained school age. It was fortunate in possessing spacious playing fields and the pupils were encouraged to participate in organised sporting activities in which Victor, being athletic, would have taken full advantage.

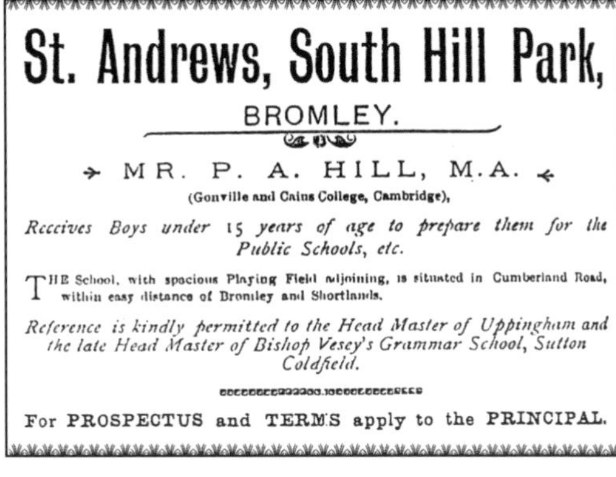

St. Andrews, South Hill Park,

BROMLEY.

MR. P. A. HILL, M.A.

(Gonville and Caius College, Cambridge),

Receives Boys under 15 years of age to prepare them for the Public Schools, etc.

THE School, with spacious Playing Field adjoining, is situated in Cumberland Road, within easy distance of Bromley and Shortlands.

Reference is kindly permitted to the Head Master of Uppingham and the late Head Master of Bishop Vesey's Grammar School, Sutton Coldfield.

For **PROSPECTUS** and **TERMS** apply to the **PRINCIPAL.**

1905 SCHOOL ADVERTISEMENT

In 1906 the family moved again, this time to 68 Granville Park in neighbouring Blackheath – Victor's parents had decided they would like him to attend Colfe's Grammar School in Lewisham Hill which was close by. Colfe's, to use the name by which it was more commonly known was, and still is, a highly respected long-established grammar school, having been founded in 1652 by the Worshipful Company of Leathersellers who remain the Trustees to this day. It catered for a total of 290 boys from mainly middle-class backgrounds, was run on public school lines and was divided into four Houses, Blue, Buff, Green and Red. A spirit of competition was encouraged with each House having its own team for various sports such as football, cricket, fives, cross-country running, swimming and shooting. There was also an Army Cadet Corps although Victor did not become a member. As was customary in those days, the school year was divided into three terms and the boys attended each weekday and also Saturday mornings. On the academic side, the usual public school subjects of English, French, Latin, trigonometry, and the sciences of chemistry and physics were taught. Natural history and architecture were also studied to a lesser degree.

Colfe's Grammar School, Lewisham

Buff House harriers, 1910. Victor is on the front row, extreme right

Victor's parents applied for their son to enter the School in October 1906 when he was nine years old, and, after passing the entrance examination, he joined the following year at the beginning of the summer term. His parents must have been very proud to watch him walking to school in his new uniform with its high wing Eton collar and distinctive grey cap, the silver embroidered badge glistening in the sunshine.

Although he later remembered his schooldays with some misgivings, Victor started off well by winning a scholarship prize in his second year, being placed third in his form, and for the remainder of his time at Colfe's he had the benefit of an annual Foundation Scholarship which would have been of great financial help to his parents.

He was keen on the sporting side of school life and at the annual sports day which was held in May at the London County Athletic Ground at Herne Hill, Victor was soon taking part in the 100 yards flat race and was a member of the gymnastic Tableau Display team. By then he was the proud owner of his own bicycle and so he was able to enter the one-mile handicap race which was included as one of the events. In 1912 Victor had a particularly busy sports day as he also participated in the Hurdles Race and was a member of the victorious Buff House team in the Harriers Cross Country Race. The report in the School Magazine, *Colfensia*, stated that this achievement was 'thanks to the fine running of Williamson H. Pool, Bennett, Davey, Wigmore and Yeates also contributed to keep the score down to 20. Scores Williamson 3, Yeates 15.'

He was now also representing the School at football, playing in the Second XI although the team's record that year was a modest one, Won 4, Lost 8.

It was on the sporting field that Victor first came into close contact with a fellow pupil, Henry Williamson, who later achieved literary fame when he won the Hawthornden Prize for Literature in 1928 with his nature book *Tarka the Otter*. Although not close friends, their friendship was to play a large part in the publication of Victor's novel *Winged Victory* in 1934. Williamson was also in Buff House and they both played football and cricket for their House teams

BUFF HOUSE FIELD CLUB OUTING, 11 JUNE 1910, TO HAYES AND KESTON. VICTOR IS STANDING IN THE BACK ROW, SECOND FROM THE LEFT

whilst Victor was also selected to play cricket for the School 2nd XI in 1912 and was in the top four of the bowling averages. Victor's all-round sporting prowess was rewarded by him being appointed Buff House sports vice-captain as well as the House cricket vice-captain. Williamson, who had the edge on Victor in the prestigious Harriers cross-country event was the House sports captain.

In the following year, his last at school, Victor had graduated to the School's 1st XI and the School Magazine analysed his batting performance:

> 7 innings, 36 runs, highest score 14 not out, average 7.2

In June of that year, shortly before he left school, he was selected to play for the School X1 against the 'Old Boys' and was by that time showing promise as the *Colfensia* reported:

> Yeates … was only with us for half a term. Was beginning to shape as a very useful steady bat. Will be a bowler.

BUFF HOUSE CRICKET TEAM, MAY DAY 1912.
VICTOR IS SECOND FROM LEFT ON THE BACK ROW

On his final sports day in May 1913 Victor must have had an exhausting time, competing in the 100 yards flat race, the half mile flat (in which he was placed third), and the 60 yards hurdles; he represented his House again in the Team race, running the 120 yards middle leg and he also won a prize in the Peg and Ring competition.

However, sport was not his only interest – he had always been interested in nature and the countryside and he joined the Natural History Society soon after starting at Colfe's and went on a number of expeditions in the surrounding area to collect specimens for further study.

Although he was a bright student and showed promise in his early days at the School, evidenced by his Foundation Scholarship, it would appear that he gradually became disillusioned with the fact that he was expected to excel in subjects in which he was not particularly interested and in some of the teaching methods employed at the School. By his final year, he was in a special commercial class known as the 'Special Slackers' which comprised those students who

School Team for the Colfe's Past & Present Pupils cricket match, 28 June 1913. Victor is on the back row, fifth from left

were not considered by the School to be destined for University life.[4] The purpose of this class was to prepare the boys for an alternative existence in the commercial world so they were taught subjects such as Pitman's shorthand, letter writing and bookkeeping and accounts. Nevertheless, he passed the Junior Cambridge Local Examinations with 2nd Class Honours and gained distinctions in French and English Grammar. He was also successful in the Senior Examinations in December 1912 with 3rd Class Honours in Spoken French which, unknown to him, would become an advantage when he was posted to the Western Front some five years later. This qualification led to the London University Matriculation during his last year at school.

By this time he had developed a keen interest in English Literature and the Classics – one which he maintained all his life. His school gave him the first opportunity to see one of his own works in print when the School Magazine in 1913 included his humorous poem *The Tourists* as one of the contributions from Buff House:

It seems there is no earthly place
Where we can rest in dream Elysian,
Without some red, round English face
Appearing near to mar the vision.
Go where we may, rest where we will,
Eternal London haunts us still.
And if this rage for travelling lasts,
If Cockneys of all types and castes,
The old and young of either sex,
Will leave their homes — whoe'er objects —
To gape at things in foreign lands
Not one among them understands,
Why, then, farewell all hope to find
A spot that's free from London-kind.
Who knows, if to the West we roam,
But we may find some friend at home
Among the blacks of Carolina,
Or, journeying in the Far East, see,
Some Mrs Hawkings taking tea
And toast, upon the Wall of China.

It was during his later years at school that Victor became friendlier with Henry Williamson, who, in his final months at Colfe's, was also in the 'Special Slackers' class. Williamson records that they did little work during classes and Victor much preferred reading literature such as Keats to paying due attention during tedious lessons like mathematics.[5]

Williamson recalled his schooldays initially through his character Willie Maddison in *Dandelion Days*, the second book in his *Flax of Dream* tetralogy which was published in 1922 and which was largely based on his experiences as a student at Colfe's. In this book he introduced a fellow student by the name of Yeates whom he described as 'dreamy' and 'pale faced', comments on Victor which he repeated later on a number of occasions; for example in his Tribute in the 1961 reprint of *Winged Victory* he recalls 'a dreamy, wild-eyed boy at school.' Yeates is first mentioned as a fellow member of Class 5b and it is possible that they were both in the same class before his final year, notwithstanding the fact that Williamson was nearly two years older, having been born on 1 December 1895. It was not uncommon for a number of the brighter boys to be promoted to a higher class and Victor may still have been regarded as a pupil of academic promise at that time.

Victor is featured again in one of his later novels, *Young Phillip Maddison*, which was published in 1953, nineteen years after Victor's death. This is the third book in the mammoth fifteen volume series entitled *A Chronicle of Ancient Sunlight* which is thought by many to be Williamson's greatest achievement. In this novel, the schooldays of Phillip Maddison (the cousin of Willie Maddison) are recounted and a boy by the name of Cundall is introduced as being a fellow member of the 'Commercial Class.' Victor in his novel *Winged Victory* had named his protagonist Tom Cundall and Williamson wrote that he deliberately chose this name in the hope that his friend's book would be remembered. Williamson was a lover of nature and an expedition into the woods with a number of his school friends (including Cundall) from the 'Commercial Class' is described in the final chapter which is entitled 'Bagmen's Outing':

> One of their number was a pale, quiet boy named Cundall, whom Phillip had taken once or twice into his preserves. Cundall was going into a bank.

Williamson goes on to recall that 'Cundall's dry sort of matter-of-fact stories' were always interesting. The adventure in the woods culminates with a visit to see a variety show at the Lewisham Hippodrome in the evening. Williamson kept a diary during this time and there are entries for Friday 11 April 1913 and also for the following Friday, showing that Williamson, Terence (another friend) and Victor visited the theatre on those days.[6] One of these shows featured the Christie Minstrels whom they watched from the sixpenny seats.

The family holidays were usually spent on the south coast at Folkestone and Victor remembered these occasions with affection:

> Folkestone. He had spent summer holidays there as a youngster. He remembered the Leas, where people walked about while a Blue Hungarian band played, conducted by one Herr Wurms ...the pier, Cardo's Cadets ...[7]

Victor left Colfe's in the summer of 1913, having obtained his matriculation at the age of 16; he later looked back on his schooldays with mixed emotions, as indeed did Williamson. In *Family Life* he writes somewhat critically of the schooldays of his character Julian, who is loosely based on himself:

> Julian had just left school, damaged spiritually and in consequence physically by the dementia of half-insane elderly schoolmasters, – the usual fate of England's sensitive youth – and was a junior bank clerk. He read Shelley ....

These jaundiced recollections are exaggerated and as has been shown, he certainly took a very active role in the sporting life at school which he must have enjoyed. After leaving he maintained his links by playing cricket for the Old Boys against the School XI in the summer of 1914. In one of his unpublished works he writes:

> ... looking back on that time [his schooldays], it presented itself to his memory as a time of almost pure delight. It is difficult for healthy childhood to be anything else but happy. [8]

Perhaps he had, therefore, like Williamson, a love-hate recollection of his schooldays.

His home life, however, continued to be difficult and he sought refuge from the friction by immersing himself in literature, poetry and music, which were great comforts to him at this time. In *Family Life* his character Julian remarks:

> He did not know that he was maddened and exhausted by the struggle against schoolmasters and his mother, a strong and unscrupulous woman who tried to dominate him entirely, using hysteria as a weapon.

On leaving school in 1913 it appears that he joined a firm of Incorporated Insurance Brokers, Albert H. Ward, which operated

CHARCOAL PORTRAIT OF VICTOR AT 18

from offices in Queen Victoria Street, in London.[9] This experience in the insurance market, although brief, was to be useful later in his life when he was looking at ways of supplementing his income during his illness whilst working for a firm of Timber and Builders Merchants. Possibly due to pressure exerted by his parents, he soon left this job and joined the Charing Cross branch of Cox & Co., a Ciy of London bank (Cox's Bank) where he was employed when war was declared on 4 August 1914.

As in all professions and industries, the call for volunteers for the armed forces (the Kitchener's Battalions) soon resulted in the depletion of male staff and the bank had to recruit female staff to alleviate its staffing difficulties. Cox's Bank had the privilege of being the bankers to the Army so it was under severe pressure to maintain its standards following the declaration of war and the resulting massive increase in the number of accounts. One of those recruited was a small, dark-haired girl with a fair complexion called Norah Phelps Richards. A friendship quickly blossomed and Victor and Norah were soon stepping out together. Norah came from Mistley, a village on the River Stour in Essex, and had made the journey to London to find work. She came from an upper middle-class background, her grandfather having owned a London brewery, W. & R. Richards, and her father, William Henry Phelps Richards, had been an accountant with the family firm. When her grandfather died, however, the brewery fell on hard times and failed and her father obtained a job as a brewer's clerk with another brewery. Some time later, after a disagreement over pay, he was forced to leave the firm and subsequently became the village postmaster in Mistley.

Banks in 1914 had been largely staffed with single young men and consequently suffered heavily by losing both volunteers and later conscripts into the army. Indeed by February 1916, 40% of all the men who had been employed in finance and commerce in July 1914 had already volunteered and enlisted.[10] Much reliance, therefore, was placed on young temporary staff and it was only natural that their high spirits sometimes spilled over into the workplace. Victor writes of these times in *Family Life*, when Kathleen, Julian's wife, recalls an episode from the time she was employed by Cox's Bank as a temporary clerk which has a ring of truth about it, and which quite probably was based on Victor and Norah's own observations and experiences:

> Then the war started, and she soon heard that Cox's Bank were taking girls on their temporary staff, and she went to see them and said that she knew all about bookkeeping. She was interviewed by a terrifying bald gentleman who held his head well back and looked down at her as from a great distance, obviously finding her very unworthy; but he gave her a job at a pound a week. Then she had a rise to thirty shillings, then two pounds, and by the end of the war she was earning three pounds per week.
>
> And it was all good fun. The ledgers were very heavy to carry about but the prettier girls got a good deal of this done for them by the younger men. Cox's was expanding *pari passu* with the army, and new staff were engaged every day, and holes were knocked through the walls into adjoining buildings to find room to accommodate them. The whole thing was too much for the stern and pompous chief clerk, and discipline went to pot. The work got done somehow, but a quarter of the day was spent in gossip, foolery, mild intrigue. The senior partner – known as Clapham Junction, because of all the lines on his face – became daily more strained and rapt and wealthy. More and more of his dependable employees went soldiering. A night staff was enrolled who hid ledgers in strange places so that the day staff was frequently flummoxed .... Clerks gossiped and flirted and bombarded each other with pellets catapulted by rubber bands. Pairs of men drifted away into corners and played odds and evens with pennies. The war was a jolly war: the first report of Jutland was the only bad news, but even that turned out to be a victory in disguise. At air-raid time a hooter was sounded and everyone was supposed to go down into the basement strong-rooms but after one experience of the contagious terror of the tight-packed smelly herd Kathleen and a few others refused to go down.

If his writings in *Family Life* are a reflection of his thoughts at that time, as he had only left school the previous year, the outbreak of the war did not interest him:

> Julian had only just passed his seventeenth birthday when war broke out, and it did not interest him. He thought vaguely that it was wicked

> foolishness. He did not particularly respect such of his friends as joined up, knowing they were only out for adventure, playing truant from work.

As the war progressed, however, Victor's attitude towards it began to change:

> ...he began to be troubled by a feeling that he ought to go too; the war was getting hold of him.

By mid-1915, Lord Kitchener's voluntary system was failing to provide sufficient recruits to maintain the army and as conscription was considered to be the last resort, one final attempt at voluntary recruitment was made, the 'Derby Scheme', named after Lord Derby who was appointed Director of Recruitment on 5 October 1915. All men between the ages of eighteen and forty-one were encouraged to 'attest' before 30 November (later extended to 25 December), that is to pledge to join up when required to do so for the duration of the war, single men being called up before the married men.

Caught up in the patriotic fervour of the time, Victor felt it was his duty to volunteer, probably against his parent's wishes and also those of his employer. Writing of Julian again in *Family Life* reinforces this conclusion:

> But the bank did not want him to go, and when he spoke of it at home his mother screamed and his father told him not to be a fool.

Two months after his eighteenth birthday on 25 November 1915, he attended the recruiting office of the Inns of Court Officer Training Corps in Lincoln's Inn and volunteered, being given an armlet denoting his enlistment. On 17 February 1916 after being interviewed, he was provisionally accepted into the OTC subject to the sanction of the Recruiting Authorities and he was instructed to present himself for final approval two weeks later on 1 March. The officer class in the early years of the war came almost exclusively from former public school pupils and being an ex-pupil of Colfe's, which was regarded as a minor public school, would have made him eligible for membership.

Under the Derby Scheme 'youths' of eighteen who wished to enlist would receive one days pay ('the King's shilling') on enlistment and

20476l

ARMLET NO. 298002

(B4694) Wt. 11366—4289 750M 10/15 H&S (R. 400/1) Forms B. 2512

Army Form B. 2512.

R 8895 Woolwich

Card No. 1087

SHORT SERVICE.

(For the Duration of the War, with the Colours and in the Army Reserve).

ATTESTATION OF

No. 10742 Name Victor Maslin Yeates Corps INNS OF COURT O.T.C

Questions to be put to the Recruit before Enlistment.

1. What is your Name? ... 1. Victor Maslin Yeates
2. What is your full Address? ... 2. ~~68 Granville Park~~ 68, Eltham Rd ~~Blackheath S.E.~~ Lee Woolwich
3. Are you a British Subject? ... 3. Yes
4. What is your Age? ... 4. 18 Years ... Months
5. What is your Trade or Calling? ... 5. Clerk Cos & Co 16 Charing Cross
6. Are you Married? ... 6. no
7. Have you ever served in any branch of His Majesty's Forces, naval or military, if so*, which? 7. no
8. Are you willing to be vaccinated or re-vaccinated? ... 8. Yes
9. Are you willing to be enlisted for General Service? ... 9. Yes
10. Did you receive a Notice, and do you understand its meaning, and who gave it to you? 10. Yes { Name D. B. Clutson Corps RSIOTF
11. Are you willing to serve upon the following conditions provided His Majesty should so long require your services? For the duration of the War, at the end of which you will be discharged with all convenient speed. You will be required to serve for one day with the Colours and the remainder of the period in the Army Reserve, in accordance with the provisions of the Royal Warrant dated 20th Oct., 1915, until such time as you may be called up by order of the Army Council. If employed with Hospitals, depots of Mounted Units, or as a Clerk, etc., you may be retained after the termination of hostilities until your services can be spared, but such retention shall in no case exceed six months. 11. Yes

I, Victor Maslin Yeates do solemnly declare that the above answers made by me to the above questions are true, and that I am willing to fulfil the engagements made.

Victor Maslin Yeates SIGNATURE OF RECRUIT.

G W E Soggers *Signature of Witness.*

OATH TO BE TAKEN BY RECRUIT ON ATTESTATION.

I, Victor Maslin Yeates swear by Almighty God, that I will be faithful and bear true Allegiance to His Majesty King George the Fifth, His Heirs, and Successors, and that I will, as in duty bound, honestly and faithfully defend His Majesty, His Heirs, and Successors, in Person, Crown, and Dignity against all enemies, and will observe and obey all orders of His Majesty, His Heirs and Successors, and of the Generals and Officers set over me. So help me God.

CERTIFICATE OF MAGISTRATE OR ATTESTING OFFICER.

The Recruit above named was cautioned by me that if he made any false answer to any of the above questions he would be liable to be punished as provided in the Army Act.

The above questions were then read to the Recruit in my presence.

I have taken care that he understands each question, and that his answer to each question has been duly entered as replied to, and the said Recruit has made and signed the declaration and taken the oath before me at London on this 25 day of Nov 1915

Signature of the Justice [illegible]

† *Certificate of Approving Officer.*

I certify that this Attestation of the above-named Recruit is correct, and properly filled up, and that the required forms appear to have been complied with. I accordingly approve, and appoint him to the ‡ INNS OF COURT O.T.C.

If enlisted by special authority, Army Form B. 203 (or other authority for the enlistment) will be attached to the *original* attestation.

Date ... Place ...

[illegible] Lieut. for O.C. INNS OF COURT O.T.C. } *Approving Officer.*

INNS OF COURT O.T.C. NO. ... 26 FEB 1917 10, STONE BUILDINGS, LINCOLN'S INN, W.C.

† The signature of the Approving Officer is to be affixed in the presence of the Recruit.
‡ Here insert the "Corps" for which the Recruit has been enlisted.

* If so, the Recruit is to be asked the particulars of his former service, and to produce, if possible, his Certificate of Discharge and Certificate of Character, which should be returned to him conspicuously endorsed in red ink, as follows, viz.—(Name) ... re-enlisted in the ... on the (Date) ...

Victor completed this Attestation form on 25 November 1915, but did not join the OTC until February 1917, after the family had moved to Lee.

then be placed in the Reserve until the age of nineteen. Victor came within this category and his service record shows one day's service on 25 November 1915 (the date he volunteered), being transferred to the Army Reserve the following day and then being posted to the OTC some fifteen months later in February 1917. In the event the Scheme was not as successful as had been hoped and conscription followed in January 1916 with the passing of the first Military Service Act which mainly affected single men; this was followed in May when the second Act was passed which applied to both single and married men between the ages of eighteen and forty-one.

D *In any correspondence this number must be quoted* 1

INNS OF COURT O.T.C.

Date 17 Feb 1916

This is to Certify *that*

Mr V. M. Yeates

has this day been provisionally accepted for membership of the above Corps and subject to the sanction of the Recruiting authorities, may present himself for final approval on day, the 1st of March 1916.

J. A. Hay

O. C. Depot.

Certificate of acceptance for membership of Inns of Court OTC

On joining the OTC as a Private at its training camp at Berkhamsted in Buckinghamshire, some thirty miles from London on 24 February 1917, he was drafted into 'C' Company and was allocated Regimental Number 10792.[11] During his three months with the Corps he was briefed on the duties and responsibilities of an officer as well as receiving basic military training, drill and practical experience of weaponry. In his application to join the OTC, in which his former headmaster at Colfe's, Mr F. W. Lucas, certified as to his good moral character, he stated his preference for a commission in the Royal Flying Corps, which indicates that he had, even then, a fascination with flying. On 27 April 1917, the Medical Officer passed him fit in accordance with the 'Special Standards of fitness for the Royal Flying Corps recommended by the Royal Flying Corps Medical Board' which paved the way for his transfer to the Flying Corps directly by way of the General List on 5 May 1917, on completion of his basic training.

Notes

1 Her mother, who described herself as Lavinia Yeates formerly Maslin, registered the birth.
2 H. Cecil, *The Flower of Battle*, Secker & Warburg, 1995, p. 44.
3 Incomplete and untitled novel known as *Family Life* deposited at the Harry Ransom Humanities Research Center, The University of Austin at Texas (HRHRC).
4 *Winged Victory*, Jonathan Cape 1961 (*WV*), p. 2, Tribute to V. M. Yeates by Henry Williamson (Tribute). All references to *WV* are taken from this edition.
5 *WV*, Tribute, p. 2.
6 Anne Williamson, *Henry Williamson, Tarka and the Last Romantic*, Alan Sutton Publishing 1995, p. 25.
7 *WV*, p. 298, when describing Tom Cundall landing at Folkestone to begin his leave. Herr Moritz Wurm's Blue Viennese Band started playing in Folkestone in 1906 to entertain visitors during the summer months. The Band proved very popular and continued to appear during the following years. In 1911 the 27-piece string band included in their varied repertoire the Grand Overture from Wagner's *Tannhäuser* and a selection from *The Chocolate Soldier*. Cardow's Cadets continued to appear at the Folkestone Bathing Establishment until 1921 – *Folkestone Herald* 15/7/11 and subsequent issues.
8 HRHRC – typescript of fragment of book entitled 'Chapter Three.'
9 *The Colfeian*, June 1914.
10 Board of Trade Survey quoted in *Britain and the First World War*, edited by J Turner, Unwin Hyman 1988, p. 104.
11 Lt. Col. F. H. L. Errington C.B. V.D. (Editor), *The Inns of Court Officers Training Corps during The Great War* (undated but probably published in 1920).

CHAPTER TWO

FLYING TRAINING

Victor's experiences during the next fifteen months of service with the Training Squadrons, the Royal Flying Corps (RFC) and from 1 April 1918, the Royal Air Force (RAF) form the backbone of his book, *Winged Victory*.

The reader could be excused for thinking that it was wholly autobiographical. Indeed when it was first published, *The Observer* of 9 December 1934 carried an advertisement for Jonathan Cape's latest publications on 'Biography and Travel' and one of the four books featured was *Winged Victory*. This did not go unnoticed and Victor commented on it, with some amusement, in a letter to his wife at the time.

Victor in the OTC, stripping a gun

On leaving the OTC, Victor, now an Officer Cadet, reported initially on 4 May to the No. 2 School of Military Aeronautics at Oxford but was immediately transferred to the No. 1 School at Reading.[1] These Schools had been established to provide technical and general training for potential officers awaiting their flying instruction. Here he would have taken advantage of his kit allowance to purchase a new khaki uniform at a cost of approximately £50, although he would still have had to wear a white band in his hat to denote his cadet status. Lectures, interrupted by periods of physical training and drill on the parade ground, took place each day covering such diverse subjects as the theory of flight, aero engines, rigging, armament, map reading, artillery observation, navigation and Morse code.

On 15 June after passing the examinations at the end of the course, he was commissioned with the rank of Temporary 2nd Lieutenant (the RFC used the same ranks as the Army) which was confirmed in the *London Gazette* of 6 July 1917. He was then posted for basic flying training to No. 4 Training Squadron (TS) which was based at Ruislip. The Squadron flew Maurice Farman 11s, or as they were more commonly known 'MF Shorthorns', a name which came into being because of their short landing skids which distinguished them from the earlier, but similar MF7s, which had longer skids and were dubbed 'MF Longhorns.'

The Shorthorn, a two-seater of French design, was an antiquated machine and a 'Pusher' type of aircraft, so called because the engine and propeller were situated at the rear, behind the crew, so it 'pushed' the machine through the air. It was generally known on the Training Squadrons as the 'Rumpty' or 'Rumpety' on account of the 'rumpus' created by the aircraft when taxiing caused by the rattling sound of its air-cooled Renault engine. The pilot sat at the front of the aircraft with the instructor behind (on active service the rear seat was occupied by the observer who was armed with a Lewis gun) and as with most Great War machines, the crew had no protection whatsoever from the elements.

Victor's flying training took place immediately when his initial instructor, Sgt. Chandler, took him up on his maiden familiarisation flight around the aerodrome for fifteen minutes on 16 June, his second day there.[2] He recounts this momentous occasion in *Winged Victory* when his protagonist Tom Cundall recalls his first flight in this primitive machine:

> ... Tom told them the first time he went up was in a Rumpty, that was to say, a Maurice Farman Shorthorn, a queer sort of bus like an assemblage of birdcages. You climbed with great difficulty through a network of

MAURICE FARMAN SHORTHORN
'an assemblage of birdcages'

> wires into the nacelle, and sat perked up there, adorned with a crash helmet, very much exposed to the wondering gaze of men. There did not seem to be any *a priori* reason why this structure should leave the ground, but after dashing across the aerodrome at forty miles an hour for some time the thing did imperceptibly and gradually climb into the air. It was very like a ride on top of an omnibus. A Rumpty was no aeroplane for stunting. The flight was a quiet trip up to three hundred feet and down again.[3]

The maximum speed of a Rumpty was a mere sixty miles an hour at sea level, so such basic aircraft which resembled the earliest flying machines had little practical use by late 1917 apart from training purposes. Flying these 'cats cradles' as Victor aptly called them, with their antiquated controls 'was a mixture of playing a harmonium, working the village pump, and sculling a boat'. Due to the fragility of the Shorthorn, flying was only possible when the weather was near perfect and consequently flights were generally scheduled for early morning or evening when the air is usually calmer. These flights were of short duration, thirty minutes or so, under 1000 feet and always in the vicinity of the aerodrome. The instructor concentrated on landings, the most exacting and accident-prone area of flying, and in his first nine days at Ruislip Victor was in the air on ten different occasions, flying a total of four hours during which time he made thirty-three separate landings.

The instructors on the Training Squadrons at this time were mainly experienced pilots who had survived a tour of active service overseas. Even in 1917, the Authorities recognised that after six months on a front-line squadron, a pilot needed time to recover from the strain of combat flying, and a spell of instructing in England would restore his mental and physical well-being, although many did not relish the job and pressed to be sent back overseas. Their aim was to get their pupils flying solo as quickly as possible. The usual procedure was for the instructor to talk to his pupil for half an hour before a flight to discuss the theory of the practice manoeuvres, followed by a thirty minute de-brief afterwards.

Victor was soon piloting the aeroplane himself, mainly practising landings, under the watchful eye of Lt. P. E. Marr who sat in the rear seat, having taken over from Sgt. Chandler as his instructor. After a total of forty-four circuits and landings covering a total flying time of 4 hours 45 minutes of dual instruction, the exciting day arrived when Lt. Marr felt confident that Victor had become proficient enough to be allowed to go solo for the first time.

On 26 June, just ten days after his first ever flight, Victor had three final flights with his instructor during the early evening, again concentrating on landings, and at the late hour of 9.25pm the momentous moment finally arrived when Lt. Marr asked Victor to take up MF A6851 alone. After a last minute briefing, Victor took off successfully and spent ten minutes in the air circling the aerodrome at 300 feet before landing safely – this was his fifteenth flight.

One can imagine the feeling of exhilaration he must have experienced after 'going solo' for the first time and he would have been keen to have a longer flight. Lt. Marr was obviously satisfied with his performance as at first light the following day (4.55am), Victor took off again for a longer flight which lasted 1 hour 15 minutes when he reached the 'eagle-baffling height' of 3000 feet: he had not flown higher than 700 feet before. He describes this in

MF SHORTHORN'S COCKPIT
'You climbed with great difficulty through a network of wires into the nacelle, and sat perked up there – very much exposed to the wondering gaze of men.'

Winged Victory as being Tom Cundall's first solo flight. Although this flight was generally successful, his instructor took him up again immediately after breakfast in a different machine (B1992) for five minutes dual control, probably to perfect his landing technique. With his confidence soaring, ten minutes later at 9.25am, Victor took off again in the same machine for his third solo flight but kept below 500 feet due to low cloud. This is how he describes the experience when writing about Tom's second solo flight:

> By this time a fairly strong breeze was blowing from the south-west, and there was a ceiling of cloud at about seven hundred feet; not the weather in which a novice in a Rumpty was likely to enjoy himself. He flew round and round the aerodrome at five hundred feet, being bumped about irksomely by the choppy air. It was a great change from the still clear atmosphere of dawn ... but an hour passed, and he might soon land. Then the engine spluttered and stopped. Tom knew one thing, that he must not stall, and immediately put the nose down into gliding position to maintain speed. The engine did not pick up. This was a forced landing, and by the time he realized the alarming truth he did not seem to have enough height to glide on to the aerodrome so as to land into the wind. There was a field in front that he must make for. The engine gave a splutter but subsided again. The field was rushing up at him. He was going down much too steeply. He was almost in the field. He was doing seventy; he would never get in. Trees were in front. The engine spluttered again. He had left the throttle open. He looked down and pulled it off, and then there was a shock and he was out of the aeroplane, lying on the

> ground a dozen yards from the remains of it. He had been thrown on his head, but the crash helmet had saved him. He must have flown into the ground; he didn't really know exactly what had happened; he found himself on the ground and the Rumpty smashed. He might have been unconscious for a little while. The nacelle was upside down on the ground with a pile of wreckage on it. He had been strapped in, but the safety belt had given; otherwise his neck must have been broken. But what a mess the old Rumpty was! One more write off. It was an achievement to smash up a Rumpty like that and not be hurt.[4]

This graphic account of the crash, in which he makes use of a succession of short pithy sentences to heighten the excitement and tension, illustrates how precarious learning to fly these antiquated machines really was during the Great War and the early years of flight.

The official report of the incident states that the crash was caused by engine failure, the pilot 'tried to land in a field but failed to flatten out' which confirms Victor's description.[5] The report also indicates that Victor was injured but his injuries must only have been slight, as he goes on to relate:

> He walked round the wreck, his own wreck. It was a good one. He ought to be dead. Was he, by the way? He couldn't see his dead body about, but it might be under the nacelle. The motor ambulance came jolting over the field towards him, and it was a relief when the orderly spoke to him, and he knew he was not a spirit. The matter ended with a fortnight's sick leave and a few words with Major Beak about his incompetence.[6]

Notes

1 The National Archives (NA), Air 76 Officers' Records. Victor's movements whilst training are taken from his record sheet.

2 These details and other later references to Victor's flights are taken from his flying logbook.

3 *WV*, p. 83/4.

4 Ibid., pp. 84/5.

5 RAF Museum, Casualty Card – V. M. Yeates.

6 *WV*, p. 85.

CHAPTER THREE

MARRIAGE

Victor, like Tom, was fortunate to be able to walk away from the crash and he was given two weeks sick leave to recover, although his injuries were probably no more serious than concussion and a twisted ankle. After leaving Cox's Bank to join the OTC he had continued to see Norah and by this time their relationship had become serious. As with many young couples during the war, the thought of being separated in a few months time once his training had been completed was unsettling. They decided therefore to take full advantage of the unexpected sick leave and marry without further delay.

In 1917 it would have been necessary for Victor to obtain his parents permission to marry as he was under twenty-one years of age. Victor alludes to this requirement in *Winged Victory* when he refers to a fellow pilot, Allen, who had been transferred to hospital in England after crashing, being able to marry as soon as he was fit 'parents permitting.' Unfortunately it seems that Victor's parents did not approve of their son, who was only nineteen years old, marrying a girl five years his senior, especially as he would soon be posted overseas. His mother, particularly, had made it abundantly clear that she felt 'her boy' should not be courting someone so much older than he was – she would have been sensitive of the age difference as she herself was, of course, fourteen years younger than her husband. It also appears that she took an instant dislike to the brown colour of Norah's eyes which she compared disparagingly with her son's attractive clear grey-blue ones. She was, however, very proud of Victor who was 'the apple of her eye' and would have been upset at the thought of Norah snatching him away from her at such a young age.

Notwithstanding these objections, the couple decided to wait no longer, and as Victor had been based at Ruislip since 15 June, he had gained the required residence qualification to enable an application to be made to the local Registry for a marriage licence. The licence allowed them to marry one clear day after the application was submitted and to avoid having to obtain his parents formal consent, Victor declared he was twenty-two years of age when completing the application form. This method of falsifying one's age to facilitate marriage was not uncommon in the heady days of wartime as the authorities did not require any proof of age when considering marriage applications. Although Victor was not religious, Norah had some religious beliefs, and the couple decided on a church wedding, choosing the impressive 13th Century St. Martin's Church in Ruislip which was quite close to the aerodrome – Victor was interested in fine architecture so that the choice of Church would have appealed to him.

On Thursday 12 July 1917 they were married, Victor being described as a 2nd Lieutenant Royal Flying Corps when he gave

St Martin's Church, Ruislip

NORAH AND VICTOR IN 1918

his address as 'The Aerodrome, Ruislip.'[1] Norah was described as a spinster with no occupation and this suggests that she had, by then, left Cox's Bank. Norah's family attended the wedding, her mother, Grace, and her sister Gladys acting as witnesses. There is no record of Victor's parents being present and in view of their objections, it is unlikely that they attended or even knew of the wedding plans.

Like many other service marriages in wartime, the honeymoon was very short and they were only able to snatch a few days together as Victor had to be back at the Training Squadron for the morning of 16 July when his leave expired. On his return, Lt. Marr, unsurprisingly, felt that Victor should have a further spell of dual instruction to regain his confidence after his crash and also to improve his landing technique. A further eight dual flights ensued incorporating twenty-seven landings before Victor was permitted to go solo again after tea on 23 July, the flight lasting 1 hour 10 minutes, when he reached an altitude of 2700 feet. A thirty minute solo flight the next morning was followed by a short dual flight with another instructor, Lt. Philcox. It appears that landing was still a problem, as in this thirty minute flight, a further ten landings were made before Lt. Marr was satisfied with Victor's progress which he confirmed by endorsing his flying logbook 'Can land a MFSH satisfactorily.' By this time Victor had 7 hours 45 minutes experience of dual control and 4 hours 5 minutes solo flying.

Having completed his elementary flying training on the Shorthorn, he was posted to No. 35 TS based at Northolt on 1 August, but a week later he moved to Wye in Kent to join No. 65 Squadron, where he stayed for two weeks having little to do. He took full advantage of this inactivity spending many a happy hour exploring the surrounding hills in glorious sunshine with two of his fellow pilots, Lts. Willis and Reeve. What lessons there were concentrated on the theory of flying and the construction of more sophisticated machines than the Rumpty. During his stay at Wye, he had only one dual flight in an Avro 504J two-seater trainer (B3160), which lasted thirty-five minutes. This took place early in the morning before breakfast on 15 August, and introduced him to flying a more advanced type of machine, when he practised turns to familiarise himself with the different controls. Tom enthusiastically recalled that compared with the primitive Shorthorns, Avros 'really were aeroplanes, and quite different to fly'.

He was soon on the move again as on 24 August he was posted to No. 40 TS which was based at Croydon for more advanced training, and he was to remain there for the next five months until he left for France. The Squadron had a number of different aeroplane types, all with rotary engines, a pupil graduating from a simple machine, such as the Avro Trainer, to the more sophisticated single-seat fighter the Sopwith Pup, and ultimately to the Sopwith Camel. The Avro 504 was the standard RFC trainer, the pupil again piloting the aircraft from the front seat, and was the backbone of many such Training Squadrons. An Avro 504J variant (C4451) had the distinction of being the aircraft in which Prince Albert (later King George VI) learnt to fly.

The Squadron's Commanding Officer (C.O.) was Major C. C. Miles, but in November he left for France to take command of No. 43 Squadron based at Auchel. His departure was an occasion for a traditional farewell party or, to call it by its more common name, 'a binge', and this was probably Victor's first experience of such a celebration, although he was to take part in many more in the months to come, as he relates in his book.

The Officers' Mess and pilots' accommodation at Croydon were situated in a large old house named 'The Dell' at Beddington, a village about two miles from the aerodrome and were quite comfortable. When the weather was fit for flying, a lorry ferried the officers from their quarters before dawn each morning and a second run was made after breakfast. As the return journey was less reliable, many acquired bicycles so that they could get back to their quarters without the inconvenience of waiting around for transport.

Life was pleasant for the trainee pilots, the Squadron having the atmosphere of a public school with little of the 'hot air' which was a feature of many such training establishments. The trainees knew they had joined the most élite and glamorous arm of the armed forces and they had the certainty of becoming officers at the end of their training. Victor was quite happy at Croydon and he considered the instructors to be a 'very decent lot'. One, Capt. J. L. Trollope, who flew with him

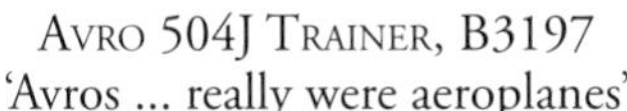

AVRO 504J TRAINER, B3197
'Avros ... really were aeroplanes'

in Avro B3146 on 20 November, was in overall charge of his training, signing his logbook at the end of each week to confirm the number of hours he had flown. Victor considered him to be a brilliant pilot, a view substantiated when he later achieved fame on shooting down six enemy aircraft in one day on 24 March 1918 whilst flying Sopwith Camel C8270 of No. 43 Squadron, when based at Avesnes-le-Comte.[2] Surprisingly, another No. 43 Squadron pilot, Capt. H. W. Woollett, repeated this remarkable feat on 12 April 1918. As Victor remarked in his essay *The Croydon Front 1917*, 'what a Squadron.'[3]

The Commanding Officer of that Squadron was none other than Major C. C. Miles, the former C.O. of No. 40 TS at Croydon. He mistakenly mentions in this essay that Major Miles became the C.O. of No. 44 Squadron and it seems that either his memory failed him on this occasion, or it was a typographical error as Major Miles and Capts. Trollope and Woollett all served with No. 43 Squadron.

The main reason for Victor's happiness, however, was that his wife had found lodgings nearby in a semi-detached house at 25 Clarendon

Sopwith Pup A6228, in which Victor made his first flight on the type

Road, Wallington in Surrey, a few miles from the aerodrome. This meant that they could be together each weekend and also in the evenings during the week if the weather was unfit for flying. These snatches of married bliss would have meant a great deal to both of them, as they knew it would not be long before they would be parted when he went to France with the danger that entailed.

After four dual flights in the Avro, he was allowed to go solo shortly before dinner on 5 September, reaching a height of 4000 feet during his twenty minute flight. His training continued with more solo flights and dual instruction – mainly practising turns and landings. The instructors at that time were not usually interested in teaching the more complicated manoeuvres such as spins and loops, leaving the trainees to learn these by trial and error once they had mastered the basic flying techniques – it was not until 20 November that Victor looped for the first time when flying an Avro. Once a pupil had become proficient in handling the Avro, he graduated to flying his first single-seat scout or fighter, the Sopwith Pup. Victor's maiden flight in a Pup took place in the afternoon of 17 December, when he attained a height of 5000 feet during a fifty minute flight which was another milestone in his training.

The Pup was a popular scout machine which had entered service with the RFC in the late summer of 1916 and soon distinguished itself in the fighting on the Western Front during the following year. It was generally considered to be one of the most pleasant aircraft of the war period to fly and had the historical distinction of being the first aircraft to land on a ship under way when, on 2 August 1917, Sqn. Cdr. E. H. Dunning landed on the flight deck of HMS *Furious*.[4]

Further practice flights were made during the following week until the welcome Christmas leave arrived, although the pressure to train pilots was such that he had only three days with his wife and was back flying again on 28 December.

The training on the Pup was the prelude to graduating to fly the most acclaimed British aircraft of the war, the Sopwith F.1 Camel (F for fighter), which was the successor to the Pup. It had, however, very different flying characteristics compared with the likeable Pup, and its reputation of being difficult and dangerous to fly would have been the main talking point amongst the pilots about to take one up for the first time. Here is how Victor/Tom Cundall describes the machine:

> They were by far the most difficult of service machines to handle. Many pilots killed themselves by crashing in a right hand spin when they were learning to fly them. ... They were unlike ordinary aeroplanes, being quite unstable, immoderately tail-heavy, so light on the controls that the slightest jerk or inaccuracy would hurl them all over the sky, difficult to land, deadly to crash: a list of vices to emasculate the stoutest courage, and the first flight on a Camel was always a terrible ordeal. They were bringing out a two-seater training Camel for dual work, in the hope of reducing that thirty per cent of crashes on first solo flights. [5]

Victor, therefore, would have been both apprehensive and excited when his instructor asked him to take up a Camel for the first time on the morning of 13 January 1918 when he was, no doubt, given the same precise instructions as Tom:

> 'Now this is what I want you to do. Take your time in running the engine on the ground, so as to get used to it, then go straight up to five thousand all out. You'll be up there in no time. You're not to turn or do anything except ease the fine adjustment back below five thousand. Climb at eighty-five. Then you can try turning to the left, all out or throttled down, just as you like. Don't be afraid of spinning.' [6]

At 10.15am Victor climbed into his Camel and after the preliminary checks and with the adrenalin flowing, he was ready for his first flight. A graphic description of this flight seen through the eyes of Tom vividly captures the nervous tension Victor must have endured:

> Tom had got in and run the engine. There wasn't any difficulty about that. He taxied out and turned round. The wind being easterly he had to take off over the hangars. He opened the throttle and the engine roared. Then it spluttered. Hell! He caught a glimpse of people jumping about with excitement. Too much petrol. His hand went to the fine adjustment. By the time he had got the engine running properly he was almost into

A Sopwith Camel in flight

> a hangar with his tail hardly off the ground. He pulled the stick back and staggered into the air just clearing the roof: if the engine gave one more splutter he would stall and crash. But the engine continued to roar uniformly. His heart, having missed several beats, thumped away to make up for them, and he felt emulsified; but he was flying.[7]

Tom, as instructed, climbed to five thousand feet and tried to turn to the left:

> What happened was that all tension went out of the controls, there was an instant of steep side-slip, and the earth whizzed round in front of him. A spin! At once his hand went to the fine adjustment to shut off the petrol.[8]

Learning to fly these unstable and often unreliable machines was fraught with danger and indeed one Second World War pilot who later became a test pilot, is of the opinion that if the Camel had been produced twenty years later it would not have been allowed to fly because of its inherent instability.[9] This characteristic, however, enabled a pilot to throw it about in combat in an unpredictable way; this was most useful when being attacked by German fighters which often had the upper hand in pure performance. It was mainly powered by a French designed Clerget or Le Rhône rotary engine – the unusual design of the rotary engine was such that the crankshaft was fixed, and the heavy cylinders revolved around it resulting in a gyroscopic effect which tried to pull the machine to the right. The aircraft got its name because of its short nose and stocky fuselage combined with an aluminium cover shaped like a hump enclosing the breeches of its two machine guns. It was only 18 feet 9 inches long, had a wingspan of 28 feet, and had a maximum speed of 115 miles per hour, with a ceiling of 19,000 feet – the Le Rhône version had a faster rate of climb and could reach 24000 feet. It had a duration of two hours thirty minutes and for armament, had two Vickers .303 forward firing fixed machine guns. It was the most famous and glamorous of the British fighter aircraft and accounted for 1294 enemy aircraft destroyed in only sixteen months of operations.

Novice flyers found the Camel difficult to master and Victor was no exception. Accidents, often fatal, were common. The hazardous nature of flying these early machines was brought home to him forcibly whilst he was at Croydon:

> He had seen George kill himself there by pulling the wings off a Pup with too much rolling. And young Fleming, who had a flair for Camel flying and took to them like an Arab right from his first flight, used to roll a Camel just over the hangars and scare everybody stiff … and then one day he broke his neck making a careless bumpy landing; such being life.[10]

Temp. 2/Lt. Thomas William George, a Scot, was twenty-five years of age when he was killed on 18 October 1917 whilst Temp. 2/Lt. Robert John Fleming, another Scot, was killed on 29 January 1918 in similar circumstances.

Victor would have been even more shocked when one of his instructors, Lt. Rupert Ernest Neve, whom he had flown with in Avro B915 on 8 December 1917, was fatally injured on 26 January 1918 whilst flying Camel B5235 when the wings collapsed whilst in a spiral dive, crashing into the front garden of a house in Purley. Lt. Neve was twenty-four years old and had been in France with No. 40

Squadron in 1916/1917 before being shot down on 9 March 1917 when his machine caught fire – but he survived by jumping clear before impact. After recovering from his injuries he retrained as an instructor, and it is ironic that this is another case of an experienced pilot surviving the rigours of operational flying, only to lose his life through machine failure whilst an instructor in England. In his essay *The Croydon Front 1917*, Victor remembers Neve:

> Other instructors I remember were Knocker and Neve. Poor Neve! He killed himself on a Camel; crashed into a Purley front garden; smashed himself completely: but I can still see him at the binge for Major Miles' departure overseas, standing there youthful, flushed, nice-looking, trying to make a speech but speechless with laughter and champagne. [11]

Victor states that he purposely used the word 'Front' in the title of this essay as the risk of death or injury during his time at Croydon was as bad as a very quiet time on a front-line squadron in France. At least four other pilots lost their lives whilst he was stationed there, so it is unsurprising that a student pilot soon became hardened to the dangers of flying even in England.[12] Indeed, the official statistics reveal the startling fact that more pilots were killed whilst training than in actual combat. Of the 14,166 pilots killed during the war, approximately 8,000 died in the United Kingdom during training.[13] These unexpected figures provoked questions in the House of Commons in June 1918 but the Secretary of State shrugged off the blame, describing the pilots as young and undisciplined.

After spending a week on the cold wintry Scottish coast at Turnberry being taught the theory of aerial fighting and the importance of gunnery practice, he passed his Gunnery Course examinations and returned to Croydon to continue flying training. By this time he had been appointed a Flying Officer – which denoted his duties and was not a rank as in the present-day RAF. This appointment was confirmed in the *London Gazette* on 10 January 1918 being effective from 18 December 1917.

Flying practice continued, mainly on the Camel, including

formation flying and some photographic work, but on 21 January Victor experienced his second crash, this time when flying a Pup (B5252) which he crashed on landing. Fortunately he was unhurt and he was in the air again two days later. By 2 February his flying training was complete, having logged 11 hours 50 minutes dual instruction and 52 hours 30 minutes solo flying of which 13 hours 10 minutes were on the Camel.

He was now considered to be a fully trained pilot and proficient enough to be sent immediately to a front-line Squadron in France, as new pilots were urgently required to replace those who had fallen during the heavy fighting in the autumn of 1917. In 1918 a new pilot arriving in France had an average of 50 hours experience of solo flying, so Victor's record was not exceptional.

Following his discharge from Croydon on 6 February, he would only have had time to say a hasty farewell to Norah before joining one of the many troopships bound for France the following day.

Ground crew assemble to deal with the crash of a Sopwith Pup trainer

Notes

1 The marriage certificate gives Victor's age as 22 years.
2 In *WV* p. 174, Victor writes that Captain Trollope had been killed whilst in fact he was shot down and wounded on 28 March 1918 and survived the war.
3 Henry Williamson, *Goodbye West Country*, Putman 1937: pp. 98/100 contain the text of Victor's essay entitled *The Croydon Front 1917* which Williamson unsuccessfully tried to get published.
4 Unfortunately Sqn. Cdr. Dunning died whilst attempting his third landing on HMS *Furious* in a Sopwith Pup (N6452) on 7 August 1917 when he overshot and was drowned.
5 *WV*, p. 25. A number Camels were adapted to two-seater machines for training purposes in mid-1918.
6 Ibid., p. 26.
7 Ibid., p. 26.
8 Ibid., p. 27.
9 Letter to the author from Wing Commander T. F. Neil DFC AFC.
10 WV, p. 30.
11 Excerpt from *The Croydon Front 1917*. Lt. Guy M. Knocker was Victor's instructor on 5 and 12 September 1917 when flying Avro 504Js (B3185 and B3231). Later that month he was transferred to No. 65 Squadron which left for France on 27 October. He is credited with two victories whilst flying with this Squadron. He returned to England after being wounded on 6 April 1918 and joined No. 63 TS.
12 Temp. 2/Lt. A. J. Maitland was killed on 22 September 1917 after spinning when flying Camel B6292, Temp. 2/Lt. J. L. Foubister from New Zealand was killed in an Avro 504 (A9769) on 8 October 1917, whilst both Temp. 2/Lt. W. Crooke and Temp. 2/Lt. J. H. Russell were killed when their Camels (B6396 and B6274) collided on 12 November 1917.
13 Denis Winter, *The First of the Few*, Allen Lane 1982, p. 36.

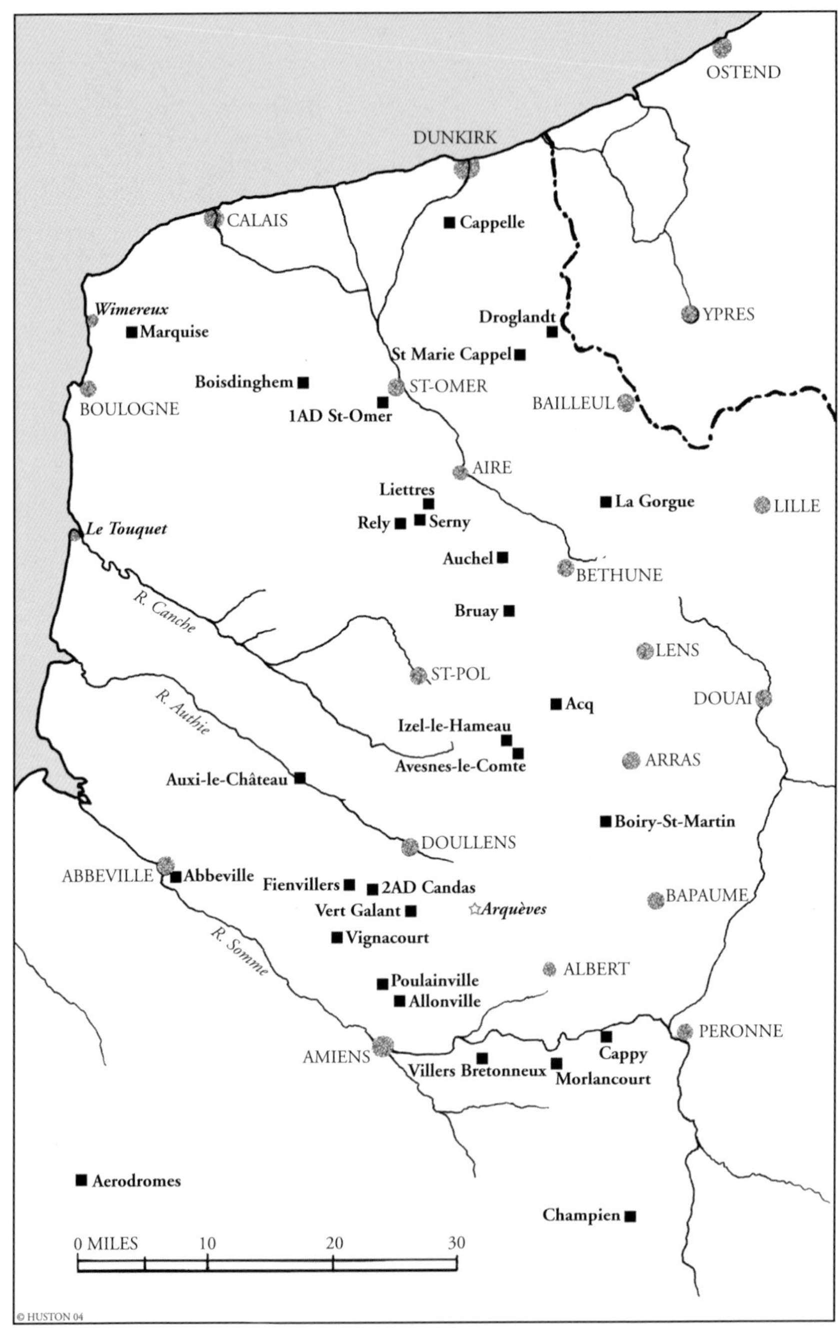

NORTHERN FRANCE

CHAPTER FOUR

THE WESTERN FRONT

The steamer docked in France, probably at Boulogne, later that day, 7 February, and Victor was sent to the Pilots' Pool at No. 2 Aircraft Depot at Candas, near Doullens, which was a transit camp for pilots and a repair depot for aeroplanes. This Depot served the Southern Front whilst No. 1 Depot at St-Omer served the Northern Sector. Here, together with other pilots fresh from training, he would have waited until a call came to replace a pilot who had either been killed or seriously wounded, or who was being transferred to Home Establishment (HE) having completed his tour of duty. This was a frustrating time as no flying was permitted and the pilots were all keyed up, anxious to know to which Squadron they were to be allocated. The usual procedure was for one of the staff to place a list on a notice board each day with the names of those who had been posted. It would have been with some relief, therefore, having been at the Pool for less than a week, to find he had to report to No. 46 Squadron at Filescamp Farm which was situated just outside the village of Izel-le-Hameau, some ten miles west of Arras. On making enquiries he found that it was a Camel squadron commanded by a Major Mealing.

No. 46 Squadron had been formed at Wyton on 19 April 1916 from a nucleus of members of No. 2 Reserve Squadron and was equipped with BE2cs. In September of that year it was re-equipped with Nieuport 12 two-seaters as a prelude to moving to France the following month under the command of Major Philip Babington, when it undertook artillery observation and reconnaissance duties. In April 1917, however, its role changed when it received Sopwith Pups and became a single-seater fighter squadron. Following the German attacks on London in May and June 1917, the Squadron was recalled to England for Home Defence duties and was based at Suttons Farm, although no enemy aircraft were encountered during its stay. Whilst there, however, the Squadron became renowned for its formation flying and also its quick reaction time, the whole Squadron of nineteen machines becoming airborne within five minutes of receiving a warning. The Squadron returned to France at the end of August, moving to Filescamp Farm on 7 September and was re-equipped with Sopwith F.1 Camels powered by 110hp Le Rhône engines in November. Major Babington returned to England on 5 December and was replaced by Major R. H. S. Mealing. His nickname was 'Standback', probably due to one of his forenames being Steinbach and also because it seems that he did not fly very often and when he did, it was usually only to test the weather conditions.

Victor left the Pool on 12 February and travelled by lorry to the aerodrome where the Orderly Officer showed him to his hut. The officers' accommodation consisted of Nissen huts, which housed four beds, one in each corner, with a stove in the centre for heating. He would have been introduced to the C.O. and asked the usual questions of how many flying hours had he under his belt and how many of these had been on the Camel. Squadrons were divided into three flights named A, B and C, each flight having six pilots, and he would then have been told that he was to be part of C Flight under the command of Capt. G. E. Thomson. In *Winged Victory*, however, he describes Tom's first flight commander as Capt. MacAndrews ('Mac'), whom, as will be shown, he based on Donald MacLaren who did not take command of C Flight until 6 April when he was promoted to Captain. The Squadron was attached to the 13th Army Wing, III Brigade.

On exploring the aerodrome, he found it to be a pleasant place, Filescamp Farm being formerly an old château with high grey walls enclosing a cobbled courtyard. There was a large orchard surrounding the farmhouse which ensured there would be a plentiful supply of fruit throughout the summer. The farm buildings housed the usual assortment of farm animals, cows, chickens, geese, ducks and numerous pigs – this is how Victor humorously described the livestock:

> The pigs were indistinguishable from English pigs, except for a greater pungency of odour, which was not their own fault. The cows, however, were less ladylike than English cows. Tom missed that air of placid and spinsterish chastity that make English cows and women so irritating to bulls and men. The chickens, too, had not been hatched in the protestant tradition, and lacked moral grandeur.[1]

At the top of a slope leading from the farm buildings and orchard, was a level piece of land making it an ideal place for an aerodrome and it was large enough to house three squadrons. The aerodrome was generally known as Izel-le-Hameau, Filescamp Farm being a part of it, and No. 64 Squadron occupied the buildings on the opposite side and was equipped with the SE5a:

> There was an SE Squadron just round the corner, more or less on the same aerodrome, and every day there was an undercarriage smashed, sometimes a complete turn-over … Most of the big Hun getters flew SEs.[2]

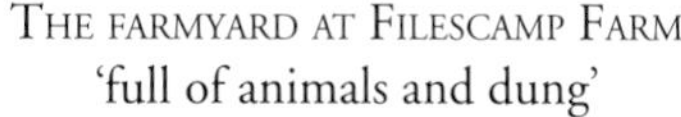

THE FARMYARD AT FILESCAMP FARM
'full of animals and dung'

THE AERODROME AT IZEL-LE-HAMEAU: MACHINE GUN PIT AT LEFT

Among the leading Allied aces who flew SEs were Billy Bishop (72 victories), Mick Mannock (61), James McCudden (57) and the South African Anthony Beauchamp Proctor who claimed 54 victories all on SE5s. A number of well-known aces had also flown from Izel, notably McCudden (whom Victor was to meet later), Bishop and Albert Ball. He also comments correctly in his book that a night bombing squadron (No. 102) was based on the far side of the aerodrome which flew FEs (Royal Aircraft Factory FE2bs).

Victor's first flight in France was on 17 February when he took up Camel B9157 for a fifteen minutes test flight when his flying ability would have been closely scrutinised by his flight commander and the other pilots. He was fortunate in joining the Squadron at this time (February 1918) as it was 'the depth of winter and the lull after [the Battle of] Cambrai' which had taken place in November 1917. Like Tom, he was not required to venture over the lines during his first month on the Squadron and he wisely took full advantage of this period of inactivity to gain further experience of flying the Camel. In his opinion it took three months on Camels to be able to fly them moderately well, by which time you were either dead, a nervous wreck or one hell of a pilot. He not only practised flying manoeuvres but also formation flying. It was essential for a pilot to be able to stay in his correct place on patrols as stragglers were the first ones to get picked off by enemy fighters and more importantly, could put the rest of the flight in danger. Pilots were also encouraged to simulate actual fighting conditions whilst on practice flights and on 21 February, Victor and 2/Lt. A. L. T. Taylor arranged such a mock combat which is recorded in his logbook 'Scrap with Taylor.' Unfortunately, this pilot was shot down the following month on 16 March and became a prisoner of war, being repatriated in December 1918.

No further flights are recorded during the next seven days which was due to a health problem as he was admitted to hospital on 25 February, returning to the Squadron three days later. His illness must only have been a minor one, however, as he was back flying again the next day, 1 March.

It was also important for new pilots to have the opportunity to practice bombing and firing at ground targets as the Camel was used extensively for ground-strafing when it carried four 20lb Cooper bombs under the fuselage:

> Unfortunately they were good machines for ground-strafing. They could dive straight down on anything, and when a few feet off the ground, go straight up again.[3]

Victor had a number of such practice flights during his first two months on the Squadron. His best bombing run was on 9 March when he recorded:

> 4 — 4 — 6 — 9

These figures represented the distance in yards which the dummy bombs landed from the target so the above score was regarded as a good one.

New pilots were also expected to collect replacement machines from the Aircraft Park at Candas and he was allocated one of these duties each week during his first few weeks with the Squadron.

In a letter to Norah's aunt Florence Bard on 3 March, he writes that he had had a quiet life since joining the Squadron three weeks earlier as the Squadron had not been busy, although it had bagged two Huns without incurring any casualties – these victories were recorded on 16 and 26 February.

It was the policy of the Allied Command for the RFC to maintain an aggressive strategy and so take the war to the enemy. The reasoning behind this approach was that it would harass the enemy's observation patrols and make it more difficult for them to fly over Allied territory, whilst at the same time assisting the work of the British observation machines. The consequence of this decision was that Allied patrols were invariably over German territory which meant that if a pilot had engine trouble, or had to make a forced landing after a combat and survived, he was likely to become a prisoner of war. The prevailing wind was also from the west and so was against Allied pilots returning to base which was unhelpful if a machine was damaged, had engine trouble or was short of fuel. No doubt these thoughts were in his mind when he had his first experience of flying over enemy terrain, with three other pilots, on a Close Offensive Patrol (C.O.P.) led by Lt. H. G. W. Debenham on 16 March. This was three days after

A Sopwith F.1 Camel with four 20lb Cooper bombs and a Flight Commander's pennant attached to the rudder

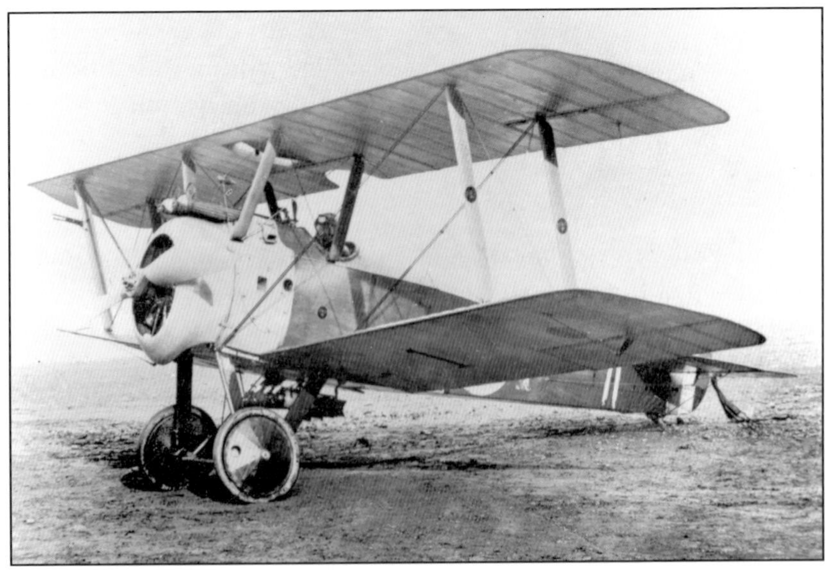

Lt. Debenham had taken him on a conducted tour of the lines. It would have been a trying flight. Not only had Victor to look out for enemy aircraft, but he had also to maintain formation with the other aircraft in the patrol and his flight commander would have carefully monitored his flying ability. He must have been relieved when no enemy aircraft were encountered, so enabling him to concentrate on his flying and keeping his position in the formation.

Like many young pilots who had barely left school when they were catapulted into a war situation, it took Victor some time to settle down to squadron life, as he comments to Mrs Bard:

> I am leading a very quiet life out here amid not very congenial companionship. They are not a bad crowd, but there is no one whom I could love at first sight, so to speak, & no one who might reciprocate such a sentiment. However, as I have plenty of spare time to do what I like, things are not so bad.

Similar sentiments were expressed by Lt. Arthur Rhys Davids, an Old Etonian and classical scholar, in a letter to his mother on 22 April 1917 in which he wrote that there were only one or two people he had any hope of being friendly with and most of them had no intellectual ambitions.[4]

Before enlisting, Victor had enjoyed a sheltered life with his privileged grammar school education and with parents who had strong opinions and probably upheld strict Victorian values. He was a sensitive young man who liked cultured pursuits such as literature, poetry and classical music and he obviously found the bawdy RFC Officers' Mess distasteful at first. This is clear from his comments in a letter written to his wife on 21 March from an Army Corps School where he was being entertained following his first crash in France:

> They are all the most perfect gentlemen, and treat me with 'unbounded hospitality.' It is so nice to be in a mess where no one swears, talks smut, or gets drunk. It is like civilisation.

He was not alone in these sentiments and many young pilots felt the same on arrival at their first squadron. Albert Ball, for example, remarked in his diary that new pilots joining his Squadron straight from school were without ideas and used foul language.[5]

The crash and his stay at the Army Corps School are recorded in *Winged Victory* when Tom comments favourably on the civilised pleasures of the Army Officers' Mess:

> Being introduced into this mess was, to one used to the R.F.C. atmosphere, something like finding oneself in the holy calm of a Pall Mall club miraculously endowed with faint but persistent Moral Purpose, after a New Year hullaballo in a Regent Street bar. Conversation was leisurely, prolonged, and decorous, and alcohol was used only in such small quantities as stimulated the larynx to this sort of talk. No one swore or discussed women. The profound purity of the mature English gentleman away from his womenfolk reigned.[6]

Like many other servicemen far from home, he soon missed female company, writing to Florence Bard that it was very strange not to see any womenfolk. Life would be horrible in a male world and on his recent short visit to hospital in February it had been nice to see one or two English women again. He would have cut an attractive figure in his RFC uniform, being of slim build, five feet nine inches tall, with fair hair, clear grey-blue eyes and pale complexion. No doubt, like Tom Cundall, he enjoyed flirting with the French women in the estaminets and also later with the nurses in the hospitals and he 'missed the gentleness of women' in the harsh surroundings of the RFC squadron.

Shortly after his arrival in France, Norah wrote to him confirming that she was pregnant – she was still living by herself at Clarendon Road – and so it was natural for Victor to be concerned for her well-being. She was missing her husband greatly and it was difficult for her to visit her parents as they lived some distance away and Victor's parents were now living in Weston-super-Mare, his father having retired from the bank on reaching the age of sixty-five. Victor expressed his concern to Florence Bard in his letter of 3 March:

> Thanks very much for looking after Norah mia to the extent I understand you have been doing. I am afraid she is having a lonely

> period just now, and she needs companionship above everything. That is to say the right kind of companionship. She seems to feel the need at the weekend chiefly.

They quite naturally corresponded frequently and it was these letters written to Norah which were to prove so helpful when, years later, he came to write his book *Winged Victory*.

Unfortunately, only two of his letters written from France have survived, the one written to Norah's aunt, Florence Bard, on 3 March 1918, and the second sent to Norah later the same month on the 21 March, to which reference has already been made. Although he felt he had been too concerned with the censor, the circumstances leading up to his first crash in France and the resulting hospitality he received from the Army Corps School are described in some detail in the letter to his wife, which even identifies the Corps School, as will be shown later. A detailed description of the crash, in identical terms but with some embellishment, is to be found in *Winged Victory* and it is reasonable to assume, therefore, that other letters written to his wife would contain descriptions of many incidents which Victor and his

OFFICERS' NISSEN HUT AT FILESCAMP FARM

Squadron experienced which he would bring into the narrative.

Although these letters would have been most useful in jogging his memory to recall the more important incidents, he looked to his flying logbook (Army Book 425) for details of the routine flights and combats which were to form such an important aspect of the book. The logbook entries, written mainly in ink, indicate the date and time of take-off and landing for each flight and initially give the serial number of the aircraft, although from 25 March this is omitted, probably due to the pressures following the German attack. There is also a comment on each flight which, although very brief, does enable many of the actions portrayed in the book to be identified, as will be demonstrated.

Notes

1 *WV*, p. 33.
2 Ibid., p. 44.
3 Ibid., p. 31.
4 Letter cited by Alex Revell in *Brief Glory: the Life of Arthur Rhys Davids*, Kimber 1984, p. 91. Lt. Rhys Davids, DSO, MC and Bar, who was accredited with 25 victories, was killed on 27 October 1917 when flying SE5a (B31) of No. 56 Sqn.
5 Cited by D. Winter in *The First of the Few,* p. 67.
6 *WV*, p. 81.

CHAPTER FIVE

THE MARCH PUSH

In *Winged Victory* Tom's first offensive patrol over enemy territory is described at the beginning of Chapter II of Phase One and recalls a low bombing 'dawn show' undertaken by C Flight which takes off just before 6.30am. This is based on Victor's second flight over the lines and his first bombing patrol which took place on 18 March when he took off at 6.25am, returning at 7.35am, noted in his logbook as 'Low bombing'. Tom is described as having been in France for two months – Victor at that time had been there for six weeks. Following this flight, as Tom's own aircraft had developed mechanical problems, he takes up a new machine, 'Y', for a test flight and he meets a fellow pilot Hudson, of B Flight, so a mock combat ensues:

> The first thing he met was a Camel marked M. That should be Hudson. He had a scrap with him over the tree-tops, in the course of which he got in Hudson's slipstream and nearly crashed with the jolt it gave him.[1]

This scrap actually took place earlier in the month on 10 March (before Victor had been over the lines) and is noted in his logbook 'Scrap with Hudson' – both pilots had taken off at 11.50am to practice combat manoeuvres. 2/Lt. Gerald Hudson was also learning the ropes having arrived on the Squadron shortly after Victor on 28 February and his own logbook also records this mock combat.[2] This is the first instance of factual events being portrayed in *Winged Victory* out of their true chronological order. Before this encounter Tom Cundall, who has been enjoying contour chasing, dives low over the aerodrome and narrowly misses an RE8 two-seater which is about to land. Enquiring later whose aircraft it was, Tom is told by his rigger that it belongs to General Mitchell who is visiting the Squadron to give them a pep talk on the expected German attack. He is described as wearing a monocle and this would be a reference to General Sefton Brancker, the Controller of Equipment and Personnel, who as Air Marshal Sir Sefton Brancker was so tragically to lose his life on the ill-fated flight of the R101 airship on 5 October 1930.[3]

A similar example of an event being included out of chronological order is the reference to Capt. James McCudden visiting the Squadron for dinner in mid-March – it is described early in the book in Chapter VI. This visit, however, can be identified as having taken place on 11 April.[4]

On the morning of 18 March Victor's logbook shows that he flew to No. 12 Squadron at Boiry-St-Martin for a Bristol F2B escort, but this had to be aborted due to the weather conditions. This entry probably prompted him to recount Tom's flight with C Flight which was assigned an escort duty for a photographic sortie although the aircraft is described as being an Ack-W. This mission was also cancelled on arrival at the aerodrome due to the inclement weather.

One of the most experienced flight commanders was Capt. George E. Thomson, of C Flight, who had been with the Squadron since July 1917 when it was equipped with Sopwith Pups. He is described as having been accredited with twenty-four Huns, this tally being very close to his accepted score of twenty-one victories. He was posted to HE on 25 March and Victor describes the traditional binge which was held in his honour in some detail. Tom wakes up the morning after somewhat the worse for wear, and learns that a bomb had been dropped on the aerodrome during the night. The Germans did attack the base but on 27 March when AMII J. E. Bentley (No. 64 Squadron) was killed and three other airmen injured.

In an attempt to achieve a decisive break-though before the Allies were strengthened by American reinforcements, General Ludendorff, the German commander, launched his offensive to drive the British 5th and 3rd Armies from the Somme at 4.40am on the morning of 21 March with an initial artillery bombardment which lasted some five hours. Victor recalls:

> A few mornings later, the twenty-first of March, the batman called Tom and Allen for C Flight's dawn job, and for once Tom did not go to sleep again. There was a tremendous racket going on; every kind of artillery seemed to be in action. It was certainly the prelude to the big German push. Thank God he was away from that rain of high explosive.[5]

It was from this day, 21 March, that Victor decided to recount the day-to-day life of the Squadron through his character Tom Cundall. It was memorable not only for the start of the German offensive and the beginning of an exhausting time for him and his fellow pilots, but it also saw his first crash in France.

This is the first reference in the book to a particular date and it is important as it enables one to compare Tom's flights on this day (and also those on many subsequent days) with the entries in Victor's logbook. Tom takes off with C Flight for the dawn job on 21 March to attack enemy infantry on the 3rd Army Front but soon develops engine problems and has to return to the aerodrome, only to find that it was plug trouble. Having had the fault rectified, he immediately takes off again to try to find his Flight but the weather had worsened with thick mist and after releasing his bombs and with his engine missing again, he turns over when trying to make a forced landing in a furrowed field near Arquèves. He is befriended by a Padre from a local Army Corps School where he enjoys their generous hospitality in the Officers' Mess whilst awaiting transport back to his Squadron.

Victor's logbook entry for that day shows that he simply took off at 6.20am and returned at 6.45am with engine trouble. He went up again at 7am and turned over on landing at Arquèves at 8.30am. In the evening he wrote to Norah on borrowed notepaper – he describes Tom borrowing notepaper before dinner whilst at the Corps School – recalling these events in detail and it is fortunate that this letter survives, as it enables one to demonstrate with certainty that Victor portrays his own experiences through his protagonist Tom Cundall.

He inadvertently dated this letter 'Thursday 21/3/17 6.30pm', an indication that he was still suffering from the after-effects of his crash. An extract from the letter shows that when he writes about Tom's experiences of 21 March he is, in fact, describing his own:

I am in a strange place just now, to wit the 5th Corps School, where Bombing & Gassing & such things are taught. It is a most excellent place, & I am being treated with the utmost courtesy by the staff people here. It came about thus: This morning we started off to drop our bombs, and when we were about over the lines my engine started to miss, so I came back and had it put right & then set out again on my own to try to find the others. I wandered up & down the lines for an hour or so without finding my flight, & then came back. I was up fairly high & by the time I had lost height & got over our side the ground was covered with a thick white mist that increased very rapidly until I was flying over an apparent illimitable sea of bright white cloud, & my engine started missing again. You may guess, my darling, that I was not too well pleased with my situation. I tried to find Arras, but either I missed it completely or it was quite covered, for I could see nothing at all. I came down low to look for rifts in the mist, and where I could see the ground it was covered with water-filled shell holes & disused trench systems: all that infinite desolation of an old battlefield. I also realized that the wind was from the west, & so drifting me towards the lines. I found a clear spot near a main road along which

A Sopwith Camel –turned over on landing!

I could see our own various motors passing, so I knew I was on the right side, and thought of landing there, but there were too many shell holes about. I then flew to the west in the hope of finding a clear spot over some fields in which I could land. After wandering about for some time I found myself over a small village, & I could see some fields near by which looked possible. On coming near the first field, I found it was sloping considerably, and I floated on a little further, coming down eventually on ploughed ground. I landed quite correctly, into the wind and with the furrows. I made quite a good landing, pancaking on to the mud & thought everything was OK, but for some inexplicable reason Monsieur le Camel turned over on his back, leaving me in the undignified position of hanging upside down. However, I undid the belt and managed to fall out.

I wandered around to the neighbouring village & found a soldier to look after my airship while I found a telephone. I went a little way along the local line to a railhead, where I tried to get through to the squadron, but the line was broken by shell fire, so I couldn't. I was recommended to try again in about an hour, when the line might be repaired. I found, however, a mechanic from a local Aeroplane Park, who got me some breakfast, & who said his people would do the necessary for me.[6] We rang them up & told them all about it, and they said I could expect transport very soon. We went back to the aeroplane & waited. After waiting some time the mechanic went away on his lorry to see why no help had come. That was the last I saw of him. While I was sitting on the machine a Padre came up to see the smash, & with him I made friends. We were both born at Dulwich, & we both said in the same breath, which is rather curious. After waiting about there for some hours the Padre suggested that I should come here with him for some lunch. Having found a guard for the machine, we came. On the way we met a tender that the Aircraft Park people had got another squadron to send with two mechanics to start me up! [7] I believe these non-combatant RFC people are absolutely mad.

However, we continued on to lunch & got a proper guard for

> the machine. After lunch I got through to the Squadron & told them all about it. So far, however, nothing has happened & I am still here, being treated like a lord.

He reassured Norah that he was unhurt and although he did not know how long 'this little sojourn' would last, it was 'a perfect heaven of rest.'

The Damage Report submitted on his machine (Camel B9197) shows that it turned over on its back and was sent to No. 2 Aeroplane Supply Depot at Fienvillers for repair, but it was so badly damaged it had to be written off.

Evidence of the effectiveness of the Squadron's attacks on the German troops on 21 March can be found in the *History of the 10th Bavarian Regiment* which states that whilst climbing high ground, the II and III Battalions 'got a rotten time … About a dozen English low-flying battle aeroplanes whizzed up and from an incredibly low height bombed our advancing troops. This caused great confusion…' [8]

A close examination of Victor's logbook entries shows conclusively that he used these extensively in describing Tom's flights during the following month of high activity and tension. Indeed all his flights from 21 March to 22 April can be identified when comparing take-off times, duration of patrols and incidents included in the 'Remarks' column in the logbook.

Following his crash, on his return to the Squadron in the early hours of 23 March, Tom is informed that he has a new flight commander, Capt. Beal:

> 'They say he's a proper hell-fire merchant, and when he goes out on low work he spends all his time at fifty feet.' [9]

Tom was to discover just how true this was in the next two weeks when he flew regularly with Capt. Beal on ground-attack missions. It is generally accepted that Beal is based on Victor's own flight commander during this period, Capt. Sydney Philip Smith, whom Victor would have already met as he had joined the Squadron on 6 March. Victor had not flown with him before, however, as Capt.

Army Form W 3347.

ROYAL FLYING CORPS.

REPORT ON CASUALTIES TO PERSONNEL AND MACHINES (WHEN FLYING).

INSTRUCTIONS: *To be rendered in duplicate by Squadrons to Wings. Wings to forward one copy to H.Q., R.F.C., through Brigades.*

No. 46 Squadron. No. 13th Wing. Date. Mar. 21st 1918

Type and No. of Machine: Sopwith Camel No.B.9197.

Engine No.: 110 H.P.Le Rhone Hakers No.35831 WD 29455

Pilot: 2/Lieut. V.H. Yeates.

Observer: ----

Duty: Low work.

Locality: Third Army Front.

Vickers guns carried, with gun Nos.: A.8403 & A.2430 un-damaged.

Camera (Yes or No): No.

Wireless (Yes or No): No.

Other appliances (bomb racks, etc.): 1 Aldis Sight 2" 1 Ring sight 5" & 1 bomb rack all un-damaged.

Where wrecked: Arquoves.

Short report as to fate of personnel and machine, and cause of casualty. Date and time of leaving aerodrome. Any reports, messages or conjectures received, stating source:

Pilot unhurt.
Left aerodrome:- 7.0.am. 21/3/18.
Crashed 9.5.am. 21/3/18.
Cause:- Forced landing on arable land owing to fog. Machine turned on back.

Total Flying Times.
Machine....50 hrs.10 mins.
Engine....36 " 40 "

DAMAGE. LONGERONS & FUSELAGE FRAMEWORK--Both bottom longerons broken rear engine bearer smashed. PLANES--T.L.H. main plane smashed, R.H.T. plane C.S. strained. ENGINE--apparently O.K.
Recommended that M/c be sent to 2 Aero.S.D. for repair.

Major,
Commanding No. 46 *Squadron.*

Remarks by Wing Commander as to whether machine is to be struck off, repaired in Squadron or recommended for transfer to A.D. for repair:

Machine to be returned to No.2.Aero.S.D. for repair.
In the Field,
23/3/18.

Lieut.-Colonel,
Commanding 13 *Wing.*

- 2 -

Q.3B/5992/A.3.

Remarks by Brigade Commander:

Headquarters,
Royal Flying Corps,
In the Field.

Forwarded.

Brigadier-General,
Commanding 3rd *Brigade, R.F.C.*

In the Field.
24/3/18.

OFFICIAL REPORT OF VICTOR'S CRASH ON 21 MARCH 1918.

Smith had been posted to the Squadron as a replacement for Capt. Thomson who, before his departure to HE, had himself taken the opportunity of introducing Capt. Smith to the enemy lines on a number of occasions.

Tom also learns that the Squadron had lost two pilots whilst he had been away although in reality there had been only one casualty, 2/Lt. G. E. F. Elliot who was wounded on 21 March.

Having written off his Camel in the crash and as he is not required for the next patrol, Tom takes up a new machine (D6080) which has just arrived from the Aircraft Park at Candas for a test flight – he chose this one because he liked the serial number – and then after lunch, he escorts a new pilot on a tour of the lines. These events are puzzling as there are no entries in Victor's logbook for 23 March and there is also no record of a Camel being allocated that particular serial number: his next flight according to his logbook was on 24 March in Camel C1572 which had been on the Squadron's strength since 12 March.[10]

Since Victor did not fly on 23 March he missed out on what was a memorable day in the Squadron's history as, notwithstanding it was engaged in bombing raids, it claimed seventeen enemy aircraft destroyed or driven down out of control. Victor records this event in his book as twenty victories (Gerald Hudson noted in his logbook that the Squadron had eighteen victories that day) and this may have been the number actually claimed but reduced to seventeen by Headquarters. Victor writes that one pilot, Jenkins, was lost – the Squadron did lose one pilot that day, 2/Lt. R. H. Edelston, who was shot down and taken prisoner. There was, however, a pilot by the name of Lt. G. D. Jenkins who was wounded in combat but this injury occurred four days later on 27 March.

On the following day, 24 March, correctly described as the Sunday before Easter, Victor had his first experience of being led by Capt. Smith on low work with two sorties, one at 11am when a total of twenty bombs were dropped and the second at 3pm which is recorded in his logbook as 'Low bombing, south of Bapaume'. On landing he reported that he had dropped his four bombs and fired one hundred

Lt. Ernest R. Watt

Lt. Cecil Marsden

rounds on massed enemy in shell holes north of Sailly-Saillisel, all the bombs bursting on the target. Both of these flights are recalled in the novel, the afternoon sortie being described thus:

> C Flight went out at three o'clock to visit the district south of Bapaume where the retreat was going on at the rate of a mile an hour, and something had to be done … There were swarms of Huns in shell holes or in the open … Bombs could hardly fail to do a lot of damage. …Taylor was definitely missing.[11]

The Squadron did lose one pilot that day from the 3pm patrol, Lt. J. D. Currie of C Flight, who had only joined the Squadron on 3 March but was fortunate in that he survived and became a prisoner of war. There was a pilot on the Squadron with the name of Taylor, however, 2/Lt. A. L. T. Taylor, who had been shot down the previous week on 16 March – this was the same pilot with whom Victor had a mock combat on 21 February. It may well be that Victor related the loss of Taylor in a letter to Norah written about this time, hence the reference in the book. A similar explanation could also apply to the loss of Jenkins referred to above.

There is, however, an alternative explanation which was put forward by one of Victor's fellow pilots, Ernest R. Watt.[12] He felt that the mixing of names, dates, nationalities and other facts was done intentionally and he quotes his own case to support this view. A pilot by the name of Watt, an Australian, is introduced in Chapter X of Phase Two and is allocated to B Flight at the beginning of May. On Tom's return from leave (Chapter I of Phase Three) he learns that Watt on his second flight over the lines, had shot down an Albatros in flames which was probably a record. He is killed later in the book. The reality was that Watt was a Canadian who had joined the Squadron on 22 March, and had got a Pfalz third time over but this was not in flames (the wings came off in a steep dive) and he survived the war. As there are a number of similar instances it does point to Victor on occasions deliberately mixing facts in this way, in some cases to disguise the true identity of a fellow pilot.

Tom hears that an A Flight pilot, Marsden, had been wounded and had been admitted to hospital. This character is a reference to Lt. Cecil Marsden who was wounded on 28 March which resulted in him being struck off the Squadron's strength.

That evening Beal warns Tom that he is on the dawn show the

PFALZ D.III – 'A very pretty aeroplane'

next morning to determine whether the line between Arras and Bapaume had altered, and this forthcoming flight again corresponds with the logbook entry. The Squadron's record of this patrol, led by Capt. Smith, shows that Victor dropped one bomb on a motor lorry which exploded just beside it, and three others on hutments around Marchies, two of which were seen to burst beside them, the remaining one was unobserved. He also fired one hundred rounds at the same targets.

Victor was flying again with his flight in the early afternoon as shown by the following logbook entry:

> 25/3/18 1.40pm Low bombing. Shot down at 2.10 by m.g. from ground.

The Squadron's Report of this patrol ends by stating starkly '2nd Lt. Yeates not yet returned' and the circumstances of his crash are graphically described in Chapter XIII of Phase One. Victor would have written to Norah following the crash and, bearing in mind the extensive use of the contents of his letter of 21 March in describing his first crash in France, it is reasonable to assume that the details of the events leading up to his second crash – which was due to machine-gun fire – then being taken as a spy, and his subsequent return to the Squadron, were based on a similar letter. Victor, like Tom, had crashed upside down in a shell-hole, and in later years he suspected that his inhalation of the gas which was swirling around was the probable cause of his tuberculosis.

After the outstanding achievements of the Squadron between 21 and 23 March in bringing down enemy machines as well as bombing enemy troops and equipment, Major Mealing, the C.O., wrote to the Headquarters of 13th Wing on 26 March:

> Could you please inform me what is the record for the number of enemy machines brought down by one Squadron in a day? Also can any Squadron beat 30 in 3 days? [13]

The reply was one that might have been expected:

> Owing to a number of Squadrons rumoured to be on service in

Date and Hour.	Wind Direction and Velocity.	Machine Type and No.	Passenger.	Time.	Height.	Course.	Remarks
13/3/18 {9.30 10.0		Camel B5247		20			From Candas
" {11-5 11-25		9195		20			Practice
" {11-40 1-10		9195		90			Visiting Lines
" {6.20 6.25		"		5			Engine Test
16/3/18 {12.15 12-25		D6407		10			From Candas
" 4.5-5.40		C1572		95			C.O.P. no E.A.
17/3/18 {11.25 12.0		B9197		35			To 59 Aerodrome
" {4.40 6.20		"	–	90		To 46 for mail	Practice
18/3/18 6.25 7.35	am	"		70			Low Bombing
" 12.15 2.25		"		20		To 12 for Bristol	Escort. Washed out
" 6.15 6.40	p.m.	"		25			Practice
21/3/18 6.20 6.45	a.m.	"		25			Returned Engine Trouble
" 7.0 8.30	am	"		90		?	Turned over landing at Arquèves
24/3/18 11-0 12-0		C1572		60			Low Bombing
" 3.0 4.5		"		60			" (South of 63 aerodrome)
25/3/18 6.30 7.15		"		45			" (Arras to Bapaume)
" 1.40				20			" Shot down at 2 mi) bagging from ground
28/3/18 9.25 10.20				55			Escort A flt. Turned over landing
Time on Camel to 28/3/18					34 h. 45 m		
" Solo					74 h. 5 m		

The page in Victor's logbook covering the eventful week in March 1918 when he was shot down and had two other crashes various theatres of war and to the general condition prevailing in this area, it is regretted that this information cannot be given at present.

Signed C.O. 13th Wing.

The main attack on the British 5th and 3rd Armies in the north on 21 March was unexpected – the Allies were expecting the Germans to attack further south – and the Allied line was soon crumbling. The situation became desperate and on 25 March, Major General J. M. Salmond, the General Officer Commanding the RFC in France, ordered additional squadrons from 9th Wing into the battle with these orders:

> These squadrons will bomb and shoot up everything they can see on the enemy's side of the line. Very low flying essential. All risks to be taken. URGENT.

The concerted efforts of the RFC in flying these non-stop ground-strafing sorties had a great bearing on the outcome of the battle and Salmond reported to Major General Trenchard, the Chief of Air Staff that evening:

> We have managed to concentrate 100 machines on the threatened line in the 3rd Army. They had orders to fly low and take every risk; nothing was to count in carrying out these duties.

By 26 March the crisis on the 3rd Brigade Front had ended and the Squadron received due recognition for its valuable assistance:

> 27.3.18
> The pilots of 46 Squadron have today been specially thanked by the Brigade Commander for their splendid work during the recent operations.
>
> Mealing C.O. 46 Sqdn.[14]

On returning to the Squadron after being shot down, Victor correctly recalls joining C Flight on an escort duty with A Flight on 28 March flying a Camel he had not flown before (C1617) and on landing back at the aerodrome, his machine turns over. Victor/Tom now had the unenviable distinction of having crashed three Camels in a week, as Tom tells the Medical Officer (M.O.) who visits him, as he had been feeling unwell:

> A week ago I turned over landing in a fog. I wasn't hurt. Three days ago I was shot down and turned over in a shell hole. I wasn't hurt – at least, beyond bruising my forehead. To-day I turned over landing on the aerodrome because of the wind up – I mean because of the wind. That was a damn silly thing to do, but I wasn't hurt.[15]

Tom is pronounced fit for flying but on the next day, 29 March, correctly described as being Good Friday, the weather is dud and no flights are possible. Easter Saturday dawned fine and the low bombing patrols resumed, Tom being on the early morning show when only two of his bombs would drop. Although there is no reference to this problem in his logbook, Victor himself did experience this difficulty on that day as the Squadron's records confirm that his bombs 'hung up' so presumably he again took these details from one of his letters.

News had come through that Robinson was being transferred immediately to another squadron as a flight commander and a binge to his honour would follow dinner that evening. This follows the facts as Lt. H. N. C. Robinson was transferred to No. 70 Squadron on 28 March, being promoted to Captain and flight commander.

The Royal Air Force was born on 1 April 1918 (which is described correctly as Easter Monday) with the amalgamation of the RFC and the Royal Naval Air Service. Tom takes part in a patrol, south of the Somme, without bombs, late in the afternoon but has to return early due to engine trouble. This again corresponds with Victor's logbook which shows him taking off at 4.30pm for a C.O.P. returning after seventy five minutes, his engine being dud.

The entry for Victor's first flight the next day shows that whilst he was on a combined escort duty and C.O.P. an Albatros two-seater was shot down. There is a description of this combat at the end of Chapter XVIII of Phase One when C Flight has the job of escorting A Flight on an unsuccessful balloon strafe when an Albatros is encountered. Although there is no mention of a balloon strafe in his logbook, the

Squadron's records do confirm that C Flight (with Victor) did fly on such a mission on 2 April when an Albatros two-seater was shot down. This is a further example of information being extracted from a letter to supplement the brief entry in his logbook. After tea Tom takes up a new Camel for a test flight and gunnery practice, which derives from the logbook entry 'Test new Y & gun practice'. This machine was C1637, delivered to the Squadron on 16 March.

The Squadron was well run and efficient and this was recognised by Army Headquarters in a 3 April communication to the C.O.:

> It has been stated a record by Army Headquarters that in all the low reconnaissance work carried out by this Squadron during the battle, not a single mistake has been made by any pilot on his information report. This constitutes of a record for a Scout Squadron.[16]

This accolade is recalled when he writes of an announcement being pinned to the notice board declaring that the Squadron had created a record by not sending in a single inaccurate report during the month of March, and it had also during the same month broken the record of bringing down the largest number of German machines. [17]

A new pilot by the name of Priest crashes heavily when his engine cuts out and he commits the elementary error of turning back in an attempt to land at the aerodrome instead of flying straight on. At first sight this appears to be a reference to a pilot with a similar name, Lt. G. R. Priestly, who ran into crops when taking off later in the year on 30 May. However it is more likely to be recalling Lt. W. J. Shorter who climbed too steeply when taking off, stalled, and spun into the ground on 24 March – evidence to support this conclusion comes from Gerald Hudson who had written on the relevant page in his copy of *Winged Victory* 'W. J. Shorter?' although it would seem that even he was uncertain after the passage of time.

During the previous two weeks Victor had flown regularly with his flight commander, Capt. S. P. Smith who, as already mentioned, is portrayed in his book as Capt. Beal. Tom is greatly influenced by Beal whom he sees on the one hand as a quiet unassuming person, but on the other as a fearless pilot who seems to enjoy the dangerous job of ground-strafing. This puts an ever-increasing mental strain on the other pilots in his flight as low-level ground-attack work, 'the great casualty maker', is regarded as one of the most nerve-racking and dangerous jobs that a pilot can be asked to perform. It is largely a matter of luck whether a stray bullet finds its target and there is little a flyer can do to safeguard himself. In a combat situation, a pilot's skill is paramount but it counts for little in low-level work:

> You could do very little to avoid machine-gun fire from the ground. The most cunning and experienced pilot was liable to be brought down, though he might feel perfectly safe upstairs, and cheerfully war against odds. Experience and cunning were everything there, and the war in the air was not too worrying once you were properly acclimatized; but machine-gun fire from the ground no one could get used to.[18]

It is unsurprising, therefore, to find Tom's nerves beginning to suffer under this stress and reasonable to assume that the description of his state of mind at this time will have been a reflection of Victor's own:

> The thought of going below two thousand feet over Hunland made him feel wrong in the bowels. That inescapable unpredictable fire from the ground was unnerving. How the devil much more of it would he have to go through? The alternatives seemed to be death or lunacy.[19]

Arthur Gould Lee, who flew with No. 46 Squadron in 1917, echoed Victor's opinion:

> The strain of waiting for that one bullet with your name on it, knowing you can't dodge it like you can archie, is quite petrifying. Trench-strafing can be a suicidal job, especially if you're rash, and the staff types who so casually order it can have no conception of what it demands from a pilot.[20]

There are only three instances in Victor's logbook of pilots being mentioned by name in connection with flying casualties,[21] the first being on 6 April when he records:

> Low work. Smith missing.

THE FOKKER DR.I TRIPLANE – 'Fearsome to look at'

A patrol of five Camels led by Capt. Smith (the other pilots being Victor, Lt. H. G. W. Debenham, 2/Lt. R. K. McConnell and 2/Lt. J. R. Coté) took off at 2.45pm on a low-level bombing and strafing mission and was intercepted by a group of enemy aircraft about an hour later. Capt. Smith is hit and crashes near Villers-Bretonneux. It is generally accepted that the victorious German pilot was Manfred von Richthofen ('The Red Baron') flying his Fokker Dr.I triplane who recorded his seventy-sixth victory thus:

> With five of my planes of Jasta 11, we attacked several enemy one-seaters at low altitude near Villers-Bretonneux. The English plane which I attacked started to burn after only a few shots from my guns. Then it crashed burning, near the little wood north east of Villers-Bretonneux, where it kept burning.

Victor, correctly identifying the date as 6 April, describes a bunch of Huns descending on Tom's patrol when Beal is hit and Tom observes him going down in a spin. He does not mention the aircraft being engulfed in flames however, so perhaps in the melée, Victor did not in fact witness his flight commander going down. The statement in the logbook that Smith was only missing, as opposed to killed, would support this conclusion as if he had seen a 'flamer' he would have presumed that Smith had not got out alive. He did not realise that it was Richthofen's Circus they had encountered, for if he had he would surely have referred to this in the book, and indeed he does state later in the narrative that Tom had never met the Circus as far as he knew.[22] Tom's machine was very badly shot up and is written off although Victor's own aircraft appears not to have been so severely damaged as he flew it again a few days later.

Capt. Smith was 22 years of age and had only been with the Squadron a matter of weeks, during which time he had been engaged mainly on essential ground-strafing duties:

> You got little credit for ground-strafing, although it was the most dangerous, nerve-racking, and perhaps most valuable work that scouts did. … He had gone out daily to confront incalculable death with risk-oblivious courage, without the stimulus of man-to-man combat; … He would be forgotten in a week. [23]

This lack of recognition of ground-strafing missions compared with the more newsworthy shooting down of enemy machines in aerial combat is also acknowledged in a conversation Tom has with his friend Seddon:

> 'After all, you don't get much thanks for dropping bombs, and you don't often see anything to shoot at on the ground that makes a good story in *Comic Cuts*. But if you come back from nearly every job saying "Lo, I have shot down a Hun" you are soon on the path of glory.'
>
> '*The paths of glory lead but to the grave,*
> *So little Eric shouldn't be too brave.*' [24]

Victor was of the opinion that had Capt. Smith been able to devote himself solely to aerial combat he would soon have acquired a healthy score and would have been awarded a DSO. The Squadron C.O., however, had recognised that notwithstanding the low work, Capt. Smith had accounted for a number of enemy aircraft and had already recommended him for an award:

> Never hesitated in going right down to verify the positions of enemy's front line, good enough example on 31/3/18 when he

Capt. S. P. Smith – 'Capt. Beal'

Maj. R. H. S. Mealing, C.O. 46 Sqn

> went down to 10 feet to trace the enemy's line from Albert to the Somme. 3 EA and 1 balloon in less than a month on the Squadron.

Unfortunately the recommendation had not been considered when he died.

Major Mealing wrote in his condolence letter to Capt. Smith's father that his son was 'wonderfully brave, perhaps too brave' which was a fitting tribute and one that Victor would have fully endorsed.[25]

Tom has pangs of conscience following Beal's death and it is reasonable to assume that Tom's emotions reflected Victor's own feelings over the loss of Capt. Smith:

> It was impossible not to feel glad that Beal had been killed, and it seemed the most horrible feeling he had ever had. He hadn't realized how much Beal had seized on his imagination as the complete hero, and how much he hated him as a menace to his own life and a reproach to his half-heartedness; or feared. Into what a vile morass of shame he had wandered when his instinctive feeling about the death of one of the bravest men he had ever known was relief! [26]

After a number of discussions with his hut-mates, however, who point out that several pilots had been lost under Beal's brave leadership, Tom recovers his composure and squares his conscience when his friend Williamson explains that it is not Beal's death but the knowledge that he would no longer have to fly with him on low-level missions which he is pleased about.

Following the halt in the German advance, General Ludendorff had called off the German offensive on 5 April, but three days later he attacked again on a ten-mile front near Armentières on the river Lys. Among the Allied forces was a Portuguese Division which was quickly overrun, the Germans taking six thousand prisoners. Victor recorded this in the form of the following reflections by Tom:

> The Germans had made a sudden onslaught on the Portuguese who were holding a sector of the line south of Armentières and had chased them off the earth. … But what were the Portuguese doing in the front line? Had Haig and Co. no idea there might be an attack? [27]

The Allied position soon deteriorated and RAF fighter squadrons were once again ordered to ground-strafe and bomb the attacking troops. No. 46 Squadron received orders to join those squadrons in the north to help alleviate the position as Victor writes:

> 'We take over a new part of the line to-morrow, Cundall. North of Arras to Nieppe Forest.'
> 'Oh,' said Tom; and then: 'That takes us on to the new push front, doesn't it?'
> 'Yes,' replied Mac, passing on.
> Tom was staggered. Another push for them to stop. The brightness went out of the evening.[28]

The situation had become so serious that on 11 April, the Allied Commander, General Sir Douglas Haig, issued his famous 'backs to the wall' Special Order of the Day. Victor refers to this when Tom sees an Order on the notice board to the B.E.F. from G.H.Q.:

> It began by suggesting that they were all splendid fellows: an ominous beginning from which the purport of the whole might be guessed. G.H.Q. evidently had complete wind up. There is no other course open

> to us but to fight it out. Every position must be held to the last man. There must be no retirement. 'With our backs to the wall and believing in the justice of our cause, each one of us must fight to the end.' [29]

Later that day it was announced that the hated bombing and ground-strafing duties were cancelled and the Squadron was detailed patrolling duties along the new line. The news was greeted with delight by the pilots, knowing that they would, at last, be released from the mental strain and danger of the constant low bombing missions and the thought of returning to comparatively safe offensive patrols was viewed with enthusiasm. It was at this point, 11 April, that Victor decided it would be appropriate to conclude Phase One, the first part of his novel.

Notes

1 *WV*, p. 37.
2 Gerald Hudson's logbook in author's possession – his entry for 10 March reads 'Fighting Yeates.'
3 Gerald Hudson obtained a copy of *WV* in the early 1960's and annotated it in a number of places. He wrote on p. 39 that it was General Sefton Brancker who visited the Squadron on 10 March 1918.
4 Hudson wrote in his flying logbook on 11 April 'McCudden came to dinner at night.' Major James McCudden VC, DSO and Bar, MC and Bar, CdeG had joined the RFC as a mechanic in 1913 and rose to become a Flight Commander with No. 56 Squadron before returning to England as a flying instructor. In July 1918 he was given command of No. 60 Squadron in France. Whilst heading to his new Squadron he was killed in a flying accident when the engine in his SE5a (C1126) cut out after taking off on 9 July 1918. He had scored 57 victories.
5 *WV*, p. 73.
6 The Aeroplane Park would have been No. 2 Aircraft Depot at Candas.
7 In *WV* Victor writes mistakenly that the mechanics were from No. 72 Squadron – this Squadron was not in fact in France at this time. It is likely that their unit was No. 70 Squadron, based nearby at Marieux.
8 H. A. Jones, *The War in the Air*, OUP 1934, Vol 4, p. 300.

9 *WV*, p. 91.
10 Serial No. D6080 was allocated to an SE5a.
11 *WV*, pp. 102/5.
12 Letter to the author from E. R. Watt dated 22 March 1974.
13 NA AIR1/1430.
14 NA AIR1/1430/204/31/28.
15 *WV*, p. 128.
16 NA AIR1/1430/20/31/28.
17 NA AIR1/204/58/35. No. 46 Squadron History states that 30 enemy machines were brought down in three days.
18 *WV*, pp. 31/32.
19 Ibid., pp. 153/4.
20 Arthur Gould Lee, *No Parachute*, Jarrolds 1968, pp. 193/4. The book is an account of the author's war service on No. 46 Squadron from May 1917 to January 1918. He continued in the RAF after the war and rose to the rank of Air Vice-Marshal, retiring in 1946. He also wrote a number of other books including *Open Cockpit* published by Jarrolds in 1969.
21 The other pilots named are 2/Lt. R. L. G. Skinner (3 May) 'Missing' and Lt. J. R. Orr (9 August) 'Killed.'
22 *WV*, p. 216. The term 'Circus' was coined by the British pilots as the German aircraft were painted in bright colours – Richthofen's own aircraft was painted bright red hence the usual reference to him as 'The Red Baron.'
23 Ibid., p. 174.
24 Ibid., p. 93. The first line of the verse is taken from Thomas Gray's *Elegy Written in a Country Churchyard.*
25 Norman Franks, Hal Giblin & N. McCrery, *Under the Guns of the Red Baron*, Grub Street 1998, p. 194.
26 *WV*, p. 175.
27 Ibid., pp. 189/190.
28 Ibid., p. 191.
29 Ibid., p. 192.

CHAPTER SIX

FIRST VICTORY

With a new line to patrol, the pilots' first priority was to acquaint themselves with the unfamiliar terrain and on the following morning, 12 April, the Squadron flew north to inspect the ground and look for distinctive landmarks. In *Winged Victory*, Tom takes off at 10am (Victor took off at 9.35am) and in the course of the flight his patrol climbs towards a number of enemy machines although no combats ensue – this flight is taken from the logbook entry which reads 'New line. Clouds. Climbed at EA.' Immediately after lunch, Tom joins C Flight to escort two RE8s from No. 5 Squadron which was based nearby at Acq on a reconnaissance mission. After the successful completion of the reconnaissance, the RE8s are escorted back over Allied territory when Mac who is leading the flight, spots two separate two-seater Albatros scouts and in the engagements that follow, both are seen to crash. It is interesting to examine this flight in some detail. The logbook entry reads:

Escort RE8s 5 Sqn. 2 Alb. Fighters

The Combat Report of this action shows that five pilots took part but MacLaren was not with C Flight on this occasion although he had been promoted to Captain and C Flight commander following the death of Capt. S. P. Smith on 6 April. The flight was led by Lt. H. G. W. Debenham, the others being Lt. A. G. Vlasto, Lt. H. L. M. Dodson, 2/Lt. R. K. McConnell and 2/Lt. V. M. Yeates. The Combat Report submitted reads:

Two Albatros Fighters
Whilst on escort to RE8s of No. 5 Squadron an Albatros

> Fighter dived on one of the RE8s to attack it crossing the front of the patrol. Lt. Vlasto dived on E.A. firing 300 rounds from 125 to 50 yards range. Lt. Debenham and Lt. Dodson then dived on E.A. firing 200 rounds apiece from 100 to 50 yards range. Lt. Debenham who was attacking E.A. from behind saw the observer standing up moving his gun into position, but before he could reply he collapsed into his cockpit as though killed and 2/Lt. McConnell then fired 200 rounds at 150 yards range. E.A. was diving steeply E. by now and 2/Lt. Yeates got in a short burst of 50 rounds at about 200 yards range. Lt. Vlasto last saw this E.A. at about 100ft. apparently going to land at Quiéry-la-Motte. Another E.A. same type dived past the patrol to let his observer shoot. 2/Lt. McConnell pulled out of his dive on the first E.A. and fired about 100 rounds at 50 yards range as it dived passed him. The observer who was standing up firing collapsed. 2/Lt. McConnell turned to see if any more E.A. were attacking and lost sight of this E.A. but it did not appear again.[1]

The flight claimed one E. A. driven down and one driven off but Capt. Thom, the Adjutant and acting C.O., reduced this claim to 'Two indecisive combats.' Victor concluded from the brief comment in his logbook that both the Albatros fighters had been shot down, as portrayed in the narrative. In reality, however, neither machine was seen to crash and the Combat Report indicates that the attacks took place whilst the patrol was still escorting the RE8s unlike the description in the novel.

These formal official reports did not record, of necessity, the tension and excitement of the pilots' experiences as Victor recalls:

> Tom was always interested in the great difference between the queer exotic reality and the terse official narrative which recorded that reality for the practical world.[2]

The next entry in the logbook, also on 12 April, shows that he took off again at 5.45pm and he wrote in the 'Remarks' column:

> RE8 crashed. Landed at 5.

THE ROYAL AIRCRAFT FACTORY RE8
'To go on active service in such an ark was an occupation for heroes ...'

Whilst walking with another pilot on the aerodrome after tea, Tom sees an RE8 crash and having recognised from the markings that it was a machine from No. 5 Squadron, he flies to its base at Acq to report the incident. This accurately reflects the entry in Victor's logbook and the records show that Lt. Lewis Mogridge and his observer Lt. R. H. Boyd of No. 5 Squadron were killed in a flying accident that day and are buried at Aubigny-en-Artois close to the Squadron's aerodrome.

Victor was very disparaging about the 'wretched' RE8s which were known throughout the service as 'Harry Tates' (after a famous comedian of the time, whose name rhymed with the aircraft's designation) and which were slow and an easy target for enemy fighters. They also had a tendency to spin into the ground and this reputation resulted in questions being raised in the House of Commons pertaining to their general safety.

Correctly describing the next three days as being dud, Victor did not take to the air again until the late afternoon on 16 April when his patrol encountered heavy cloud, forcing it to return after forty minutes. Low work returned the following day after only five days respite, but the weather once again worsened and the flight returned with their bombs still intact. Again, due to the inclement weather no flying was possible during the next forty-eight hours. All these events are correctly recorded in the novel.

The Squadron was successful in the late morning of 21 April in shooting down an Albatros scout and two balloons as Victor's logbook indicates:

COP 1 Alb. Scout. 2 Balloons.

This combat is accurately portrayed in *Winged Victory* when Tom's friend Seddon is credited with a Hun and two balloons are also destroyed, but in reality MacLaren was the successful pilot. Later that day a rumour began circulating that Manfred von Richthofen had been killed: this was confirmed the following day. Victor accurately relates the report that the German had been shot down by Brown, a Camel pilot who was a flight commander with a former naval squadron (No. 209) although recent research has since established that Richthofen was killed by machine gun fire from the ground. He writes that as far as he knew, Tom had not encountered Richthofen or his Circus but, as has been shown, in all probability Victor met the

The Albatros D.Va
'In the spring a brighter war paint decorates the flying Hun'

Circus on 6 April when Capt. Smith was lost.

On 29 April Victor left on a practice bombing flight at 11. 25am and had a score of 15-18-10-16, these figures again being the distance in yards his bombs landed from the target. The records of the Squadron show that Victor crashed Camel B9271 on landing that day and although he was again uninjured, the machine was so badly damaged it was sent to the Repair Park, and not returned to the Squadron until 2 July. It is surprising, therefore, to find that the crash is not mentioned in his logbook as the bombing practice run is shown. It is quite possible, however, that like Tom, he had a further flight later in the day which resulted in the crash which he failed to record. On his return, he would have been told that 2/Lt. E. J. Smith when on a low bombing mission had been seen to spin into the ground just inside the British lines when hit by machine gun fire.

These events are faithfully recalled in Chapter VII of Phase Two when Tom is left behind from a patrol, and on its return he learns that his friend Smith had spun into the ground having been hit by ground fire near the front line. Tom then goes up for some bombing practice and has the same indifferent score (which he blamed on the wind) as mentioned above except that Victor writes that the distance from the marker was in feet rather than yards. Tom takes off again for some firing practice in windy conditions when his engine misfires, and on landing the machine turns over on its nose causing the wrath of his flight commander. As mentioned above, Victor's logbook does not record this flight, so to have included the crash in the correct context and date order, he will have again extracted the information from one of his letters to Norah.

On the following day, 30 April, C Flight with Tom, takes off at 11.25am and encounters two LVG two-seaters which are shot down, one by Mac and the other, which was engulfed in flames, was a joint effort in which Tom was involved. Although Victor did not fly on 30 April and the Squadron did not claim any victories that day, this action appears to correspond with his morning flight of 3 May as the date is in chronological order in the narrative, having identified his crash landing and 2/Lt. Smith's death as occurring on 29 April.

2/Lt. E. J. Smith who was killed on 29 April 1918

2/Lt. R. L. G. Skinner who was shot down and killed on 3 May 1918

On Tom's second flight at 4.30pm the patrol engages a number of Pfalz and five are claimed although in reality no enemy aircraft were shot down during the afternoon sortie on 3 May. A Pfalz, however, was shot down by Lt. Vlasto during the morning patrol at 1.30pm that day. The remarks in Victor's logbook for these two patrols run into one another, which may be the reason why the reference to the combat with the Pfalz is described as being during the afternoon patrol rather than the morning one. The entries read:

3/5/18
11.25/1.25 COP. 2 2Seaters. LVG. Vlasto Pfalz & Balloon. Skinner missing.
4.30/7.50 COP. No EA. Trenches. Forced landing next field.

This is the second occasion Victor refers to a casualty by name in his logbook, the pilot being 2/Lt. R. L. G. Skinner who was shot down in flames at 1pm. In his book, however, he portrays Tom's friend Seddon being shot down in flames that day, although it is interesting to note that he actually records a pilot named Skinner being killed in early

April. Tom's friend Williamson is initially missing but turns up later in similar circumstances to that of Lt. J. R. Coté, who had to make a forced landing when his aircraft (B5585) was badly damaged during the morning patrol although he was uninjured.

According to the logbook entry Victor suffered a forced landing on the afternoon patrol but as this accident is not recorded in the Squadron's records, any damage to his aircraft must have been slight and repaired on the Squadron — he flew the same machine (C1637) until 11 May when he crashed again near the aerodrome.

A further pointer to 3 May is the comment by Tom's batman that Seddon's death was the second in two days, Smith having been killed the previous day. The records do show that a pilot Lt. L. C. Hickey was killed on the previous day (2 May), whilst 2/Lt. E. J. Smith had been killed only three days earlier on 29 April.

The Combat Report submitted by Victor and MacLaren for their victories on their morning patrol on 3 May indicates that MacLaren got an LVG in flames and then:

> Later Capt. MacLaren engaged two more two-seaters NW of Don at 14000ft diving on one from the rear. Capt. MacLaren fired 50 rds at 50yds range. 2/Lt. Yeates also fired 50 rds at 150yds range. E.A. then attacked a Camel which dived away from it. On seeing this Capt. MacLaren again dived at E.A. firing another 50 rds at 50yds range. The right hand wings came off and E.A. crashed hopelessly.[3]

It will be seen that although the two-seater which crashed was not a 'flamer' and no aircraft were shot down from the 4.30pm patrol unlike the description in the book, the other events portrayed would seem to be largely based on fact and Victor's own experiences of 3 May.

Writing in the next chapter, however, Victor records that the date was May Day, 1 May, i.e. two days before the events described above. He then goes on to describe a patrol in which Mac shoots down an Albatros, and then on finding a two-seater, Tom dives down with his flight commander and sees it crash to the ground, one of its wings collapsing. This description also accords with the Combat Report of

W6180—778 20,000 9/16 HWV(P1484/1) Forms/W3348/2
10432 M1079 30,000 11/16

Army Form ~~W.~~ 3348.

50

Combats in the Air.

No.123.

Squadron: No.46

Date: 3-5-18.

Type and No. of Aeroplane:
Sop. Camel B.9153, C.1637.

Time: (1) 12.30 pm.
(2) 1.o/c pm.

Armament:
2 Vickers.

Duty: O.P.

Pilot: Capt.D.R.MacLaren. M.C.
2/Lt.V.M.Yeates.

Height: (1) 12000 ft.
(2) 14000 ft.

~~Observer~~:

Locality: (1) ~~[illegible]~~. S. BAILLEUL
(2) N.W. DON.

Two E.A. destroyed.

Remarks on Hostile machine:—Type, armament, speed, etc.

(1) L.V.G. 2 Seater
(2) Supposed Halberstadt 2 Seater.

— Narrative. —

S. BAILLEUL

Whilst on O.P. ~~near [illegible]~~ Capt.MacLaren saw an E.A. 2 seater working N. of Line at 12,000 feet. Capt. MacLaren attacked, dived firing 75 rds. at 50 yds. range. E.A. half rolled underneath him, and made a slight turn, from that fell into a spin and 2000 ft. down burst into flames.(Confirmed by Pilots of No. 41 Squadron.) Later Capt. MacLaren engaged two more two-seaters N.W. of DON at 14,000 ft. diving on one from the rear. Capt. MacLaren fired 50rds. at 50 yds. range. 2/Lt. Yeates also fired 50rds. at 150 yards range. E.A. then attacked a Camel which dived away from it. On seeing this Capt. MacLaren again dived on E.A. firing another 50 rds. at 50 yards range. The right hand wings came off and E.A. crashed hopelessly at T 17 d, Sheet 36, approx.

D.R. MacLaren.....Captain.

V.M. Yeates.....2/Lieut.

Major,
Commanding No. 46 Squadron. R.A.F.

Combat report of Victor's first victory, on 3 May 1918

3 May quoted above except that it was an LVG and not an Albatros which MacLaren shot down earlier. It would seem, therefore, that Victor has based both of Tom's combats of 30 April and 3 May on his own experiences of 3 May. Tom later recalls seeing a Summary of Work of the 1st Brigade to which No. 46 Squadron was then attached, in which his 3 May combat was included:

> Later the same pilot (Captain MacAndrews) attacked another E.A. this time a two-seater, NW of Harnes. He and Lt. Cundall fired many bursts into it. The right-hand planes were seen to fall off, and the E.A. crashed at Estevelles. [4]

RAF Headquarters' staff produced weekly Communiqués of the air activity which were mainly prepared from the Combat Reports submitted by the pilots, and these were circulated amongst the squadrons on the Western Front. Although written in a formal matter-of-fact way, the pilots christened them after a popular children's comic, *Comic Cuts*. Victor had referred to these when writing about Tom agonising over Beal's death, comparing the less newsworthy but courageous low-level patrols with the more glamorous pursuit of shooting down the Hun:

> ... there was no red triumph of broken or burning enemies reeling down the skies to be entombed in the perky officialese of *Comic Cuts*.[5]

Victor's success of 3 May was his first victory and was included in the Communiqué for the week 29 April to 5 May:

> Later Capt. MacLaren engaged two more E.A. two-seaters, diving on one from the rear and firing 50 rounds into it from 50 yards range. 2 Lt. V. M. Yeates, of the same squadron, also fired 50 rounds into this E.A. Capt. MacLaren then dived on the E.A. again, firing another 50 rounds into it. The right-hand wings came off and the E.A. was seen to crash.[6]

It can be seen that the wording of this Communiqué is very similar to that of the Combat Report on which it was based and also the Summary of Work quoted by Victor to which reference has already been made.

Capt. D. R. MacLaren (r) with fellow Canadian Lt. J. H. Smith at Izel in front of an engine from a Gotha

Victor did not fly again until 6 May when he went up for a thirty minute practice flight before lunch. This was followed by a Squadron show led by MacLaren after tea when the weather had cleared. They found a Hun two-seater unusually on the Allied side of the lines which is noted in the logbook, and the ensuing combat is described quite vividly at the beginning of Chapter XI of Phase Two, the aircraft being shot down by Mac and Tom. It was notable as it was one of the new DFWs, a type Tom had not seen before. Victor describes the observer being shot and the machine spinning and burning before crashing. This corresponds with the known facts, as the Combat Report submitted indicates that the observer collapsed in his cockpit and the machine (described as a new type DFW) went down 'rolling and spinning, emitting volumes of black smoke and crashed to pieces'. This success also appeared in the weekly Communiqué for the week 6 – 12 May showing the victory being shared by the five pilots on the patrol, Capt. D. R. MacLaren, Capt. C. J. Marchant, 2/Lt. J. H. Smith, 2/Lt. V. M. Yeates and 2/Lt. H. T. W. Manwaring.

Soon after landing Victor took off again in search of the remains of the downed enemy aircraft – the entry in his logbook reads, 'Search for remains up N'. He records Tom and Mac looking for the crash site but without success.

May was proving to be an eventful month as Victor had already had a share of two victories, both being mentioned in the *Comic Cuts*, and had experienced a forced landing without injury. The action continued three days later on 9 May, when he had his second forced landing in the month which was closely followed by a further crash two days later – both of these occurrences are covered in *Winged Victory* although in reverse order.

The narrative describes Tom, after lunch, buzzing a group of Canadians who are holding a sports day at the far side of the aerodrome, when his engine stops which results in a stall and his subsequent crash. These events can be identified from Victor's logbook as having taken place on his 2.45pm flight on 11 May, the logbook entry being 'Crash Izel.' The report of the accident which he submitted states that he was on a practice flight in Camel C1637 when he crashed near the aerodrome at 3.15pm.[7] The cause of the crash was a sudden fall of pressure due to a breakage of a pipe to the

A CAPTURED DFW C.V
' – a nice looking, very splitarse bus'

Sopwith Camel C1659 'W' which Victor was flying on 9 May 1918 when he suffered engine failure which resulted in a forced landing.
The aircraft was undamaged and was flown back to the Squadron the following day by Lt. H.G.W. Debenham, seen here standing by the machine. He usually flew this aircraft, in which he recorded two victories.
Five days later Lt. C.H. Sawyer crashed the machine on landing. It was subsequently rebuilt at the Repair Park at Marquise and renumbered F5938.

mechanical pump – Tom discovers that his engine failure had been due to a broken pressure pipe. Victor was again fortunate to escape injury as the machine was so extensively damaged that it was struck off the Squadron's strength and scrapped.

In the morning, as his new Camel was not yet ready, Tom borrows Dubois' machine as it was his day off. The ensuing patrol sees Miller bring down a triplane and on his next flight after tea, Tom has to make another forced landing when his engine stops. On the following day Tom and Dubois visit the site to recover the machine and after rectifying the engine fault, Dubois flies his aircraft back to the aerodrome.

The forced landing can be identified as having taken place on 9 May, i.e. two days before Victor's crash at Izel referred to above, a further example of factual events being included out of their strict chronological order. In reality Victor was flying Debenham's aircraft (C1659) that day as it was his day off and a triplane was shot down by Lt. Dodson on the morning patrol. On the early evening patrol Victor's logbook indicates that he made a forced landing at 7.50pm and the records show that Lt. Debenham, like his character Dubois, retrieved his machine the following day, 10 May, and flew it back to the Squadron.

As a result of his earlier crash at Izel when his machine was damaged beyond repair, Tom is allocated Camel D6585 which is described as being brand new. This is correct, as a machine with this serial number had only been delivered to the Squadron a few days earlier on 4 May and Victor took the number from his logbook entry of 14 May which reads 'Test new D6585.' [8]

Victor now sends Tom on two weeks leave which is a fitting break in the narrative to close Phase Two. Tom needs a rest from the fighting and his nerves by this time are jagged. Like many other servicemen both before and after, the sight of seeing his native England again after months away fills him with emotion:

> He had forgotten how lovely England was. All this incredible, jocund, casual beauty … it was difficult to keep back tears. He resented the emotion, fought it, called it murderous, deceitful. If it had been a dull and rainy evening — but it was useless. The emotion constricted his throat; it seemed deep and real; all his other feelings appeared shallow and meretricious in the shock of discovering how unquenchable, how real was his love of England.[9]

Notes

1 NA AIR1/1223/204/5/2634 Combat Report.
2 *WV*, p. 286.
3 NA AIR1/ 1223/204/5/2634 Combat Report.
4 *WV*, p.275.
5 Ibid., p. 174.

6 Christopher Cole (editor), *Royal Air Force Communiqués 1918*, Tom Donovan 1990, Communiqué No. 5.
7 NA Report on Casualties to Personnel and Machines (When Flying).
8 Ray Sturtivant & Gordon Page, *The Camel File*, Air Britain Publication 1993.
9 *WV*, p. 298.

CHAPTER SEVEN

THE STRESS OF COMBAT FLYING

On 16 May the Squadron moved north from Filescamp Farm, Izel-le-Hameau, to an aerodrome south of St-Omer, officially called Liettres, although it was generally known as Estrée-Blanche, after the larger of the two villages. This is recalled at the beginning of Phase Three in *Winged Victory* when Tom, returning from leave on 27 May, travels to his old base at Izel only to find that the Squadron has departed. Victor, however, had still been on the Squadron when this move took place, as he did not start his leave until 6 June. Interestingly the Squadron moved again whilst Victor himself was on leave, transferring from Estrée-Blanche to Serny on 17 June. It is quite possible that Victor had gone to Estrée-Blanche on 21 June when he returned from leave only to find that the Squadron had left four days earlier, which prompted him to write of Tom travelling to his former aerodrome at Izel on his return to France. He sent Tom on his fourteen days leave, therefore, three weeks earlier than himself and this may have been because he felt the book was, by this time, quite long (300 pages) and it made a natural break in the story-line to bring Phase Two to an end.

On Tom's return to the Squadron, Victor reverted again to his logbook to record Tom's flights to 6 June, the date when he himself went on leave. In the notebooks in which he wrote *Winged Victory*, Victor began to insert dates when writing this section of the book. He inserted '27 May' at the beginning of Chapter I of Phase Three, being the date in the story when Tom returns to the Squadron from leave, with Chapter II being prefaced by '28 May.' He entered each day from 27 May to 7 June, and the insertion of dates at this juncture was done to assist him in keeping track of the date order in the narrative as he was not adhering to the strict chronological order of the events referred to in his flying logbook.

In the published book, however, the first date actually mentioned in Phase Three is towards the end of Chapter II, 1 June, and it is not until Chapter VIII that we find the next date quoted which is 23 June. This latter date is significant, being the date when Victor made his first flight on returning to the Squadron from leave, and many of his later patrols can be identified in the following chapters.

Tom's first flight, therefore, prefaced '28 May' in the manuscript, is with C Flight on the dawn show. The patrol meets a number of enemy scouts and in the resulting scrap Mac shoots down an Albatros. The logbook entry for 28 May shows that Victor took off at 5.30am and landed at 7.30am, although there is no mention of an enemy aircraft being shot down. An examination of the Squadron's records, however, confirms that an Albatros was indeed shot down at 6.50am by MacLaren so Victor, once more, has obtained this additional information from one of his letters. Tom's second flight that day is at 7.30pm when the whole Squadron is airborne but everything is quiet and no hostile aircraft are seen. This accords with the records which state that fifteen aircraft were on patrol, but there was no enemy activity.

The action portrayed under the date of '30 May' in the manuscript, however, would appear to relate to a combat which took place earlier in the month on 15 May. C Flight takes off at 11.30am and towards Armentières, a large formation of eleven Pfalz is encountered. In the melée that follows, five are shot down. Tom is accredited with one of these, Mac claims two with Baker and Cross each bringing an aircraft down. In reality, the records do show that five Pfalz were shot down that day, Capt. MacLaren and Lt. Vlasto were each credited with two victories whilst Victor had the remaining one to his credit. His logbook entry for 15 May states briefly:

11-30 / 1-15 C.O.P. 5 Pfalz scouts down.

but he describes Tom, after shooting down the Pfalz, having to switch over to gravity feed following pressure problems. Although not referred to in his logbook, Victor experienced similar difficulties himself on this patrol as is evidenced by the following extract from the pilots' Combat Report:

> 15/5/18
> Lt. Yeates who had pressure trouble at first, having switched on to gravity dived on a Pfalz which was turning under him firing a long burst from 100 to 30 yards range. E.A. went down vertically turning erratically obviously out of control. The pilots were unable to follow machines down owing to the presence of other E.A.

The Report also confirms that eleven enemy aircraft were encountered and five were destroyed. The only small discrepancy between the account in the book and the factual report is that in the book, the pressure problem occurred after the combat whilst the official report indicates that Victor shot down the machine after rectifying the fault. Again it can be assumed that the detailed account of the encounter was gleaned from one of his letters.

Victor was by now one of the more experienced pilots on the Squadron, having been in France for four months and having survived the 'March push.' On 1 June he had his first opportunity of acting as flight commander, leading C Flight on two patrols at 6.35am and 7pm which are noted in the logbook although no enemy aircraft were seen. These flights are recalled towards the end of Chapter II of Phase Three – Tom is leader on two identical patrols when Mac has a day off although no enemy aircraft were in range. The narrative also dates these correctly as occurring on 1 June.

On the following day, 2 June, Tom goes over to the aerodrome at Rely to collect his aircraft, which had been borrowed by another pilot who had made a forced landing following engine trouble, and afterwards he flies around the battlefield. Although the logbook entry for 2 June reads 'From Rely', the records show that Victor did not fly his own aircraft that day, but simply collected a rebuilt Camel (B5409) from the Aircraft Issues Section at Rely and ferried it back to the Squadron, the flight lasting a mere fifteen minutes.

Victor was now faced with a dilemma as there were no entries in his logbook for the next two weeks, since he himself had been on leave between 6 and 20 June. To solve this difficulty, he reverted to the events which took place earlier from 18 May to 31 May, which he had not related before, as Tom is portrayed as having been on leave at that time. Under the date of 4 June in the manuscript, therefore, he picks up the story again by describing correctly the events of 18 May which was an uneventful day, Tom having two patrols when no enemy aircraft were encountered.

Tom's engine is playing up the next day, and although he again has two patrols, no hostile aircraft are seen which corresponds with the remarks in Victor's logbook of 19 May. On the following day, however, Victor saw some action. During the early morning Squadron show, although his engine was still not running properly, he witnessed B Flight shooting down two two-seaters. In the afternoon, MacLaren increased his score by shooting down another two-seater and was also accredited with one balloon and shared another with Victor and Lt. J. R. Coté. These events are related in Chapter III of Phase Three, although Tom is described as shooting down the second balloon himself, whilst Victor was only accredited with a one third share. Attacking balloons was a dangerous occupation as they were heavily defended with a circle of anti-aircraft batteries and pilots did not relish such attacks. As Victor wrote:

> Tom found that his mouth was dry and foul. The way the Huns protected their balloons was wonderful. It was miraculous that they had all got away. The sky had been full of death.[1]

He had expanded these thoughts in a further paragraph which was ultimately omitted when he edited the manuscript for publication:

> A balloon strafe was never a pleasant job as it aroused the black hating heart of Archie and his balloon-protecting assistants' dysphoric bursts. Not only did he put up a barrage and bombard you individually having your height to a millimetre, but added to his terrors with quick firing pom-poms and with flaming onions, queer bubbles of smoky

> phosphorescence that come floating up as though you were in a glass of champagne; or little strings of flaming onions. If you touched one you were down in flames. These terrors could not stop a determined attack, but they certainly took all the pleasure out of it; it seemed impossible that a man could get through all that stuff more than once in a lifetime.

When Tom lands he has been out for nearly two and a half hours and this corresponds with the entry in the logbook for 20 May, which shows Victor taking off at 4.05pm and returning at 6.25pm, a flight time of two hours and twenty minutes. Victor comments that there were two casualties that day but in reality no pilots were lost.

At the beginning of Chapter IV of Phase Three, prefaced by 7 June in the manuscript, Tom is again acting flight commander, and on his first job at 8am a formation of Pfalz is seen, and then the patrol encounters an LVG which is shot down in flames. Tom feels for the crew of the solitary two-seater and the failure of the Pfalz to come to their rescue:

> 'You bloody skunks,' he yelled at them. Christ almighty, what were they doing up there, leaving that wretched LVG to look after itself? [2]

Victor's Combat Report of this flight which took place on 22 May confirms the victory, the enemy aircraft going down in flames,

A captured L.V.G. C.VI

W6180—778 20,000 9/16 HWV(P1484/1) Forms/W3348/2
10432 M1079 30,000 11/16

Army Form W. 3348. 39

Combats in the Air.

No. 135.

Squadron: No. 46

Date: 22nd. May. 1918.

Type and No. of Aeroplane: Sop. Camel B.2522 - D.6585 - D.6424 - C.1675.

Time: 9.20 a.m.

Armament: 2 Vickers guns each.

Duty: Off. Patrol.

Pilot: Lt. A.G. Vlasto. Lt. J.R.Cote.
~~Observer~~ Lt. V.M. Yeates.
Lt. N. Bruce.

Height: 7,000 feet.

Result. 1 E.A. destroyed.

Locality: West of ESTAIRES.

Remarks on Hostile machine:—Type, armament, speed, etc.

L.V.G. two-seater (new type)

— Narrative. —

Whilst on O.P. at 9.20 a.m. and L.V.G. two-seater was observed flying S.W. over ESTAIRES at 7,000 ft. The patrol got into the sun and Lt. Vlasto dived on E.A. firing 70 rds. at 200 to 150 yds. range. Lt. Yeates then dived firing a short burst. Lt. Vlasto dived again, firing 50 rds. at 100 yds. range. The Observer who had been firing, ceased as though hit. Lts. Yeates, Cote and Bruce then dived firing about 100 rds. each, at 150 to 100 yds. range. E.A. was diving rapidly East at this time. Lt. Vlasto dived a third time on E.A!s tail, firing a short burst of about 50 rds. at 100 yds. range. E.A. went down steeply giving out clouds of smoke and was later seen by Lt. Manwaring to burst into flames. E.A. was last seen going down very steeply in flames at about 3,000 ft. Patrol was unable to follow the L.V.G. down owing to the presence of numerous E.A. scouts assembling above them.

..................Lt.

..................Lt.

..................Lt.

..................Lt.

On e decisive combat.

Major,

Commanding No. 46 Squadron. RAF.

COMBAT REPORT FOR C FLIGHT'S SUCCESSFUL LVG ENCOUNTER ON 22 MAY 1918 although it appears that Lt. Vlasto was the leader of the patrol. The victory was officially shared between four pilots, Vlasto, Victor, Coté and Bruce. The Report also confirms that due to the presence of other enemy aircraft the flight was unable to follow the LVG down to where it crashed.

The weather closed in during the morning of the following day and Mac rounds up a number of his fellow C Flight pilots, taking a tender to St-Omer to have lunch at the Treille d'Or. This was a popular estaminet with the officers and Gerald Hudson recalled dining there on a number of occasions. As was usual, the wine flowed freely, and they were surprised when the weather cleared up and C Flight was required to fly a patrol. Tom takes off in a drunken haze and after avoiding a number of enemy triplanes, he finds himself over a German aerodrome where he attacks a two-seater just becoming airborne. His luck holds, and he manages to get back to base intact where he reports his success and concocts a report of the attack on the aerodrome at Cardin. Mac, who was leading the patrol, is successful in shooting down a triplane. Victor's logbook does not record this attack and as he is not accredited with another victory until 3 August, it would appear that this account is fictional, although it may have been based on an actual event, possibly by one of his fellow pilots. In reality a number of triplanes were observed on Victor's patrol of 23 May, but none were destroyed although MacLaren shot down a Pfalz as noted in his logbook.

HOTEL DE LA TREILLE D'OR
GARAGE & STABLES
16, RUE D'ARRAS
SAINT-OMER
ROGÉRÉ-MERLIER

At this point in the narrative, i.e. late May, Victor recalls a binge taking place to celebrate Mac being awarded the DFC. MacLaren did receive this distinction, but not until some three months later in August – it was gazetted on 21 September 1918. If such a celebration did take place towards the end of May, it is more likely to have been for the award of a bar to his MC which was received that month. Victor describes Mac celebrating this honour with a number of his fellow Canadians in St-Omer when he returns to the aerodrome somewhat the worse for wear. MacLaren, however, was a teetotaller, so it is strange that Victor relates this incident and it would seem that he deliberately departed from factual events or alternatively, MacLaren did, for once, let his hair down.

On another visit to St-Omer, Tom meets a 'snubbed nosed' former No. 46 Squadron pilot, Lt. Marsden, who having recovered from wounds, is awaiting posting. He hopes he will not be returning to the Squadron as he does not like Camels with Le Rhône engines – he was eventually posted to No. 210 Squadron. This description fits with that of Lt. Cecil Marsden who was wounded on 28 March when he was shot down on the British side of the lines and suffered concussion. Victor had referred to this pilot in Phase One whom he described again as a 'snubbed nosed Midlander' (although he actually came from Darwen in Lancashire) and who was in hospital having been injured by a bullet in his left arm.

On the following day Tom has two patrols, the morning one uneventful due to poor weather, whilst during a successful evening patrol with B Flight, a group of six Pfalz are encountered which are shot down by B Flight. These flights are based on the logbook entries of 27 May which show that the morning patrol was dud. The comments for the 7.50pm flight read 'B Flight – 2 Pfalz' which indicate that only two enemy aircraft were accounted for by the joint patrol, which is confirmed by the Squadron's records.

A few days later, Tom takes off with the Squadron to bomb a Hun aerodrome but he encounters serious problems when suddenly his windscreen is shattered, he loses his engine cowling and his prop stops. He manages to glide into the nearby aerodrome at Serny, where No. 22 Squadron which flew Bristol F.2B fighters was based, and here he meets up with Lt. Christie whom he had known from his training days at Croydon. Victor's logbook entry for his flight on 30 May states simply 'Tappet rod' but again the detailed description of the incident fits the known facts. The official Damage Report of 30 May states that the cylinder tee piece broke, the clip tore loose smashing the cowling and damaging the two top planes and the port top longeron, the pilot (Victor) being unhurt. The Camel (D6585) was sent to the

Repair Park, rebuilt, and subsequently renumbered F5949 on 26 June. By coincidence, this rebuilt aircraft was eventually delivered to No. 80 Squadron on 8 August, the day before Victor joined that Squadron, although he did not fly it again. The Lt. Christie referred to would appear to be a reference to Lt. H. L. Christie who was a pilot on No. 22 Squadron at this time. Victor then relates an interesting anecdote concerning a pilot by the name of Biheller whom he had known from his time with No. 65 Squadron, who took off from Wye and supposedly landed in Holland. He was subsequently declared a German spy although Victor writes that Tom could not understand why a German spy should want to land in Holland. This incident is based on the flight of Lt. Walter Biheller, an instructor, who took off from Wye on 19 January 1918 on a test flight, and according to his own account, became lost in cloud and subsequently had to land in Belgium but escaped to Holland where he was interned.[3]

The first patrol the next day is allocated to A flight when Griffith, a Welshman, has engine trouble and stalls whilst taking off at 9am sustaining severe head injuries. This incident would appear to relate to a crash which had occurred the previous day, 30 May, when Lt. G. R. Priestly also received serious head injuries when he crashed into crops on take off and was hospitalised, his Camel (D6601) being a write-off. He had been born in Belfast and this could be another instance of Victor disguising a personality by altering his name and nationality.

Due to his own machine having been severely damaged the previous day when he made the forced landing at Serny, Victor had to use another aircraft, D6603 (one in which MacLaren flew later gaining eight victories) on the 9am patrol on 31 May. This was also giving trouble, so he, like Tom, had to return after dropping his bombs, for adjustments to the engine.

The evening sortie was an eventful one. Victor describes Tom's flight, led by Miller, joining a group of SE5s before encountering a mixed group of seventeen Pfalz and Albatros scouts and a hectic dogfight develops. Tom gets a Pfalz, Baker an Albatros and Miller an Albatros and a Pfalz and the scrap is totally successful. MacLaren in fact led this patrol, and although the logbook entry merely states:

'C.O.P. Scrap. SEs' the Combat Report submitted by Victor and MacLaren does confirm that they met seventeen enemy machines, claiming one out of control and two driven down. These claims were reduced by the acting C.O., Capt C. J. Marchant, to one decisive combat (MacLaren – an Albatros) and two indecisive combats. The SE Squadron involved can be identified as No. 64 Squadron, which was still based at Izel, their records showing that they had four victories accepted from this encounter. Victor records that six German machines had been claimed by the SE Squadron but this number may have been reduced to four certain victories by its C.O.

Victor returned from leave on 21 June and so he was able, from this date, to again use his logbook entries in chronological order as the basis for Tom's subsequent flights. Although the Squadron had moved from Estrée-Blanche to Serny on 17 June, Victor does not record this move in *Winged Victory*. The reason for this may have been that he did not spend much time at Serny as for most of July he was in hospital and shortly after being discharged, was posted to another squadron.

Two days after Victor's return, the Squadron was ordered to take part in a new job of 'wireless'. This necessitated two pilots being at a constant state of readiness to take off immediately an enemy observation aircraft had been detected by Wing from bearings of radio waves, telephoned to them by special receiving stations. His logbook shows that over a four-day period, he had five flights resulting from such reports although only one hostile machine was encountered. Victor quotes Tom taking off at 9.25am on 23 June, meeting an LVG which disappeared in cloud, and then flying again after dinner landing shortly before 9.30pm, which corresponds exactly with the logbook entries for that day. Tom's fellow pilot, Moore, did not return from the morning flight, which is a departure from the facts, as the Squadron did not lose a pilot that day. A similar flight took place the next day, with Tom having no flights on 25 June and just two quiet patrols the following day.

The influenza epidemic was sweeping through France at this time and Victor relates that after a visit from the Wing M.O., all the sufferers were sent to hospital, depleting the Squadron's fighting capability considerably. The reality of the situation was that during the four days 18/21 June, thirteen pilots, one half of the Squadron's strength, were admitted to hospital due to sickness, being discharged approximately five days later. It was not long before Victor succumbed to the illness and he describes Tom feeling unwell and visiting the M.O. He is told that he is suffering from P.U.O., which was short for 'Pyrexia of Unknown Origin', which at this time implied influenza. He is forbidden to fly and ordered to have complete rest. From an inspection of Victor's logbook, it appears that he went down with the illness on or about 27 June, as there are no entries from 26 June until the last week in July. He was hospitalised on 5 July when he was admitted to No. 1 Red Cross Hospital at Le Touquet, generally known as the Duchess of Westminster Hospital.

He describes Tom being sent there with three of his fellow pilots, Miller, Jones and Hole. This is close to the facts, as four pilots entered hospital at the beginning of July, Lt. J. H. Smith and Lt. H. Dodson on 2 July whilst Victor and Lt. F. H. Cave were admitted on 5 July. Although in all probability the four of them did not travel together as in the narrative, they would have met up with each other on arrival. Lt. Cave is probably referred to as 'Hole', whilst the circumstances surrounding Miller's hospitalisation, being diagnosed as suffering from tuberculosis, and his subsequent transfer to England and repatriation would appear to be based on Lt. Smith. He, like Miller, was a Canadian, and was invalided to hospital in England on 10 July suffering from what was thought to be bronchitis and was not to fly again, being sent home to Canada in June 1919.

THE DUCHESS OF WESTMINSTER HOSPITAL (FORMERLY THE CASINO DE LA FORÊT)

Victor wrote that Tom thought TB was an illness which affected geniuses like Keats and Mozart, and Henry Williamson romantically expanded on this in his Tribute in the later editions of *Winged Victory* when writing that Victor had suffered 'the usual poet's sickness, which killed Keats, Flecker, D. H. Lawrence, Richard Jefferies; bright blue eyes, fair hair, pale, thought-sculptured face, life ebbing away under a steadfast will to truth.'

As Victor recalled, the Hospital was an attractive white building which was formerly the Casino de la Forêt. It had one hundred and thirty beds and was reserved for wounded and sick officers. From Victor's description, life was quite pleasant apart from the early 'lights out' ruling and the to-ing and fro-ing of the nurses during the night. After a five day stay, the Hospital doctor declared that he was still run down and on 10 July Victor was sent to recuperate in the more bracing air of the No. 14 General Hospital at Wimereux, a coastal resort near Boulogne. This Hospital was formerly the Hôtel Splendide, an imposing building on the promenade, and was part of the large No. 14 General Hospital complex. Tom is also sent there to convalesce, where he shares a room with a young man, a fellow RAF officer, by the name of Skelton who had left Charterhouse less than a year before. He shares Tom's passion for good literature and a passing friendship develops.

THE SPLENDIDE HOTEL AT WIMEREUX

In March 1935, Victor's publisher Jonathan Cape, received a letter from a former RAF pilot who was then working in Brazil addressed to 'Dear Yeates-Cundall' which they forwarded on to Norah. He wrote that he had just finished reading *Winged Victory* and that he recognised the 'young man' at the Hospital in Wimereux as himself, and that the only discrepancy in Victor's account was that he had left Charterhouse eighteen months before and not, as stated in the book, less than a year before. His name was J. E. L. Skelton (another instance of Victor using a pilot's real name) who had been wounded on 15 September 1917 when flying as an observer with No. 20 Squadron and, after retraining, had joined No. 13 Squadron as a pilot on RE8s.

After a week's stay at Wimereux, Victor was pronounced fit and on 16 July he was sent to No. 1 Aeroplane Supply Depot (A.S.D.) based at Marquise, to await a posting: he was hoping to return to his own Squadron although he had been struck off its strength on entering hospital. He describes Tom finding the A.S.D. a dreadful place, the food was poor, the tented accommodation filthy ('Even the earwigs must be uncomfortable'), and one was expected to practice firing machine-guns during the day which he felt was a waste of time, as firing on the ground was completely different from firing in the air. The only consolation was that the camp was set in pleasant countryside and after enjoying the scenery during a solitary walk he muses:

> In this smiling valley the certainty grew up in his mind that the earth was too pleasant a place to leave yet if he could help it.[4]

Eventually his posting came through – he was to return to his old Squadron – and the welcome driver arrived as he flamboyantly recalls:

> He was Orpheus come to release him from the plutonic regions behind the battle front, where fighting men were cattle and organizers prevailed.[5]

Victor arrived back at his Squadron on 23 July having been absent, like Tom, for almost a month. Tom was anxious to hear what had been happening whilst he had been away and his friend Williamson told him they had lost three pilots – in fact two pilots had been shot down in Victor's absence (2/Lt. H. L. Cross and Lt. A. J. Cyr) – and the new impressive Fokker D.VII biplanes were operating on their front which Victor was soon to encounter.

The weather was unfit for flying on the first two days following his return, and the Squadron began preparing to say farewell to Major Mealing, who was returning to England on completion of his tour of duty, having served as the Squadron's C.O. since December 1917. The usual binge took place after the formal dinner on 24 July when the guest of honour was again General Sefton Brancker, complete with his monocle. Victor recalls this event by describing the arrival of General Mitchell with his eyeglass attending the farewell dinner for the C.O., Major Barlow, on Tom's second day back, so mirroring the facts. Major A. H. O'Hara Wood succeeded Major Mealing as C.O. of the Squadron.

On 25 July Victor had his first flight since returning to the Squadron when he took off with C Flight at 5.20pm for an Offensive Patrol, but ended up flying alone as the others had to return due to mechanical problems. Tom has the same experience when he takes off at a similar time, 5.30pm, with three other pilots who all have to return to base with engine trouble. On landing Tom reports to the office that no E. A. had been seen and is introduced to the new C.O., Major Yorke.

Victor himself experienced engine trouble on the dawn patrol on the following day, 26 July, when he returned to the aerodrome at 6.20am noting in his logbook:

> O.P. Engine trouble. Press. Prop. Off.

He describes Tom having the same misfortune on his next flight when he too arrived back a little after six o'clock:

> When he had landed he saw that the little propeller that worked the mechanical pressure pump had come off.[6]

After another dud day due to rain, Victor had two flights late in the day on 28 July, the first at 4pm being a bombing patrol on Estaires and the second at 7.45pm during which a two-seater was seen near Bailleul but escaped. These flights are faithfully recorded in the text as is the one on 29 July, when he officially went out to test his guns but stayed out for more than an hour enjoying himself contour chasing before trying them out on Merville Square.

Victor's next job was to lead the following morning's patrol to escort two-seater DH9s on a reconnaissance flight, and it was on this mission that he had his first encounter with the new Fokker biplanes.

The events of this flight are accurately recorded in the book and deserve to be examined in some detail together with their aftermath. His logbook entry briefly states:

> Escort. 18 E.A. 5 Fokkers

whilst his Combat Report gives the detail:

> 18 Fokker Biplanes
> Whilst on Special Mission with DH9's, Lt. Yeates with his patrol saw 2 formations of 9 E. A. scouts one above the other. The E. A. formation climbed into the sun. Lt. Yeates climbed parallel with them and the E. A. who were 1000ft above the Camels at 18000ft suddenly dived away N. Lt Yeates dived after them and fired 200 rounds at 200 yds range, but could not follow them owing to presence of other E. A. Lt. Sawyer fired 50 rounds at long range at another E. A. No result was observed.

He describes Tom leading a patrol to escort one DH4 (and not a DH9) when he spots a circus of eighteen Fokker biplanes, which keep their distance, and the escort is accomplished successfully.[7] His flight then encounters a patrol of five Fokkers which dive towards them but flatten out without making contact. Tom watches them carefully but suddenly they dive away with Tom and his flight in pursuit. Tom then notices a large group of aircraft flying towards them and sensing a trap, breaks off the engagement only to find that the formation is a squadron of SEs. He waggles his wings at them twice to warn them of the enemy aircraft but his signs are ignored, much to his disgust, and the SEs fly on without attacking. Later, on reporting to the office after returning from an uneventful afternoon sortie, he finds the new C.O. in an aggressive mood and Tom is criticised for breaking off the engagement with the five Fokkers during the morning patrol. The Major tells Tom that he had been in the air that morning and the Fokkers had dived down on him. Tom should have seen his solitary Camel below and have gone down to assist, and it was no thanks to him that he wasn't shot down. The C.O.'s guns had jammed and he had to splitarse about to shake them off. He had also noticed that the SEs had not taken up the attack and had reported them.

It is probable that this exchange took place, as the report submitted by Major O'Hara Wood reinforces Victor's story line:

> Whilst looking for wireless machines at 11.15am Maj. O'Hara Wood who was at 9000ft over Estaires, saw 12 Fokker biplanes, two of which were below him. He dived on these two firing 10 rounds at 50yds range when his guns went out of action. Just then two more Fokkers dived on him and he manoeuvred back to the lines being driven down to 50 ft, his guns meanwhile being useless. The E. A. pursued to the Fôret de Nieppe and then turned round. Five SE5s were patrolling behind Estaires during the combat and should have seen the E. A. attacking but rendered no help.

Tom discovers later from the Armament Officer that there were no obvious signs that the Major's guns had jammed and although it must be conjecture, it is quite possible that this revelation was also based on fact.

On 31 July Victor had a very exhausting day as C Flight was again on wireless duty and he went up no less than five times flying a total of 5 hours 25 minutes, a record for him. Enemy aircraft were seen on two occasions, the first on his second sortie east of Locon, and the second near Bailleul on his early evening flight but in both instances the enemy machines fled on the Camels' approach. These events are faithfully recalled under the correct date when Tom has five flights although his total time in the air is slightly exaggerated to 6 hours 30 minutes. Unsurprisingly he is described as tired and aching.

At this juncture, the death of the Squadron's new C.O., Major Yorke, is brought into the narrative. He is killed in a mid-air collision

Lt. F. H. Astle, Armament Officer

Maj. O'Hara Wood, C.O. 46 Sqn

when leading the Squadron and Tom witnesses the incident. This event relates to the flying accident which took place on the morning of 4 October, when Major A. H. O'Hara Wood was in collision with 2/Lt. L. L. Saunders over St. Quentin, resulting in the death of both pilots. From an eye-witness account submitted by Capt. J. L. Leith, it appears that Major O'Hara Wood suddenly executed a sharp turn through 180 degrees and collided head-on with 2/Lt. Saunders coming from the opposite direction. In Victor's account the circumstances are similar, in that Major Yorke made a sharp right hand turn, clipping Smith's tail-plane and both machines fell to the ground. Smith is described as a youngster from England who had only been over the enemy lines once before, whilst the real casualty, Saunders, was a Canadian who had joined the Squadron at the beginning of August from No. 70 Squadron so he was a pilot of some experience. Victor attached the blame for the collision on the C.O., which appears to be supported by Capt. Leith's report, but the subsequent official inquiry concluded that it was a pure flying accident and neither pilot was at fault.[8] Victor was back in England in October, so he must have learnt of the collision from former colleagues in France.

Continuing his patrol, Tom spots two two-seaters and one is shot down which corresponds with the Combat report submitted by Victor and two of his fellow pilots, Lt. J. Taylor and Lt. C. H. Sawyer for 1 August, Taylor being the victorious pilot.

Victor's final victory took place in the early evening of 3 August when a patrol, led by Lt. R. K. McConnell, met a group of five Fokker D.VII biplanes east of Lens, three of which were shot down with Victor claiming one of them. The Combat Report submitted by Victor, McConnell and Sawyer describes Victor's role:

> 5 Fokker Biplanes
> … Lt. Yeates after attacking several E. A. at long range, saw another E. A. coming straight towards him nose on. Lt. Yeates zoomed up and the E. A. did a right hand stalling turn, being fired on all the time from between 100yds and 50yds range. E. A. went into a slow spin. All three machines were seen crashed on the ground.

This scrap, which was included in the RAF Communiqué for the week 29 July to 4 August, can easily be identified in the text which quotes the correct date. Tom takes off with his patrol at 6pm and finds a bunch of six Fokker biplanes, and meeting one coming towards him he is forced to zoom up above it before getting it in his sights and shooting it down. Three victories were confirmed from this skirmish, Tom claiming two, the wreckage being viewed on the ground. Both the Combat Report and logbook entry, however, state that only five Fokkers were encountered, so it is puzzling why Victor referred to Tom meeting six enemy machines.

Victor's next flight was after tea on 4 August, when an enemy scout and two two-seaters were seen but no combats ensued, which corresponds with Tom's flight that day. There were no jobs the following day due to heavy overnight rain which continued throughout the day, although it brightened up in the evening. Tom then went up for a joy ride which was spoilt when it began raining again, and he had a hairy moment when he just missed a slag-heap which loomed up through the mist. Again this description is taken from the brief remarks in

Victor's logbook, 'Caught in rain – no jobs.'

After having a day off, Tom is due to lead his flight on the dawn patrol on 7 August for wireless duty, but the bad weather persists and the flight is unable to get airborne until the evening which corresponds with Victor's logbook entry for that day.

The Amiens offensive began on 8 August when the Allies attacked along a twenty-mile front between Morlancourt and La Neuville on the Avre, and the RAF was heavily involved. Victor had only one flight that day, before dinner at 6.30pm, and although the patrol saw seven E.A., none were within range so no combats ensued. He was fortunate, as the RAF suffered more casualties on that day than on any other day of the war.[9] Victor describes Tom seeing the Germans retreating and comments that at last the Allies were winning the war on the ground – Ludendorff later wrote that this was 'the black day of the German army in this war'.

On the following day, 9 August, Victor writes that instructions had come through for the Squadron to move on to Vignacourt, to another Wing and Army, Amiens being correctly described as being some twelve miles to the south-east. On first sight this is puzzling, as No. 46 Squadron did not move until 14 August when it was transferred to the aerodrome at Poulainville (not Vignacourt) under the command of 22 Wing, 5th Brigade. However, Victor and a fellow pilot, Lt. J. A. R. Coté, were posted to 22 Wing on 9th August and joined No. 80 Squadron, which was indeed based at Vignacourt, the same day.

There had been three No. 80 Squadron pilots killed on the first day of the battle (8 August) and as they would have been in need of experienced pilots, No. 46 Squadron may have agreed to send Victor and Coté, as they had both been officially struck off the Squadron's strength when they entered hospital in July, when replacement pilots would have been received.[10]

Victor now deliberately departs from his own experiences in the narrative, as Tom stays with the same Squadron throughout the book. The reason for this may have been that he was already shaping the ending with the death of Tom's close friend Bill Williamson, and to have portrayed his own posting to another Squadron would have been an added complication. The final five chapters, however, cover the three weeks during which Victor flew with his new Squadron before being sent back to England.

Following the death of Major Yorke, Victor portrays the replacement C.O., Major Ling, as an Australian, affectionately called 'the Digger' who is well liked. Did he have in mind the line 'Bells go Ding-a-Ling, Ling' when he chose this name as he based his character on the real C.O. of No. 80 Squadron at this time, Major V. D. Bell, who was also an Australian, and popular with the pilots?[11] An interesting departure from the facts, however, is that Victor describes him wearing a white ribbon denoting Antarctic exploits, a reference to the Polar Medal. Neither Major Bell nor any of the Squadron's pilots had received this medal but it is reasonable to assume that to have mentioned such a rare award, Victor must have met someone during his time in France who had been awarded the medal.[12]

The aerodrome at Vignacourt was uncomfortable and inferior to those Victor had been used to. The officers' accommodation, for example, was in tents which were hot and dusty. Two other squadrons shared the base, No. 8 Squadron, which was equipped with Armstrong Whitworth FK8s ('Big Acks'), and later in August, No. 20 Squadron which flew Bristol F.2B fighters was also stationed there.

Tom travels to a nearby aerodrome at Havernas to visit another Camel Squadron, and although there is no record of an Allied aerodrome at this location it is possible that a number of pilots were billeted in this village, as there were several aerodromes in the vicinity.

On arriving at Vignacourt on 9 August, Victor joined B Flight and was immediately in action as shown by his logbook entry for that day. He started a new page with this entry to mark his posting to No. 80 Squadron although, surprisingly, there is no specific mention of the move. The entry reads:

> Bombs behind Morlancourt. Orr killed.

The Squadron's role at this time was supporting the army in the battle around Amiens when Morlancourt was captured after heavy fighting. The pilot referred to in the entry was Lt. J. R. Orr, and it is probable that Victor was flying with Orr at 6.30pm when he was shot down, hence the reference in the logbook. Unusually, Victor did not enter the time and duration of this flight, but as he had only arrived at the Squadron that morning, it is reasonable to assume that his flight would have been late in the day. However, as the Squadron's records for this period are missing it has not been possible to verify this. This is the third and final occasion where Victor mentions a casualty by name in his logbook, and this time the entry states that the pilot was killed, unlike the previous entries which indicated that the pilot was simply missing. The certainty of the outcome reinforces the conclusion that Victor saw his fellow pilot go down.

This incident is related in the book when Tom, on his first flight from Vignacourt, takes part in a low-level bombing patrol around Morlancourt with a pilot named Brindley who, like Orr, is shot down and killed by machine-gun fire from the ground. However it is pertinent to note that there was a pilot on No. 80 Squadron by the name of 2/Lt. V. G. Brindley, who flew with Victor on several patrols during August. Brindley was killed in similar circumstances by machine-gun fire later in the month on 30 August, whilst Victor was still in France. As 'Brindley' is not a common name, this appears to be a further example of Victor purposely mixing names in factual events in the narrative. He also describes a number of pilots taking a tender to La Chaussée to swim in the Somme and it is likely that Victor relaxed in this way as the village is close to Vignacourt.

Most of Tom's remaining patrols can be identified from the entries in Victor's logbook for August, for example after a practice patrol during which Tom introduces new pilots to the front line, C Flight dives on a formation of eight Fokker biplanes which retreat at speed. This is taken from the entry of 13 August, 'O.P. 8 F.B.'

An unusual accident is recalled whereby a pilot by the name of Smith collides with an Ack-W and crashes in flames:

> As he was practising diving on the aerodrome an Ak-W flew across below him at about two hundred feet. He hit it amidships, cutting it in two.

> The Camel crumpled and burst into flames ... Smith was an unlucky name in that squadron. The two pieces of the Ak-W floated down, and the pilot was not quite killed; the back seat, where it was struck, was not occupied.[13]

This relates to the death of 2/Lt. G. Smith of No. 80 Squadron who, when flying Camel F5956, collided on 15 August with an AW FK8 (B4163) of No. 8 Squadron (which as already mentioned was based on the same aerodrome), and went down in flames close to the airfield. The pilot of the FK8, 2/Lt. L. G. Kesterton, was injured which accords with the extract quoted above, although he was not flying alone but with an observer 2/Lt. H. N. Ullyott, who was killed. As this incident is not noted in the logbook, this is another case where a letter to his wife has provided the relevant details. Victor comments that 'Smith' was an unlucky name on the Squadron as during his time with No. 46 Squadron, two pilots named Smith had been killed (Capt. S. P. Smith and 2/Lt. E. J. Smith). This was, therefore, the third occasion when a pilot of that name whom Victor had known had died, albeit he was now flying with No. 80 Squadron.

With the Allied advance continuing despite strong resistance, the squadrons on the Somme front were ordered to assist the Army by bombing strategic targets such as railways, transport and troop concentrations. This resulted in heavy casualties, not only from machine-gun fire from the ground, but also from the new improved Fokker D.VII biplanes which are considered by many to have been the best fighter of the war:

> It had been impossible lately with all the casualties to have days off; to take a lot of raw pilots among the Fokkers would be murder; the experienced men had to stick it. The squadron would have to be rested soon, or go back north, else the experienced men would be dead or gibbering. Yet they had been only ten days on the Somme front. The horrors of ground-strafing, of continually fighting machines by which they were altogether outclassed had made this time as wearing as the previous three months.[14]

The new Fokker machines were certainly making their presence felt, and rumours began to circulate that, in an attempt to counter this menace, Major Miles' Squadron (No. 43) was to be equipped with the new Sopwith Snipes, and Mac would be returning from leave to command a Snipe squadron. Victor was correct in that MacLaren was on leave at this time (from 2 to 23 August) and Snipes did begin to arrive in France during August and were allotted to Major Miles' Squadron, although MacLaren returned to No. 46 Squadron and continued to fly Camels.

Tom/Victor hated this low work reminiscent of the March offensive and the stress again began to take its toll. Many pilots found it difficult to adjust to the extremes of flying two or three sorties a day and the constant risk of being killed, with the safe haven of the aerodrome where they had little to do, but where the danger of the next flight was always in the back of their minds:

> The evenings weren't so bad, but they were drawing out disgustingly, and the thought of the next day and the day after was always lurking in the shadows of the mind when one was on the ground. … on the ground there was depression, reaction from the over-excitement of fighting, and weariness.[15]

THE FOKKER D.VII
'Very fast, splitarse, and marvellous climbers'

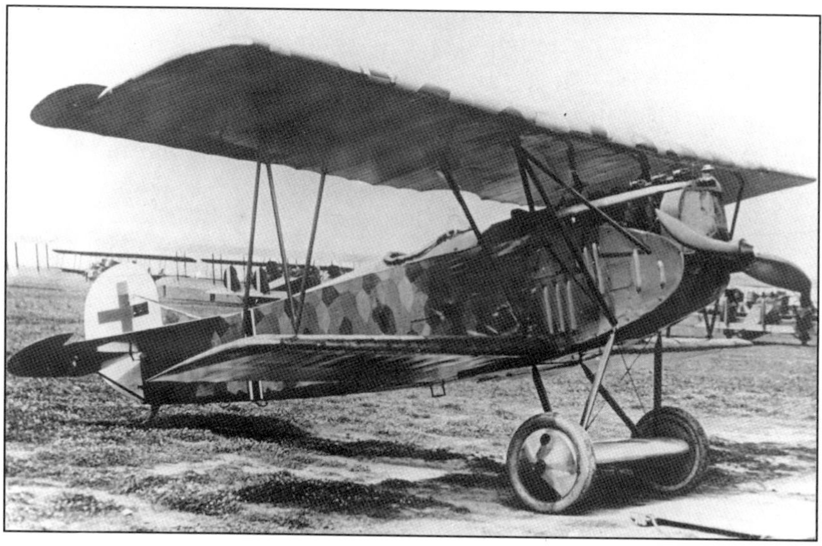

The continual strain of these daily patrols made sleep difficult and preyed on his mind, especially as his tour overseas would be completed at the end of the month when he would return to England and be able to see Norah again.

Victor had written to Mrs Bard in March that the weather was playing an important part in his life:

> As my leisure or forced activity depend almost entirely on the weather, that trite subject of conversation has become of vital importance to me.

As the exhaustion took hold, dud days caused by mist or rain were looked forward to:

> By eleven o'clock it was raining steadily, and had obviously set in for the day. There was a general rising of spirits. Rain at last, thank God; half a day's rest and perhaps a peaceful night.[16]

One of the RAF songs of the period captured these sentiments in its first verse:

> *I left the mess-room early, just on the strike of nine,*
> *And greatly to my horror the weather promised fine.*

In an attempt to relieve these pressures, Tom turns to drinking more heavily, especially on binge nights. It is unlikely that this reflected Victor's own habits as he would want to ensure that he was fit to fly the next day. Indeed another No. 46 Squadron pilot, Lt. W. T. Burkitt, felt that these descriptions of heavy drinking did not fit the facts, as the pilots were usually too exhausted to partake in regular binge nights.[17] However, they did let off steam to relieve the strain on occasions, especially when there was something to celebrate such as a promotion or someone leaving the Squadron to return to HE. As Victor recalled, being rowdy in the mess was a relief to the nerve-wracked and a diversion for the sane.

The tension gradually heightens during the last chapters of the book with a sense of foreboding as Victor prepares for the climax with the loss of Tom's friend Williamson. He describes vividly how the constant killing and the fear of death gradually erodes Tom's state of mind:

> It was impossible for him to go on any longer and not be killed. He couldn't be missed by bullets for ever. A Fokker would get him or a machine gun on the ground. He would certainly be killed if he went on; he could feel death in his bones. He would be shot down in flames. Oh Christ. He sweated at the thought of it and groaned and turned over….[18]

These fears were very real, and would have mirrored Victor's own mental state at that time. Many pilots felt the same, Lt. Burkitt, for example, wrote that he considered *Winged Victory* gave a very clear picture of the steady deterioration of their mental well-being during this period.[19]

In the safety of their hut, the pilots were alone with their thoughts which naturally turned to home:

> In the quietness young men, sick of fighting, ill with unacknowledged ravages of excitement and fear, dreamed of past times that seemed perfect in happiness; or imagined the joy of going home, wounded, on leave, on Home Establishment, or after the war. Peace: if peace returned to the world it was difficult to imagine that anyone would ever find anything to grumble about; no one could help being happy in peace time. And, this one ended, there would be no more war.[20]

Victor correctly comments that Bapaume had been recaptured when describing Tom/Victor's bombing patrol near Peronne, which from his logbook took place in the afternoon of 29 August. On his morning flight Tom had encountered a Sopwith Dolphin, which dived at him out of the sun causing his nerves to leap as he thought it was an enemy machine. This flight was prompted by the entry in the logbook which notes that Victor met a Dolphin on the morning patrol.

Victor's final operational flight took place on 30 August, when he took off at 11.20am on a low bombing mission near St. Pierre-Vaast Wood which lasted ninety minutes. This is described in *Winged Victory* as Tom's last flight when his friend Bill Williamson is shot down and killed. In reality, as mentioned above, No. 80 Squadron did lose one pilot that day, Lt. Brindley, who was shot down and died of his wounds earlier that morning.

The death of his close friend and confidant is the final blow to Tom's mental state, and the doctor orders no more flying, a month's leave and HE. Victor writes that the Squadron was moving forward to Allonville the next day but Tom would not have to go, as a tender would be taking him to Boulogne and to the hospital at Wimereux in the morning. In reality, however, the whole Squadron took off at 1.10pm on 31 August for the ten minute flight to their new aerodrome and although there is no entry in his logbook, the Squadron's records do indicate that Victor flew his Camel D9433 to Allonville with the rest of the Squadron.[21]

Tom had done 163 operational sorties, or 'jobs', totalling 248 flying hours, and many writers have assumed, mistakenly, that this was Victor's own record and indeed even Williamson thought this was the case as is evident from his Tribute. These figures in fact represent roughly the number of flights Victor made in France (including practice flights) and the total number of hours he had flown solo, including those in England whilst training. An examination of his logbook shows that Victor actually flew on 110 operational flights and had flown a total of 188 hours during his seven months in France.

He had been shot down once (by machine-gun fire from the ground), had four forced landings and had crashed three times whilst attempting to land back at the aerodrome and all these events are faithfully described in the narrative.

He had shot down two enemy aircraft himself, had a share in three other successes, and had with Capt. MacLaren, brought down a balloon in flames.[22] The term 'ace', a description Victor would have derided, is used to define a pilot who had shot down at least five enemy machines. As the British treated a shared victory as a whole victory for each of the individual pilots where more than one was involved, Victor is regarded as one of the aces of the war. The Germans, however, did not use this method, only crediting one pilot with a kill in a shared victory situation. It is puzzling, therefore, to find Victor mistakenly putting forward the opposite view in that it was the Allies who credited a victory to only one pilot (or it was split up into fractions between all those who shot at the aircraft), the German pilots each being credited with a kill when a victory was shared. A possible explanation of this contradiction could be that as the British for the duration of the war did not officially keep a record of an individual's victories, the squadrons and the pilots would keep their own scores and some, such as No. 46 Squadron, may have allocated fractions when a victory was shared. The Germans on the other hand were keen to publicise their aces and maintained records, but perhaps the British pilots at that time were under a misapprehension as to their method of scoring, as it would be out of character for Victor to have got the facts reversed.

Victor like Tom was admitted again to No. 14 General Hospital at Wimereux on 3 September where he enjoyed the luxury of:

> ...a world of unfamiliar amenities: a bath to lie down in, electric light, clean sheets, a plastered room, unmilitary food, cleanliness. He had escaped from the wilderness of dirt, chaos, death.[23]

Victor/Tom was diagnosed as suffering from an illness known as 'Flying Sickness D' (D for debility), which was caused by the stress of too much war flying, and two days later he embarked on a steamer for Dover to start a month's sick leave. Two months earlier when he went on leave, he had been elated to be back in his native country, but this time England's 'casual, opulent beauty' no longer evinces any emotional reaction, so profound are the changes caused by his experiences in France:

> Green hedgerows again between green meadows and cornfields where reapers were busy. Beyond Ashford, the Weald. This was England. Wandering lanes, hedged and ditched; casual, opulent beauty; trees heavy with fulfilment. This was his native land. He did not care.[24]

Notes

1 *WV*, p. 321.
2 Ibid., p. 324.
3 NA Air 76, Records of Officers. A somewhat controversial account of this flight, which he wrote in 1918, appeared in the January 1995 issue of *Saga Magazine*. He died in 1932.
4 *WV*, p. 386.

5 Ibid., p. 389.
6 Ibid., p. 396.
7 In the typed copy of *WV*, Victor had originally shown the aircraft as a DH9 but he had altered it to a DH4.
8 NA AIR1/1430/204/31/45 Personnel Casualties.
9 Forty-five RAF aircraft were lost on 8 August 1918.
10 The three No. 80 Squadron pilots who became casualties on 8 August were 2/Lt. H. E. Hudson (KIA), 2/Lt. G. Wignall (POW), and Lt. T. S. Nash. (DofW).
11 The badge of No. 80 Squadron depicts a bell in recognition of the outstanding leadership of Major V. D. Bell during his time as C.O. of the Squadron.
12 There were a number of Polar Medal recipients who subsequently served in the RAF including F. H. Bickerton, T. Gran (a Norwegian), T. O. H. Lees and C. H. Meares. I have been unable to trace any of these as having served on No. 46 Squadron or No. 80 Squadron during Victor's time with these squadrons.
13 *WV*, p. 429.
14 Ibid., pp. 430/431.
15 Ibid., pp. 120 & 277.
16 Ibid., p. 327.
17 Letter to the author from W. T. Burkitt dated 10 May 1974.
18 *WV*, p. 437.
19 Letter to the author from W. T. Burkitt dated 10 May 1974.
20 *WV*, p. 335.
21 NA Air1/1820/204/198/2 No. 80 Squadron Record Book.
22 See Appendix E.
23 *WV*, p. 454.
24 Ibid., p. 456.

CHAPTER EIGHT

SQUADRON PILOTS

There are sixty-two pilots named in *Winged Victory* and as already mentioned, a number of these can be identified with those who served with Victor on No. 46 Squadron or No. 80 Squadron during the seven months he was in France.

In some cases the pilot's real name is used; in others the pilot can easily be identified as the name is similar to his correct one, and in further instances a purely fictitious name is used. This was a practice used on occasions by Henry Williamson; it has already been seen that when describing his schooldays at Colfe's in *Dandelion Days*, Victor was referred to by his correct name (Yeates) and this may have influenced Victor when he was writing his book.

Two pilots are introduced by their real names in the first chapter, Thomson (A Flight commander) and Robinson. As mentioned earlier, Capt. G. E. Thomson flew with the Squadron at this time (although he was in command of C Flight), Victor describing the binge which was held in his honour before he returned to England in March. Unfortunately, Capt. Thomson was killed shortly afterwards on 23 May 1918 when, flying with No. 7 Training Depot Station (TDS) at Port Meadow Oxford, his machine burst in flames soon after take off. Victor records this:

> After tea there came with the mail news of another death, the death of Captain Thomson. He had gone, after his leave, to Castle Bromwich to do some instructing, and the first time he went up his machine came to pieces in the air. Poor old Tommy! This news was far more depressing to the people who knew him than Richthofen's death was encouraging.[1]

Thomson had been awarded the MC and DSO, and was the second

Above: l to r: Lts. M. M. Freehill, R. K. McConnell and H. N. C. Robinson
Left: Lt. Gerald Hudson in flying kit

highest scoring No. 46 Squadron pilot with twenty-one victories.

Lt. H. N. C. Robinson, who had joined the Squadron in July 1917, was awarded the MC in March 1918 and later on the 28th of that month was promoted to Captain and posted to No. 70 Squadron. Victor correctly describes Robinson being transferred to another squadron which was again celebrated with the traditional binge.

A little later in the narrative, Debenham makes his appearance. This pilot would have been named after Lt. H. G. W. Debenham whose career was unique, as he was a 'founder member' of the squadron having joined in April 1916 when it was formed. He had originally flown as an observer but when the Squadron was re-equipped with single-seater Sopwith Pups in April 1917, he was transferred with the other observers 'much to their disgust' to No. 21 Squadron which flew RE8s. Soon afterwards, however, he returned to England and retrained as a pilot before rejoining his old Squadron in November 1917. In the March offensive Victor writes that he goes missing, but in reality Debenham was posted to No. 208 Squadron in May 1918 as a flight commander and survived the war.

A pilot whom Tom had known whilst training at Croydon, Jenkins, is portrayed as being shot down towards the end of March whilst watching his Hun go down after a combat. This character is based on Lt. G. D. Jenkins who was wounded on 27 March and although he is not recorded with a victory that day, he had been successful in shooting down an enemy aircraft earlier that month on 6 March. He had previously been an assistant instructor with No. 40 TS at Croydon whilst Victor was in training so they would have known one another from that time.

Reference has already been made to Victor's mock combat on 10 March with 2/Lt. Gerald Hudson who is portrayed as the Squadron's pianist who 'could play quite well' and:

> He had served as a Tommy in the infantry: the experience had smashed his development as a sensitive aesthetic young man with a passion for playing on church organs that drove him into even ugly red-brick suburban churches … .[2]

Hudson had served in the army before transferring to the RFC and was an accomplished pianist, his love of music being rewarded after the war when he was appointed organist at the Cathedral in Barbados, where he was also the local representative of the Royal College of Music. He obtained a copy of *Winged Victory* when it was reprinted in 1961 and made notes on several pages referring to the events he recalled. Victor writes in his book that Hudson was wounded, whilst in fact he was struck off the Squadron's strength on 20 July when he entered hospital, probably due to influenza, as there is no record of him being involved in a flying accident. After a spell of leave, he was posted to No. 204 TDS at Eastchurch where he retrained as an instructor and remained there until the end of the war.

In describing the Nissen hut at Filescamp Farm which he shared with three other pilots, Tom recalls a trip to Doullens when a table was purchased which cost the occupants, Tom, Williamson, Seddon and Johnson, whom he mentions was by then deceased, a great deal of trouble. The reference to Johnson would fit the facts as, although his injuries were not fatal, a 2/Lt. T. L. Johnson was seriously wounded on 11 March which would have been the approximate date around which Victor was writing.

A few pages later, his character Williamson comments when

2/Lt. J. W. Muir, Lt. H. P. Blakely, 2/Lt. G. D. Falkenberg.
Capts. D. R. MacLaren, C. J. Marchant, Lt. P. W. S. Bulman mc (seated)

returning from a low job that Muir had failed to return. This would have been a reference to 2/Lt. J. W. Muir who was killed on 12 March whilst strafing enemy troops. Similarly a pilot called Taylor is introduced and goes missing towards the end of March. 2/Lt. A. L. T. Taylor was shot down on 16 March, became a prisoner of war and was repatriated in December 1918.

In Chapter XI of Phase One, Skinner and Orr go to Candas to collect new aircraft. Although there is no record of a pilot by the name of Orr serving with No. 46 Squadron during the war, Victor may have wished to name one of his characters after Lt. J. R. Orr, who as mentioned earlier, served with No. 80 Squadron. Orr was killed on 9 August as noted in Victor's logbook, although the character in the novel survived. Skinner is described as a sandy young Scot, and will have been named after 2/Lt. R. L. G. Skinner, who came from Callander in Scotland. Victor had written in his logbook that Skinner went missing on 3 May which relates to the date in the text when Tom's friend Seddon is killed. The narrative suggests, however, that the death of his character Skinner occurred earlier at the beginning of April.

In a letter he wrote to Henry Williamson, although there is some doubt as to whether it was actually sent, Victor comments:

> ...I think of *Winged Victory*. I think of Tom Cundall & Bill Seddon & Beal. I think, these are real people. There has been nothing like them in this century before. They must be unforgettable.

One could conclude from this extract that, together with Tom Cundall whose exploits were mainly based on his own experiences, Seddon and Beal, in Victor's eyes were the two other main characters of the novel and were based on the actual pilots, 2/Lt. Skinner and Capt. Smith, Bill Williamson not being mentioned as this character was fictional.

Another No. 80 Squadron pilot referred to by his correct name is 2/Lt. V. G. Brindley who was probably flying with Victor when he was shot down on 30 August. As we have seen, a pilot with the same name is killed during Tom's first flight from Vignacourt.

Victor was one of the relatively few married pilots in the war and another one was 2/Lt. E. J. Smith, who had married his fiancée Alice

Heaton on 14 March 1918. After a few days honeymoon, he left for France and joined the Squadron seven days later on 21 March. Victor, naturally, would have been missing his wife dreadfully, and it is probable that the two young married men were drawn together by a common bond. Victor describes this pilot as one of Tom's hut-mates under his correct name of Smith. He was newly married and came from Huddersfield in Yorkshire – in reality he came from nearby Bradford:

> Tom spent a good deal of time talking to Smith, who had a wife and was interested in nothing else. He had been married only six months, very little of which time he had been able to spend domestically, and he was aching so much to get back to his wife that life was hardly bearable, separated ineluctably from her, faced by imminent death. There was nothing to be done about it; Smith knew well enough that it was one of those situations that a man has to face with such force as he can bring to bear; but it eased him a little to make moan once into a sympathetic ear, though moaning was very other than his usual mien.[3]

Victor had been married eight months (Smith for six weeks) at the time he was writing and the sentiments expressed in this passage were no doubt a reflection of his own feelings. Unfortunately 2/Lt. Smith lost his life whilst on a low bombing patrol on 29 April and this accords with the narrative when the correct date can be ascertained.

Another pilot referred to by his correct name is Marsden to whom reference has already been made. The circumstances described whereby he is wounded in March, and on recovering is awaiting a posting to a squadron, are similar to those of 2/Lt. Cecil Marsden who was wounded on 28 March and was subsequently posted to No. 210 Squadron.

Canadian pilots distinguished themselves admirably in the war and the RFC/RAF owe them a huge debt of gratitude. By March 1918 there were, on average, five Canadians on each RFC squadron, so that almost one quarter of all Squadron pilots on the Western Front were Canadians, and a disproportionate number of these were among the highest scoring Allied pilots.[4] Victor recognised this:

> Tom's own notion was that the Canadians were very much to be thanked

Lt. Richmond Viall, an American pilot, with his Camel

2/Lt. Nigel Bruce, victim of a collision with a fellow pilot

> for this [British air supremacy], and, much as he disliked their national expletive, he was very glad he was on their side when it came to a scrap.[5]

There were a number of Canadians with No. 46 Squadron in 1918 and two, Burkitt (or Burkett) and Watt are referred to by their correct names in the book. Lt. W. T. Burkitt joined the Squadron on 29 March, having previously served with No. 210 Squadron, and he returned home at the end of June. Victor, however, wrote him out of the story following a leg wound. Lt. E. R. Watt is described as a tall and massive Australian and is shot down by a Fokker: in reality he was a Canadian who was indeed tall in stature but survived the war.

A number of other pilots mentioned in the book are named after those whom Victor would have known from his time with No. 46 Squadron and who were wounded, killed or became prisoners of war. When a pilot went missing Victor, not unnaturally, assumed he had been killed as he would have no way of knowing otherwise, although in a number of cases the pilot survived the crash and became

Lt. M. M. Freehill

Lt. Gerald Hudson ready for take-off

a prisoner of war. It seems clear that he wished to record their sacrifice and so depicted them in the book, although the approximate dates of the casualties taken from the text in some cases are quite different from the correct ones. A pilot by the name of Sawyer appears in Phase One and shortly afterwards he is wounded in the air and crashes. Lt. C. H. Sawyer joined the Squadron in May 1918 and claimed six victories before he spun into the ground on a practice flight on 8 October 1918, when Victor had already returned to England. Similar cases, again of No. 46 Squadron pilots, are 2/Lt. H. L. Cross (prisoner of war 19 July 1918), 2/Lt. N. Bruce who was killed in collision with a fellow Squadron pilot (2/Lt. A. A. Partridge) on 19 September 1918 (again when Victor was no longer in France), 2/Lt. C. E. Thorpe (prisoner of war 14 August 1918), and Lt. R. Moore who was killed on 12 August 1918.

Turning now to pilots whose names have been altered but can be identified, as has already been revealed the first obvious one is Tom's Canadian flight commander, MacAndrews. This character is based on Lt. (later Major) Donald Roderick MacLaren who was born in Ottawa and who had joined the Squadron on 23 November 1917. Although slow to make his mark, his first victory not being until 6

March, he rapidly built on this success and became the fifth highest scoring Allied pilot of the war with fifty-four victories, all when flying Camels with No. 46 Squadron. This made him the leading Camel pilot of the conflict. By the end of the war he had been awarded the DSO, MC and Bar, and the DFC. He was not only a brilliant pilot, but a fine leader who looked after his flight:

> He was a Canadian, a dangerous man, a born fighter. His efficiency was tremendous, and he was a first-rate leader. He saw everything in the sky within ten miles, never led his flight into a bad position, and he was very successful at surprising unsuspecting Huns, often miles and miles over Hunland.[6]

Lt. Richmond Viall, one of the American pilots on the Squadron who arrived in France in July 1918, endorsed Victor's praise:

> MacLaren our flight commander was absolutely terrific. He took wonderful care of his fliers in the air, and on the ground too for that matter. I just cannot say enough for MacLaren. He was a friendly sort of chap, and was an absolutely uncanny pilot in his tactics.[7]

After the war, MacLaren was given a permanent commission in the RAF but chose to leave the service as he realised that commercial aviation was the way forward. He became a pioneer in this field in North America with the formation of Pacific Airways, the forerunner of Canadian Airways, and was the very first pilot with Trans Canada Air Lines, now Air Canada. He died in 1988 and a bronze bust to honour his war record and his contribution to Canadian aviation was unveiled in 1996 in the concourse at Vancouver International Airport.[8]

The second pilot easily identified is Tom's other flight commander, Capt. Beal who, as mentioned earlier, is based on Capt. S. P. Smith. It is clear from reading the book that his death left an indelible mark on Victor. He had written in his logbook 'Smith missing', the first of only three occasions when he referred to a casualty by name. He was a very brave pilot who led low ground-strafing patrols with little apparent concern for his own, and often his fellow pilots' safety.

A married French Canadian called Dubois joins the Squadron in late March and is described as coming from a place where there were two rivers but which was nevertheless named Trois Rivières. This fishing town is situated where the St. Maurice and St. Lawrence rivers meet and is so named because they divide into three at the point where they flow around two islands. This pilot is based on Lt. J. A. R. Coté, a bachelor, who was posted to the Squadron on 29 March and, like the character Dubois, came from a small town near to Trois Rivières. Confirmation of this assertion can be found from a close examination of the notebooks in which Victor wrote the novel. To assist him in keeping track of the pilots in each of the three flights, he listed their individual names in several places. On one occasion he inadvertently wrote 'Coté' and, realising he had written the pilot's real name, crossed it out and wrote above it 'Dubois.' He describes Dubois becoming ill with influenza and as he fails to recover, he goes away to hospital, pale and quiet, having hardly spoken for days. This will have been close to the facts as Lt. Coté was admitted to hospital on 5 June, again on 21 August and finally on 24 October where he sadly died from influenza four days later.

Another Canadian is Miller, a tough ambitious pilot who was admitted with Tom to the Duchess of Westminster's Hospital at the beginning of July where he is diagnosed as having tuberculosis and is sent back to England for treatment. It is likely that Miller is based at least in part on Lt. J. H. Smith, also a Canadian, who joined the Squadron on 3 March 1918 and is accredited with eight victories. He was with Victor in the hospital in Le Touquet and was invalided to hospital in England with P.U.O. on 10 July.

Franklin who flew initially with A Flight, appears early in the book and subsequently leaves the Squadron in July on being made a Flight Commander. Gerald Hudson thought this character was a portrait of Lt. M.M. Freehill who had joined the Squadron on 26 January 1918 and in the September was promoted to Captain and transferred to No. 80 Squadron.

A pilot introduced at the beginning of the book is Allen, so it is reasonable to assume that he was on the Squadron at the end of February or the beginning of March 1918. Tom gets on well with Allen, who is engaged and who feels strongly that he should remain faithful to his

Lt. A. G. Vlasto

2/Lts. G. W. Williamson and R. E. Lindsay, with pup at Izel

fiancée. He is reported missing towards the end of March after five jobs and is presumed dead. A few weeks later, however, Tom receives a letter from Allen's fiancée and is delighted to hear that Allen has survived and is in hospital in Manchester recovering from his injuries. It is probable that Victor based this character on 2/Lt. R. E. Lindsay who had joined the Squadron on 26 February and was wounded in combat on 27 March, crash-landing away from the aerodrome. He was repatriated and admitted to hospital in Whitechapel, London on 4 April with gunshot wounds to the leg. The dates of Lindsay joining the Squadron and being wounded are similar to those in the book although he was in hospital in London and not Manchester. This discrepancy could be another case of Victor deliberately altering the facts or simply a lapse of memory with the passage of time.

One of the pilots in C Flight with whom Victor flew regularly was Lt. A. G. Vlasto who lived in London and was from a wealthy Greek shipping family. It is likely that he had Vlasto in mind when creating his character Moss, as he comments that no one took gambling seriously 'and the stakes were so low that they could not have interested a wealthy young man like Moss.'[9] This probability is strengthened by the comment made when Moss was leaving the Squadron that he had shot down two Huns simultaneously – Vlasto achieved two victories on 15 May both being timed at 12.45pm. He was posted to HE on 15 July 1918.

Victor portrays the Squadron's armament officer, Chadwick, as having served originally in the infantry then, after transferring to the RFC and becoming a pilot, he had a serious crash which resulted in him being found a ground job as he was no longer fit to fly. Early in July, as he was conversant in French, he takes ten days leave in Paris rather than returning to England. This officer is based on the Squadron's real armament officer, Lt. F. H. Astle who, like Chadwick, had originally joined the Army (the Cheshire Regiment) but retrained as a pilot with the RFC. As a result of a flying accident in January 1917 he had been regraded Bii which meant that he could no longer serve as a pilot or observer, being only fit for ground duties. His records show also that he had a conversational knowledge of French and he did take his leave in Paris during the first 10 days of July as Victor described.[10]

The character Bill Williamson cannot be identified as being a portrait of any particular pilot and is wholly fictitious although, interestingly, a pilot with the same surname, 2/Lt. G.W. Williamson, served on the Squadron for a short time towards the end of February 1918. Henry Williamson, as will be shown, suggested the outline for the flying novel, the friendship of two pilots and how the strain of combat flying affects them. Victor created the character of Bill Williamson to act as Tom's friend when he accepted the suggested story-line. Their friendship blossoms as the book progresses and Williamson becomes a steadying and stabilising influence for Tom in times of stress when he is feeling particularly low. He also acts as the foil for some of Tom's more outspoken and controversial viewpoints in their many debates.

During his final four weeks in France when he was with No. 80 Squadron, Victor flew on a number of occasions with a Canadian, F. J. Tanner who, although holding the rank of Major, flew regularly.

This pilot is introduced in the book as 'Major Bob' and is correctly described as a Canadian whom Tom admired as he had chosen to forfeit his seniority to continue flying.

It is clear, therefore, that many of the characters in the book are based on actual pilots and this view was substantiated by a former No. 46 Squadron pilot, A. A. Partridge, who wrote that it was 'such a true record of what went on at that time, and the characters, disguised but easily recognised.'[11]

Notes

1 *WV*, p. 217.
2 Ibid., p. 223.
3 Ibid., p. 136.
4 W. A. Bishop (72 victories), Raymond Collishaw (60), Donald R. MacLaren (54) and W. A. Barker (50). There were also six other Canadians with more than 30 victories. In late 1916, Canadian industry built a flying school and aircraft factory to train pilots in Toronto and by 1918 it was providing 200 pilots a month for the RAF.
5 *WV*, p. 50.
6 Ibid., pp. 16/17.
7 Interview in US Cross & Cockade Journal, Autumn 1961.
8 The sculptor was Raoul Schreiden, a former Royal Canadian Air Force pilot. The wording on the plaque reads:

MAJOR DONALD RODERICK MACLAREN
1893 – 1988
D. S. O. M.C. & BAR, D.F.C.
CHEVALIER OF THE LEGION OF HONOUR
CROIX DE GUERRE
THE 4TH RANKING CANADIAN ACE OF WW1, AND
A MEMBER OF CANADA'S AVIATION HALL OF
FAME. IN 1924 HE ESTABLISHED THE FIRST
FLYING SERVICE ON THE WEST COAST, AND
LATER RECOMMENDED THIS SITE FOR THE FUTURE
LOCATION OF VANCOUVER INTERNATIONAL AIRPORT.
AIR FORCE OFFICERS' ASSOCIATION

9 When A. G. Vlasto died in 1935 from TB he left a substantial estate of £142,743.

10 NA Air 76 Officers Records.

11 Letter to the author dated 27 October 1974. 2/Lt. A. A. Partridge joined No. 46 Squadron in August 1918 and was seriously injured in a mid-air collision when flying Camel C8342 on 19 September 1918. The other pilot, 2/Lt. N. Bruce flying Camel F2172, was killed.

CHAPTER NINE

CIVILIAN LIFE AND THE WRITING OF *WINGED VICTORY*

By August 1918, Norah had returned to Mistley to be with her parents as the birth of her first child was imminent and she had no definite news as to when her husband would be posted to HE. She was both relieved and delighted, therefore, when she learnt that he was safe and returning to England with four weeks leave, albeit sick leave, as this would enable him to be with her when their child was born. Victor arrived in Dover on 5 September and reported initially to the London District Hospital in Marylebone, where the doctors confirmed that he was suffering from Flying Sickness D caused by the 'stress of service' and immediately sent him on one month's sick leave. He arrived at his in-laws' home shortly afterwards, just in time to be present when Norah gave birth to a healthy baby girl, Mary Joan, on 17 September. Two days later Victor proudly registered the birth in Harwich, describing himself as a 'Lieutenant RAF', although he also added his civilian occupation of bank clerk.

On his return to England he was attached to the South-East Area Command, and on the expiration of his leave, he was instructed to report to No. 54 TDS at Fairlop, near Ilford. This unit was one of a number established to train single-seater fighter pilots and Victor, like many other experienced pilots on completion of a tour overseas, was posted there with a view to becoming an assistant flying instructor on Sopwith Camels. The TDS was equipped with two-seater Avro 504Ks as well as Camels. He was still weak from his illness, however, and on 15 October, within a week of arriving at Fairlop, he was admitted to the RAF Central Hospital in Holly Hill, Hampstead, London and this resulted in a further period of sick leave.

He returned to the TDS on 7 November when his sick leave expired and remained there until 6 February 1919 when the station closed and the unit disbanded. He was then posted to No. 50 TDS based at Eastbourne which also trained Camel pilots. Although there are no individual entries in his logbook for this period, he noted that he flew an additional thirty hours at Fairlop to 1 February 1919. As Eastbourne is not mentioned it can be assumed that he did not fly whilst he was stationed there. He had then flown a total of 300 hours – 288 hours had been solo of which 248 had been on Camels.

When the war ended on 11 November 1918 there was no requirement for further pilot training or indeed pilots and on 23 May 1919 he left the RAF. The records officially recorded that, like many others, he was 'Transferred to the unemployed list.'

He had now to make a decision concerning his future and whether he should continue with his pre-war career in banking. Like so many young men scarred by the experience of war, he found civilian life unsettling and decided against rejoining Cox's Bank. It is probable that he felt somewhat guilty about making this decision as he wrote in *Family Life* about his protagonist Julian:

> Julian went to see his bank about returning to work. A job would be found for him when he was demobilized. His salary, including bonus, would work out at about three pounds a week. Julian said this was useless, he wanted to get married, and the bank could go to hell. This wasn't very nice of him as it had been paying him five pounds a month all the time he was away, but he was full of war-fever and regarded the bank as a profiteer and stay-at-home.

Victor loved flying and as there was a surplus of machines on the market at cheap prices, he became involved in a venture to take commercial aviation to Spain which he hoped would lead to the establishment of a regular air service to England. He alludes to this in *Winged Victory* when Tom discusses plans for the future with his friend Williamson:

> We'd take out a couple of Avros; they'll be giving them away with a pound of tea as soon as the war's over. Then we can hire a field near Madrid and give joy rides to wealthy Spaniards. Five pounds for a quarter of an hour.

> Fifty per cent extra for a loop. They'd jump at it. Then we might get a fat government contract to start an air force.[1]

As the money he had saved whilst in the RAF and the gratuity received on leaving the service were insufficient to finance the project, he had to borrow further funds from his parents, his in-laws and Norah's aunt. He was to be the pilot, whilst his partner would look after the other aspects of the business. To enable him to travel to Spain to explore the project he had to obtain a passport, and a joint family one, which included Norah and their nine-month old daughter Mary, was issued in June 1919 in which his profession is shown as an aviator. He was, however, still concerned that he had falsified his age on his marriage application as convenient inkblots have obliterated his age and the year of his birth on the appropriate page in his passport. Blots also made it difficult to determine Norah's age. It can only be assumed that Victor did not want anyone who might see the passport to know their true ages, but it is unclear whether the effacement was made before or after his visit to Spain.

He left for France and Spain in July 1919, visiting Paris whilst he was in France. It is probable that it was on this visit that he learnt the shattering news that his partner, whom he had entrusted with the money, had absconded with all the funds for the project. This was a devastating blow, as not only had he lost all his own savings, but his relatives had also lost their investments. This catastrophe left him very short of money and having already turned his back on a banking career, he was forced to look elsewhere for a means of earning a living. It was important for him to find a job as soon as possible to support his family, especially as Norah was pregnant again, and he eventually found a position in the offices of Gliksten, a firm of Timber Merchants in London. It appears that he had at least two temporary addresses in London at this time, 15 Duke Street, WC2 in 1919 and 48 Boyne Road, Lewisham in 1920, which suggests that he lived in London during the week for his work, returning to Mistley at the weekends to be with his family who continued to live with Norah's parents.[2] A second daughter, Joyce, usually known as Joy, had been born on 26 September 1919 in Ipswich and this addition to the family meant the need for a place of their own became more important, the situation becoming urgent at the beginning of 1922 when Norah became pregnant once more.

They could not afford to purchase a property outright so looked around for rented accommodation. They eventually found a reasonable flat occupying the top two floors of a three-storey, end-terraced house, 22 Wemyss Road, Blackheath, the ground floor and basement being occupied by other tenants. This was to be their home for the next nine years. The accommodation was not ideal – the kitchen was on the landing for example – and became even more cramped when their third child, Guy, was born in the summer of that year. Victor's salary was only modest and with three young children to feed and clothe, the family's budget was tight, with little left for luxuries. Despite this, like many other 'middle-class' families of the day, they employed a maid, Elsie, who had previously worked for Norah's parents in Mistley. Victor also acquired a motor cycle and sidecar, but after a near accident this was discarded on Norah's insistence and exchanged for an open top Morgan three-wheeler, which was generally regarded as a rather rakish machine. With the family increasing, however, the Morgan became impractical and a French Peugeot was acquired, a rare motor car in those days. It is probable that the family received some financial assistance from Norah's parents, as it is unlikely that Victor's salary would have been sufficient to cover these comparative luxuries.

22 Wemyss Road, Blackheath (r)

Unfortunately Victor's health had been gradually deteriorating and by the late 1920s he was finally diagnosed as suffering from tuberculosis (TB), which came as a shattering blow. It was not unusual for P.U.O. contracted in France to develop into TB in later years and the illness was quite common among First World War combat pilots. Lt. A. G. Vlasto, for example, one of Victor's fellow C flight pilots, was found to have the disease at about the same time and died shortly after Victor on 1 March 1935.

When his employer became aware of the diagnosis, Victor was prohibited from working indoors in the office for fear that he might pass on the illness to his fellow workers. The Company, however, sympathetically offered him a position as a commercial traveller which he accepted for the obvious financial reasons although selling goods on commission was not to his liking. As his new job entailed travelling to see customers to try to obtain new business, with help of a loan of £60 from his mother, he later changed his car for a larger more suitable model, a Morris Cowley. It was now much easier to take the family out for runs in the country and also visit his in-laws at Mistley where he was often prevailed upon to take his in-laws out for excursions, as he humorously recounted to Norah whilst he was convalescing:

> I am to take your Bright Little Father out for a Drive this afternoon. His overcoat & hat are being aired before a mighty fire in preparation for this great occurrence. Tomorrow I shall take out Hain; I am an Institution for Airing the Aged.

The children liked visiting Norah's parents as they could stroll down to the estuary and watch the boats being unloaded. Indeed, when his daughter Joy was suffering from bronchitis, she was taken to Mistley to recuperate in the cleaner air and Victor, visiting her at weekends, took her for long walks in the countryside which she still fondly recalls. Victor had a love of the English countryside which comes across repeatedly in *Winged Victory*, for example when describing the delights of seeing England again on starting his leave.

Money, however, was still very short, and it was whilst they were living in Blackheath that he attempted to supplement his income by acting as an Insurance Broker working from home, but this venture does not appear to have been very successful.

V. M. YEATES,
INSURANCE BROKER.

ALL CLASSES OF BUSINESS PLACED WITH
LLOYD'S AND LEADING COMPANIES

22, WEMYSS ROAD,
BLACKHEATH, S.E.3.

LETTERHEAD USED WHEN VICTOR WAS TRYING TO SUPPLEMENT HIS INCOME BY WORKING AS AN INSURANCE BROKER

By 1931 he was having enforced periods in hospital for treatment and he would have been disappointed not to have been at home when Joy heard that she had won a scholarship to the Eltham Hill High School for Girls. He wrote to her from hospital:

My dear Joy

Someone who's prosperous, indeed! (said he snorting)

I used to go into Elmstead when I was young as you. I believe the idea was to find eggs in nests, but I don't think I ever did.[3] Woods are quite attractive enough without eggs – like trees. Especially when they are Private. They are private because of the Norman Conquest, I think. What other reason? All property is theft.[4]

My father wrote to me yesterday and he congratulated me about you and your old scholarship that you are feeling so uppish about.

I shall be glad to see you if you come next Sunday, and I will introduce you to my sparrow if he will show himself. I am afraid he has three wives.

By all means write when you feel so disposed.

Yours affly
Victor

For relaxation, Victor enjoyed smoking a pipe and would listen to classical music on Sunday afternoons on the wireless, his favourite composers being Bach and Mozart. His wife, also musical, was a member of the local music society and played the piano at a nearby picture house from time to time, which helped the family's financial position. He also liked to play bridge and was a member of the local chess club, his interest being fostered through his long-time friendship with Captain Arthur Edward Dickinson who lived nearby in Blackheath. Captain Dickinson, who was sixteen years older that Victor, was a tall, imposing and distinguished-looking figure over six feet in height. During the war he had been a Captain in the Royal West Kent Regiment and had insisted on retaining the use of his army rank when the war ended. He was employed as the secretary to the Earl of Crawford and Balcarres and lived with his unmarried sister, Kate, who was five years his junior, and her nurse/companion. Through the Earl's connections, Captain Dickinson was able to obtain tickets to take Victor's children to London Zoo which usually included a 'zoo tea' and they eagerly looked forward to these treats. He was fond of the children and invariably gave them sardine sandwiches for tea on the family's frequent visits. Shortly after the war, Captain Dickinson became engaged to a lady who sadly died before they could marry and he found it difficult to recover from the shock. Wounds suffered during the war still troubled him and he was often in pain. Tragically, these caused depression which resulted in him shooting his sister and then taking his own life on 26 October 1931 – his sister was also in poor health with heart problems and it was thought that he was worried about how she would manage if she had to live by herself. The inquest recorded that Captain Dickinson, who was fifty years of age, murdered his sister and then committed suicide whilst of unsound mind brought about by war wounds.

In *Family Life*, Victor based one of his main characters, Major Robert Kelsey, on Captain Dickinson whom he portrays as a rather tragic and sorrowful character. Major Kelsey, who insists on being called Major, is the secretary to a Lord Crossman and lives with an unmarried sister and her companion. His fiancée also dies shortly after they become engaged and although there is no indication in the unfinished work as to how the story would end, it seems very likely that this character would, true to life, meet the same fate as Captain Dickinson.

His untimely death brought unexpected benefits to the Yeates' family since under his will, as his sister had predeceased him, one half of his estate passed to Norah. Victor had known Captain Dickinson since he was a boy when they were neighbours and it was presumed that the bequest had been left to Norah, rather than Victor, as he knew Victor was very ill. Some thought, however, that he benefited Norah as he was extremely fond of her, which may have been nearer the truth as his will was made in 1927, when Victor's illness would not have been so acute.

Whatever the reason, Norah received some £800 from the estate and as the family now had the resources to achieve their ambition of owning their own house, they began looking for larger accommodation which was by then urgently needed as their fourth child, Rosalind had been born on 8 April that year. They eventually found one to their liking, a semi-detached house, 569 Sidcup Road, Mottingham, London SE9, a new property which, importantly for the growing family, had a large garden at the rear in which the children would be able to play safely, and they moved there in late 1931. Norah, with her inheritance, was able to put down a sizeable deposit towards the purchase price of £875, the balance being left on mortgage.

As his condition worsened and he became weaker, Victor realised that he would soon be unable to continue travelling for his employer

569 Sidcup Road, Mottingham (r)

Molly, Norah, Guy, Victor and Joy in the garden at 569 Sidcup Road
Rosalind, their youngest child, was probably asleep when this was taken.

and he became increasingly worried about the future of his wife and their four young children. He decided to try his hand at writing which he could do whilst he was convalescing and eventually he completed a novel which he called *Adjustment*, and which Henry Williamson was later to describe as a sort of Ulysses. It is a meandering story – it begins with his main character, Tom Cundall (he did of course also use this name for his main protagonist in *Winged Victory*), a former Great War Camel pilot, walking into a London café and over a cup of coffee he muses over the past and dreams of the future. He recalls his days in the RAF by describing Victor's own flight of 30 July 1918 when he failed to notice a patrol of Fokkers diving on his C.O. from whom he was later to receive a dressing-down. He then proceeds to recount the flight in which the C.O. is killed in a mid-air collision and both these incidents are to be found in *Winged Victory*, the C.O. being Major Yorke. The story then goes back in time to the 16th

Century and the exploits of one of his forebears, Thomas Cundale, before conveying the reader into the future with the hope of a better and just world.

Having finished the novel he looked around for help in getting it published and his thoughts turned to his school friend, Henry Williamson, who was by then a celebrated writer having had his widely acclaimed nature book *Tarka the Otter* published in 1927.

Williamson had enlisted in the army in 1914 as a Private, was commissioned the following year, serving on the Western Front. He was demobilised in September 1919 and his wartime experiences deeply affected his thoughts and writings throughout his life. They had met on just two occasions since leaving school, once dining at the Café Royal in late 1916 when they had rather too much to drink and again in 1919 in Blackheath when they discussed the literature of Richard Jefferies and Compton Mackenzie.[5] On 19 March 1933 he wrote to Williamson via his publisher, and asked him for his advice on the novel he had just completed, reminding him that, as he was one of Williamson's characters in *Dandelion Days*, he could hardly refuse.

Williamson was probably flattered by this approach and in acknowledging a copy of the typed manuscript which followed shortly afterwards, he, somewhat rashly, congratulated Victor on his 'magnificent' book and assured him he would be able to arrange for it to be published when it would be a success. Privately, however, Williamson, with some justification, was not impressed with the overall story although he was enthusiastic about the flying scenes. In his critique which followed, therefore, he suggested to Victor that he should write a book about the RFC for which he was, of course, well qualified.

He suggested the outline framework for the proposed novel, two friends on a squadron becoming to rely on each other and the effects on them of the increasing strain of war flying. Not surprisingly, Victor was both shocked and hurt to receive this negative appraisal so soon after Williamson's encouraging first response. He replied on 2 May from Colindale Hospital, where he had been admitted at the beginning of April, that he was not keen on this suggestion, as he felt he should write on a subject which interested him. He was disappointed that Williamson had not recognised the main thrust of *Adjustment*, which was the improvement of moral conditions.

Despite these misgivings, however, he bowed to the experienced writer's advice and immediately began writing the 'flying novel', and had by then already completed the first chapter, which he mentioned in the postscript. As he still had faith in *Adjustment*, notwithstanding Williamson's adverse comments, he asked him to submit the manuscript to a publisher to see whether a more favourable response would be forthcoming.

Although Victor admired Williamson as a writer, he detached himself from some of his more unconventional beliefs and actions, writing to Norah on 4 May:

> I asked W.....son to send the other stuff ['*Adjustment*'] to a publisher & see what happens. The poor fellow is as mad as ever, I'm afraid. I tried to hint that he is a genius as well. One should always pay back compliments.

As he had not received any response by the second week in May, he became irritable, due partly to the dismal conditions in the hospital, complaining to Norah:

> I should have done better to have sent the thing to a publisher myself. Perhaps. I don't know. See how the flying stuff goes.

Williamson eventually sent the manuscript to Putnam & Co Ltd (who had published a number of his own books including *Tarka the Otter*) but they too were not impressed. Whilst acknowledging the 'writer's gift' and agreeing with Williamson that Victor showed a rare sensibility and power of expression, Mr Charles Huntington of Putnam's was of the opinion that it would not be in his best interests to launch him with such a book. He conceded, however, that it contained thoughts and conceptions which if handled differently could form the basis of 'a masterpiece' which was encouraging, and he would like to have a talk with Victor if he ever came to London.

He continued by saying that at the most difficult time ever known in publishing, it would be wrong to write a book on flying in the war. Williamson after some thought, sent Victor a copy of this rejection letter but told him to ignore the disheartening comments and encouraged him to continue writing. Nor did he advise Victor to meet the publisher as he wrote that he had better plans for the flying novel.

Colindale Hospital was near to Hendon Aerodrome and it was whilst he was there that he witnessed the crash, on 1 May, of Pilot Officer Viscount Knebworth, the Unionist member of Parliament for Hitchen, of 601 City of London Squadron of the Auxiliary Air Force. Viscount Knebworth was practising for an air display when flying a Hawker Hind and both he and his passenger Leading Aircraftman Ralph Harrison lost their lives in the accident.[6]

Victor soon realised that his letters from France which Norah had faithfully kept, would be invaluable in re-creating the day-to-day life of the Squadron. He wrote to his wife from hospital on 4 May:

> As you know, I am trying to do the war in the air. There is a lot of material, besides frantic endearments, in the letters I wrote to you from the front. If you will kindly dig those from France out of the tin in the bottom bureau drawer, I will endeavour to extract their material. Bring them with you when you come. …And then all aboard for fame and fortune!

She must have taken the letters on her next visit as five days later he was writing again:

> I have been very busy scribbling and reading all those letters, between the lines where I could. I had far too great a respect for the censor. I ought to have kept a diary. However there is something. What a lot of bosh there is in them. A very young man was he.

By this time he was already writing the third chapter and he went on to say that although he was 'as dull and sleepy as ditchwater', he intended to finish it that evening. Even at that early stage he was obviously determined to keep up the momentum in his writing.

When the book was published he acknowledged the great debt he owed to Norah for keeping all his letters by inscribing the copy which he gave to her:

> To N. P. Y. with love
> (and after all it is her book, for I couldn't have written half of it if she hadn't valued my letters from the front sufficiently to keep them through fifteen difficult years)
> VMY

WINGED VICTORY

To N.P.Y. with love
(and after all it is her book, for I couldn't have written half of it if she hadn't valued my letters from the front sufficiently to keep them through fifteen difficult years)
VMY.

As a typewriter would not have been available in hospital, he began writing his novel in three-penny lined school exercise books and it is quite remarkable to find how few changes were made when comparing this hand-written first draft with the published version. The novel was completed in neat, legible handwriting using a number of these exercise books, and on completion of each chapter it was then typewritten and sent to Williamson for comment. Williamson praised the work and encouraged Victor to continue. Although many of his war experiences would still be ingrained in his memory, the letters to his wife from France, his logbook and a map of the area which he had brought back with him, were the main sources of information, especially for the day-to-day descriptions of squadron life and flying action.

He found it difficult to write during his stay at Colindale Hospital – he commented that it was a 'crossword puzzle and solo whist place' – and eventually he discharged himself against medical advice and returned home. He set up a study in the lounge at the back of the house, which was out of bounds to his children whilst he was working. He did his writing on a bureau, typing the hand-written manuscript using an elderly Adler typewriter.

The London County Council was sympathetic towards his condition and arranged for a wooden hut to be erected in the garden of his house in Sidcup Road so that he could take advantage of the fresh air when the weather was favourable. The Council also arranged convalescent breaks on the coast in Eastbourne, Ventor in the Isle of Wight, and later in Bournemouth. He had spent three months at Eastbourne with No. 50 TDS in early 1919 but now the circumstances were more tragic, as he wrote despairingly to his wife:

> My dearest Pet,
> This is an awful life. Here I do nothing but cough, cough, cough. I can eat all right but this is almost worse. I feel half dead with it. What did Eastbourne air do for me in 1919? If good, I expect it was the beer. And of course it is a most unmitigated bore being here.

His mother was able to visit him during his stay at Eastbourne as she was now living on the south coast in Bournemouth, and on one occasion she took him to the local theatre to see a play, *Marry the Girl,* although apparently the visit aggravated his cough.

With the urgent need to support his wife and their four young children, Victor drove himself hard, writing each day for several hours. By August he had written some 70,000 words and by the end of that month he had completed Phase One of what he envisaged would be a trilogy. He posted a copy to Williamson who expressed the view that it should be the first part of one volume, which was accepted. Phase Two, which was completed by November, was thought by Williamson to be exceptional and he passed this on to the publisher Jonathan Cape who was well-known to him, having also published a number of his books.

After reading the manuscript and swayed by Williamson's enthusiasm, Cape had high hopes that the flying novel might rival T. E. Lawrence's *Revolt in the Desert* which Cape had published successfully in 1927. He wrote to Victor on 17 November expressing willingness to publish the book when complete and setting out the royalty terms, 12½ % on the first 3,000 copies sold, 15% on the next 5,000 and 20% on the remainder. The formal Memorandum of Agreement was signed on 20 November and knowing of Victor's financial difficulties, Williamson assisted by giving him £50, later

23.

On the next day, ~~being~~ Saturday the sixth of April, rain spread over northern Europe in the early hours of the morning, and in places continued all day. In London, for instance, those with ~~sons~~ relatives in the R.A.F. hoped that this would be a real day's rest for them, + bore with patience ~~this~~ the damping addition to the horrors of week-end shopping; but in Picardy it cleared up in the afternoon, and there was plenty of flying, for the enemy was making yet another assault on the defences of Amiens, and there seemed very little reason why they should not carry them, ~~and~~ unless it might be their own exhaustion ~~or fear of too sharp a salient~~. The Allies' reply was to ~~concentrate large numbers of aeroplanes on~~ the attack was to bomb from the air more intensely than ever. The clouds had lifted to some ~~two~~ three thousand feet, so that machines of all descriptions could be used. When C flight arrived at the scene of action soon after three o'clock, ~~there was~~ air ~~seemed~~ quite

A TYPICAL PAGE FROM ONE OF THE EXERCISE BOOKS IN WHICH VICTOR STARTED WRITING *WINGED VICTORY*.

The page is headed '23' (Chapter 23 of Phase One) but appears in the book as Chapter XXII as the original Chapter 18 was omitted from the published version. It shows how he edited the manuscript by deleting words without affecting the story line: 'hours of', 'for instance' and 'seemed quite' were removed from the text on this page.

reimbursed by the publisher, which he said would be an advance on the royalties payment and Cape agreed to make a further advance when the entire manuscript had been received.

The title of the book caused some problems and took months to resolve. Victor originally thought of *Aircraft over Chaulnes* but this was soon replaced by *This Tassel Gentle*, which refers to a male hawk, and is taken from a speech of Juliet's in Act Two, Scene II of Shakespeare's *Romeo and Juliet*:

O for a falc'ner's voice,
To lure this tassel-gentle back again!

Although this was the title shown in the Memorandum of Agreement, in his letter of 17 November Cape commented, unsurprisingly, that it was not a good title from a sales point of view and asked Victor to consider alternative titles. Victor suggested *P.U.O.* but this was also considered too obscure and unsuitable. Williamson from the outset favoured *A Test to Destruction*, but Victor rejected this suggested title (Williamson in fact used it himself in 1960 for the eighth volume in his *Chronicle of Ancient Sunlight* series) and put forward as an alternative *High Adventure*. When this was also discarded Victor suggested *Wings of Victory*, which was the title he used in the typed copy of the manuscript. He asked Jonathan Cape if this was satisfactory, and realising the problem the title was causing, enquired 'Am I more bother than other of your writers?' However he soon had misgivings about this title also, and wrote to Cape in April 1934:

> What I am writing about is title. *W of V* seems to me rather horrible now. Can't it be *WINGED V.* which isn't so bad? [7] Or if that's not available, there's a Keats phrase … Huge cloudy symbols of a High Romance,[8] you remember. Ironic. And you could comment in blurb thus: Major YB is reported in *Cry Havoc* to have said 'Many young pilots etc (whatever he did say; I haven't the book but you'll know) blub blub': here is the presentation of the romance.
> What do you think? *High Romance*. Wife says it won't do. Public wants something direct, not ironic. What a life. But blurb might make it simple enough for public.

The quotation to which Victor refers in support of his suggested title *High Romance* is contained in Beverley Nichols' book *Cry Havoc!* which Jonathan Cape had published in 1933. Francis Yeats-Brown, a right wing journalist and former army officer who had written a best selling book *Bengal Lancer*, poses the following question in a conversation with a pacifist:

> 'Supposing you were a young airman, couldn't you at least see the romance and excitement of it even though you were killing?'

It was not until late in April that the title question was finally resolved when *Winged Victory* was agreed upon, although a reader cannot escape the irony of this title.

Williamson visited America in February 1934, when he met his New York publishers, Harrison Smith and Robert Haas who, on the strength of his strong recommendations, accepted Victor's forthcoming book unread.[9] This was exceptional considering it was by an unknown author although Jonathan Cape had agreed by then to publish it in England. Harrison Smith wrote to Victor on 12 March that he was looking forward to seeing the book with 'the greatest pleasure' and that Williamson's 'enthusiasm for it is unbounded'. A formal Agreement followed which covered the distribution of the book in the USA and provided for a royalty of 10% on the first 3,000 copies sold, 12½% on the next 2,000 and 15% thereafter. Most importantly, the publishers made an immediate advance of $500 on account of future royalties, which would have been most welcome at that time.

Like Jonathan Cape, they too were unhappy with the title which had been shown in the Agreement as *A Test to Destruction* (showing Williamson's influence), and they raised this matter with Victor in their letter of 2 May:

> I look forward to reading WINGED VICTORY, if we are to call it that, with excitement but no trepidation. We are still bothered about the title and Williamson is against WINGED VICTORY which he thinks banal. But I think his suggestions are worse, not because they are banal but because they are bad titles. A title after

> all is a label and I see no reason for giving one to your book that would be forbidding or confusing.

No better alternative title was forthcoming, and so it was agreed that the English title would be used as this could help to sell more copies in America if the book became a success in England.

Williamson was reading the proofs of the book, which he described as 'a beautiful and balanced transcript of reality', on his way back to England from America, and he refers to the title problem in *The Linhay on the Downs* which was published in November 1934. He wrote that it was originally going to be *A Test to Destruction*, but that everyone looked blank and didn't know what it meant except for the author and some of his friends, who had already been tested to destruction. It was therefore changed to *Winged Victory* which was somewhat ironic to former RFC pilots. He did not mention, however, that the author himself was not keen on *A Test to Destruction*, which was the main reason for the revised title.

In appreciation of the help he had initially received from Henry Williamson, Victor named one of the two main characters in the book after him – although it was in no way intended to be a portrait of Henry. In addition, in acknowledgement of his continued help and encouragement, he decided later that it would be a fitting tribute to include a dedication to Williamson, and in view of this, he became concerned whether he should change the character's name. He queried this with his publisher, and Cape agreed that it would be preferable if the name was changed, and suggested 'Williams' as an alternative. No alteration was made, however, and 'Williamson' appears as one of the main characters in the book so the objection cannot have been thought to be of lasting importance.

In February 1933, Williamson had caused something of a stir by publishing *The Gold Falcon* anonymously and he subsequently sent a copy to Victor which he inscribed:

> To the Tassel Gentle from the Gold Falcon [10]

He suggested that the dedication in *Winged Victory* should not name him but should be made 'To the author of *The Gold Falcon*'

The author Henry Williamson, pictured here circa 1934

which would help to increase the sales of the book. Williamson later explained that if *Winged Victory* was also published anonymously with his suggested dedication to the anonymous author of *The Gold Falcon*, the public would think that he had written it and so buy more copies of the book, the real author's name being released later.[11] Obviously Victor would not have entertained this odd suggestion, and Williamson himself seems to have had second thoughts about it as after he wrote it, he asked Victor to ignore these remarks.

By February 1934 the book was complete and he sent off Phase Three to Williamson for comment. He was most upset to receive Williamson's response which indicated that he had rewritten parts of it and had also re-arranged the last chapter suggesting Victor should cut out some of the 'economic talk.' Victor replied in great anguish and horror that this was wrong and that he did not care about the art of writing as his book was true, it was life. Although he was willing to consider Williamson's recommendations as to where amendments were needed, he felt strongly that he must make any alterations himself, as the book must be his own work. He accepted the need for revision, however, and went through the final part again making a number of improvements but mainly in his own words. Although a comparison of the last few chapters of Phase Three of the manuscript with the published version does highlight a number of minor alterations, some in Williamson's hand, none are in fact major revisions. An example of Williamson's influence can be seen from the following passage taken from the final chapter. Victor originally wrote:

> They gave him drink. He went to the tent and slept soundly for two hours. But it was hell to wake up to the desolate tent
> He drank tea. The thing was gaining on him: the lead in his belly was beginning to melt and burn. He would have a rotten night.

Victor accepted Williamson's revision so it now reads:

> They gave him drink. He went to his tent. He slept, but it was hell to wake up in the desolate tent.
> He drank tea. The thing was gaining on him; the glass in his belly was beginning to move and pierce. He couldn't face the night alone. [12]

In his Tribute, Williamson gives the impression that he had rewritten the last chapters of the book, and Victor himself wrote in the copy he presented to Henry that 'H.W. cut my ending into shape' which leads one to assume that much of the final part was Williamson's work.[13] Apart from such small alterations as illustrated above which were made mainly in the last chapter to heighten the impact of Williamson's death, there is no evidence of wholesale revision. As Williamson subsequently admitted to T. E. Lawrence (Lawrence of Arabia), Victor put much of the original wording back which he thought was to the book's detriment.[14]

The continuous pressure of forcing himself to write each day, often when he would have been feeling quite ill, began to take its toll and it is surprising that this is not reflected in his writing. He did, however, bare his soul to Williamson on occasions which gives an insight into how ill and frustrated he must have been:

> God. I feel bad. I've got a cold and my pathway is downwards. I'm doomed more surely than you. I can't think, can't write, I'm not doing anything at all but rot. I must get to Africa. Don't mind my grumbling, but this disease is so damned exasperating. You build up and build up patiently until you don't feel so bad, and then you get a damned cold and are back again where you were six months ago in a few days. You haven't the energy or the breath to go out and get warm in cold weather, and if you sit about indoors you catch cold for certain.[15]

Again, in February, just before Williamson set sail for America Victor wrote:

> Farewell, farewell, farewell. Thou goest to the warm south. O fortunate tu! I sit here and cough and cough and cough. If the Great-hearted British Public won't buy my BOOK, it puts on the black and condemns me. No use, Wingless Victor, 'twill say. Get under the earth. Toot toot (trumpet of doom).[16]

Victor was by this time signing his letters to Williamson 'Wingless Victor', a rather tragic name in the circumstances. He wrote to

Williamson that if the book sold really well, would he spend some time with him in the Transvaal, where his brother-in-law Cedric Richards was manager of a gold mine, and where they could shoot big game. On receipt of these letters Williamson became very concerned with Victor's worsening condition, and generously offered him a loan to enable him to spend some time in Africa where the warmer, healthier climate would be of benefit, but perhaps unsurprisingly, the offer was not taken up.

Books had been of great comfort to him all his life and when he entered hospital in April 1933 he asked his wife to bring him the *Oxford Book of Poetry* on her next visit. He was fond of Boswell, writing to Norah:

> Being in hospital I do appreciate Boswell. He is always readable. Listen to this 'though I can by no means approve of confounding the distinction between lawful & illicit offspring …I cannot help thinking it laudable to be kind to those of whose existence we have, <u>in any way</u>, been the cause'. I ask you.[17]

He had already referred to his appreciation of Boswell in *Winged Victory* when Tom remarked that 'Boswell was the only book in the world likely to triumph over a queasy stomach'.

Cape asked Victor to write a blurb for the book but, somewhat surprisingly, he replied that he had no wish to do so. Williamson obliged, indicating that he had collaborated in the writing of the novel. Victor objected to this statement as he considered 'collaborated' was too strong a word. An acknowledgement of his help and guidance would be covered in the dedication:

> To
> HENRY WILLIAMSON
> at whose suggestion this book was begun, with whose
> encouragement and help it was written and ended.

Williamson also wrote a blurb for the American edition which Harrison Smith thought was overwritten – Victor sent a copy to Norah whilst he was convalescing, commenting:

> I enclose it [the blurb] in case you would like to read the extraordinary remarks. Smiling fortitude is a lovely touch – so touching.

In the event, Williamson's wording was not used, as the blurb which appeared on the dust jacket of the American edition was identical to that in Cape's edition published three months earlier – although it is not clear whether this also was Williamson's work. Victor's American publishers, at his request, sent Williamson a cheque for $60, representing a fee for writing the blurb which, although not used on the dust jacket, may have been the basis for other publicity material. Williamson however refused to accept it, and thoughtfully passed it on to Victor.

Williamson, who regarded himself as a poet, romantically wanted Victor to be advertised as one also, as he considered some of his prose, like his own, had a poetic quality. Victor objected, not having written any serious poetry, but Williamson continued to refer to him as a poet in later writings. Victor had jotted down some verse for amusement on occasions – Williamson for example, included a poem in *Goodbye West Country* which he had found on the cover of one of the exercise books in which *Family Life* was written.[18] Another piece of verse, written with the war in mind, was scribbled on a letter:

When I consider how the toiling years
Bring to world more pain and pain's infliction
And cruelty increased by growing fears
And goodness check'd by evil insurrection
When for the schooling of poor naked man
I see prepared engines of huge destruction
And wealth misused and money misapplied
And knowledge slave to damned misdirection
Then in despair back in myself I cringe
And study to maintain a selfless ease
And   *life.*

Victor's publisher was of the opinion that the book was too long and suggested some pruning. Some six thousand words were deleted – achieved by omitting odd words here and there which did not alter the meaning of sentences, and by excluding a number of paragraphs which was done without affecting the story-line. A question also arose over Chapter 18 of Phase One which included a debate on profiteering, and it was finally agreed that the whole chapter should be omitted, as the gist of the conversations had been covered in other parts of the novel.[19]

It would appear that from the outset, Victor had reservations about the structure of the book and he expressed some lack of confidence in correspondence with Williamson, who he felt, must find the book dull. He had also written of his apprehension to his wife:

> I have about finished proof-reading. Now for the whizz, if any. It is rather horrible to me in print in many places – clumsy, obscure, dull. It is a relief to think that you liked it. Perhaps I have read it ten times too often.

A charcoal portrait, sketched when Victor was eighteen, adorned a wall in his house in Sidcup Road and he suggested to Cape that it could be used as a frontispiece, but this was rejected as Cape indicated that it was unusual to have a frontispiece in a novel.[20]

The doctors prescribed complete rest and relaxation as the only way to combat his illness, but this proved impossible as he was anxious for his book to be published without any delay. He had driven himself to the limit, 'all hard slogging and chipping words out of my breastbone', a phrase which Williamson liked and one which he was to use himself in several of his later books.[21] It is hardly surprising then, that the demands he had made on himself during the latter twelve months eventually took their toll. In mid-April Victor was admitted, exhausted, to a convalescent home, Pineville, in West Cliff Gardens in Bournemouth where it was hoped the fresh sea air would be beneficial. He could not relax completely, however, as he was still correcting the proofs, the book having been sent to the printers the previous month.

His mother, who quite naturally was very concerned for her son, contributed towards the cost of the nursing home fees, and as she was still living in Bournemouth they were able to see much more of one another. Although now in her late sixties she looked younger and was very proud of the fact that her hair had not turned grey, in marked contrast to Norah's hair which had been grey for many years. Victor would have been thinking of her when writing *Family Life* as Mrs Felce, Julian's mother, remarks:

> 'Did you ever see such hair in a woman of my age? Not a grey hair in my head; in spite of all the worry I have. That's the funny part of it. I'm nearly worried into my grave first by one thing, then by another, and yet my hair keeps its wonderful colour.'

He had driven down to Pineville in his car and so when he felt well enough, Victor and his mother were able to enjoy day trips together – one such trip was a visit to Beaulieu which she thoroughly enjoyed. His father Augustus had died on 21 December 1933, and his mother was at this time dealing with the probate requirements, which she considered an ordeal to which he referred in a letter to Norah in April 1934:

> My mother is well except for some questions from the Probate people which she has to answer. She says it gives her diarrhoea to have to answer questions.[22]

He recalled his mother's feelings when writing about Mrs Felce again in *Family Life*:

> As the sole legatee and executrix she could not avoid bothersome correspondence with solicitors; she regarded the inquisition into her husband's financial affairs and the demand for death duties as utterly wicked, devised solely for torturing and impoverishing a poor wretched widow.

Although well meaning, Lavinia, who described Victor as 'the best son in the world', was still somewhat difficult to deal with, and it is understandable that Victor became exasperated with her at times. When he was in the sanatoriums she often sent him small gifts; one, a new dressing gown was useful, but another was less so:

> I suggested to my mother that she might like to send me [Boswell's] *Tour in the Hebrides*, & she responded with an American funny

> book! I have composed a letter for her today, but find it a little wearing to think of suitable remarks, and I am afraid I may not always be successful.[23]

Again he writes to Norah:

> I had a hysterical letter from my mother this morning. I wish she would calm down. In spite of my earnest entreaties, she has bought a book on old churches, with fifty pictures. She says 'I bought it for you', and then asks if I would like it. [24]

He had not given up hope on his first attempt at a novel, *Adjustment*, and in April, he referred to it in a letter to Jonathan Cape:

> Look, I'm knocking another novel into shape, only it won't go. Shape I mean. I wonder if you'd read it soon; I should like your opinion as to its publishability before the success or flop of the other affects the issue.

Cape rejected the book, but not submitting to failure Victor sent it off in June to another publisher, Arthur Barker Ltd, in the hope of a more favourable response. Although it was again rejected, they recognised his writing potential as they stated they would be very interested to see anything else that he might write, if he was not under contract to anyone else.

On 23 February, just before he departed for America and whilst the book was being finalised, Williamson mentioned the 'marvellous' book about the RAF entitled *A Test to Destruction* to T. E. Lawrence, with whom he regularly corresponded, and told him something of Victor's tragic circumstances.[25] He again described him as a great poet, and later that month forwarded one of Victor's letters 'merely for interest'. He asked Lawrence whether he would read a proof copy when available and help it on its way by giving a quote which Cape could use in its publicity material – this, as he later admitted, was somewhat premature, as Lawrence had not at that time read the manuscript. A proof copy was sent to him, however, in May and in his reply to Williamson with his 'review' of the book he wrote that he had been 'delightedly' reading *Winged Victory* and thought it admirable.[26]

He then continued with a critical analysis, commenting that he thought the 'purple' passages were too long so a reader tended to skip them, there were too many rare words of classical origin and many of the ideas expressed in the book related to the 1930s rather than those which were current in 1918. The descriptions of flight amongst the clouds and the development of the characters were pleasing as was the final chapter which was masterly. He assumed that much of the book was reality including the scenes in the hospitals. Having served in the ranks of the RAF as a humble aircraftman himself, first under the assumed name of 'J. H. Ross' and later as 'T. E. Shaw', he thought it was a pity the 'other ranks' were not mentioned more but, quite correctly, added a rejoinder that officers rarely had any contact with them. Although he felt the book was being published too late for it to be a financial success, he regarded it as 'An imperishable pleasure'.

In April, Victor was invited to a house party hosted by Messrs. Jonathan Cape for their authors and it was here that he met one of Lawrence's RAF friends, Gregory W. M. Dunn, whose book *Poems – Group One*, with Lawrence's help, had been published by Cape earlier that year. [27] Dunn had been asked to review *Winged Victory* for Cape's in-house magazine *Now and Then* and after reading a proof copy, he wrote to Victor later that month suggesting that Victor had been too modest about the book at the party, as he found it wholly praiseworthy. Although he suggested a couple of small amendments to the text which were accepted, Victor was pleased with Dunn's appraisal and replied:

> I am glad you liked my stuff. I was a little afraid my old memories of flying might seem faded and unreal to a present flyer … I was told I was writing too diaryishly and must not write the truth so much as The Truth. Well, well. [28]

Dunn arranged for Cape to send Victor a complimentary copy of his book of poems on receipt of which Victor replied that, although he had not had chance to read the book carefully, he loved 'his flooding warm-in-the-chest making rhythms.'

On 24 June 1934 *Winged Victory* was finally published priced at ten shillings and sixpence (52p) – it had been anticipated it would cost seven shillings and sixpence (37p) but as Cape explained, it was now a long book which justified the higher price. Everyone concerned had high expectations that it would be a success and so provide some badly needed funds for Victor and his family.

THE PLAIN DUST WRAPPER OF THE 1934 ENGLISH FIRST EDITION

Notes

1 *WV*, p. 392.

2 In the Air 76 Officers Records at the NA his address is shown as 15 Duke Street, WC2 in May 1919 whilst 48 Boyne Road, Lewisham is quoted as his address in *The Inns of Court Officers Training Corps during the Great War.*

3 One such occasion was on 10 April 1913 when he accompanied Williamson and another school friend, Smith, on a visit to Elmstead woods – see *Henry Williamson Society Journal* No. 38, Summer 2002, p. 26, 'A School-boy's diary 1913.' See also *Young Phillip Maddison*, p. 404, 'Cundall now took charge; this was his country; the Elmstead woods were his preserves.'

4 Tom also remarks to his friend Seddon 'But there's a saying, all property is theft.' *WV*, p. 208. The French political theorist Pierre Proudhon (1809-1865) gave the answer 'property is theft' to the question posed by his famous essay *What is Property?* (1840). He described the ownership of capital as the right of exploiting the labour of others without just reward and advocated that the ideal state should be brought about by progressive reductions in interest and rent.

5 *WV*, Tribute p. 2.

6 Victor referred to this accident in a letter to H. Williamson, quoted in *WV* Tribute, p. 2.

7 The title *Winged Victory* had been used by Norman Leslie for his novel of a bomber squadron pilot in WWI which had been published three years earlier in 1931 by Thomas Nelson & Sons Ltd.

8 The quote is taken from John Keats poem *When I have fears.*

9 Harrison Smith and Robert Haas had published Williamson's *The Gold Falcon* in 1933.

10 Copy of *The Gold Falcon* in possession of Joy Vowles.

11 Anne Williamson, *Henry Williamson, Tarka and the Last Romantic*, p. 173.

12 *WV*, p.451.

13 Daniel Farson in *Henry, An Appreciation of Henry Williamson*, Michael Joseph 1982, p. 195, writes that Henry re-wrote the last chapter himself as Victor was too ill to do so.

14 T. E. Lawrence *Correspondence with Henry Williamson*, Castle Hill Press 2000, p. 162, letter from Williamson to Lawrence dated 26 May 1934.

15 *WV*, Tribute, p. 4.

16 Ibid., p. 7. Victor had written in his letter 'O fortunate tu.' but Williamson had altered this to 'O fortunatus tu!' when he quoted from this letter in his Tribute.

17 Letter to Norah dated 1 May 1933.

18 H. Williamson, *Goodbye West Country*, p. 47.

19 See Appendix A.

20 This charcoal portrait was included as a frontispiece in the Reprint Society edition of *WV* which was published in 1963. It had also appeared on the inside rear flap of the dust jacket of the 1961 and 1962 reprints published by Jonathan Cape.

21 Radio broadcast 21 March 1936 printed in *The Listener* 25 March 1936; *The Story of a Norfolk Farm*, Faber and Faber 1941 Chapter 2 when describing the writing of *Salar the Salmon*; Preface to 'Tales of Moorland and Estuary' in *Collected Nature Stories*, Macdonald 1970, p. 306 when again referring to *Salar the Salmon* 'It seemed dull to me, 'every word chipped from the breast-bone' as V. M. Yeates wrote of himself whilst writing, at Eltham in Kent, his classic *Winged Victory*.'

22 Letter written to Norah on 18 April 1934 from Pineville, West Cliff Gardens, Bournemouth.

23 Letter to Norah dated 1 May 1933.

24 Letter to Norah dated 'Probably 4 May' [1933].

25 T. E. Lawrence was at this time known as T. E. Shaw but he is here referred to by his more well-known name 'T. E. Lawrence.'

26 The Personal Tribute which Williamson wrote for *John O'London's Weekly* published on 26 January 1935 quoted from correspondence with T. E. Lawrence. Williamson stated that Lawrence had written 'I read it for seven nights … .' and 'How fortunate is the R.A.F. to have collared one of the most distinguished histories of the War, and how creditable that it deserves it.' These quotations were strictly incorrect, as T. E. Lawrence had written 'I have spent the evenings of rather more than a week in delightedly reading *Winged Victory* …', and 'How fortunate the R.A.F. has been to collar for itself one of the most distiguished histories of the war! And how creditable that it deserves it.' The Tribute, without the first quotation, also appeared in *Goodbye West Country* (1937) in which Williamson remarks that he had been admonished for the misquote by A. W. Lawrence, T. E. Lawrence's younger brother, who had commented that he [Williamson] did not have 'a scholar's eye.' The correct quotations appeared in Williamson's *Genius of Friendship – T.E. Lawrence*, Faber & Faber, 1941.

27 Two copies of Dunn's book of poems were found in Lawrence's library in Clouds Hill on his death. One was inscribed 'For T. E. Shaw from G. W. M. Dunn. For the only encouragement I ever received.'

28 Cited in Stephen F. Clarke's Clearwater Books 'Spica' Catalogue 1986.

CHAPTER TEN

A PERSONAL WAR

Fourteen months had elapsed from Victor's acceptance of Henry Williamson's suggestion of a flying novel to its publication, during which time his health had gradually deteriorated. What he had envisaged as a trilogy was now a long book – possibly too long – as he himself acknowledged.[1] He had pushed himself hard to complete it which had resulted in a relapse and the stay at the nursing home in Bournemouth.

It is part autobiography, part fiction and part history, and as he wrote in the copy that he gave to Williamson, his main difficulty was to 'compromise between truth and art'. He achieved his objective admirably as the reader immediately recognises that it rings true, not surprising considering that it is largely his own story and faithfully reproduces the life of a fighter pilot in 1918. Fellow pilot Ernest Watt confirmed this, stating that 'actually Yeates had many facts, more than you would think'. Williamson himself wrote that Victor had lived through all but the final three chapters, but apart from the death of Bill Williamson, much of the action described in these chapters is based on reality.[2] It is very moving and one begins to relate to Tom from the first page, the style of writing leading the reader to empathise with his thoughts and emotions day-by-day as the strain begins to take its toll, culminating in his breakdown. As one reviewer aptly put it in a letter to Norah:

> … he obviously put so much of himself into his book. … Whoever reads the book will, I am sure, know something of its author.[3]

He had set out to write a book which was true to life as he had experienced it on the Western Front but it is in no sense a glorification of war, in fact quite the reverse, it is an indictment of war and an anti-war book. It is perhaps the only book on the air war which describes and explores the darker side of a pilot's experience, living with the fear of not only being killed, but also the fear of losing one's nerve under the psychological strain. He adeptly develops this anxiety so that a reader senses a growing romantic feeling of doom overcoming his hero as the months pass. This culminates at the very end of the novel when Tom's friend Williamson is killed the day before they were both due to return to Blighty on leave, and Tom, heartbroken, is sent home both physically and mentally broken.

This is the only highpoint, as he chose to recount the routine life and comradeship of a group of pilots sharing the same hut on a fighter squadron during a seven month period in 1918 through the eyes of his hero, or perhaps anti-hero, Tom Cundall, whose exploits are largely based on his own experiences. The main characters in this group are skilfully developed, so that one soon begins to relate to them, their fears and ambitions; they seem like real people. The reader feels a deep sense of sorrow, therefore, as one by one they are lost and replaced by new pilots fresh from training.

In order to portray how the cumulative effect of the daily fighting affected the pilots, their weariness with the conflict and their agony at the loss of their friends, it was necessary, as he explained to Williamson, to include much detail as the book 'was to be an exact reproduction of a period and an exact analysis and synthesis of a state of mind'. So it is almost inevitable that he would describe *The Camels are Coming*, the first of the very popular 'Biggles' books by W. E. Johns, written as an heroic adventure story, as being 'super-bunk.'[4] His book had to be factual and he was very dismissive of flamboyant stories of air warfare far removed from reality, as is evident from his comments on such a short story:

> Why the devil was such stuff published? What a rotten trade authorship was; spreading misconceptions and lies.[5]

An insight into his thoughts when compiling his novel can be gleaned from a letter he wrote to Williamson in January 1934 as it was being completed:

> You say I musn't let things happen as in life. I MUST. Art is selection, not alteration. ... There is no meaning whatever in events that are not as-in-life, unless we want to use words for rhythm and decoration, like late Joyce, but that seems to be plastic art, not literary. [6]

Written some fifteen years after the event, although true in essence, some of 'the bitter wisdom of retrospect' has crept into a number of the debates as he himself admitted.[7] He acknowledged this in a letter to Norah when he had just srarted writing:

> All history is contemporary history. I mean, we see the past in terms (so to speak) of the present.

There are two main themes running through the book which mirrored Victor's own thoughts and emotions during the war. First his increasing disillusionment and bitterness with the war itself, the generals and the politicians at home. He gradually comes to recognise the senselessness and hypocrisy of the conflict which results in his distrust of all declarations of patriotism. Initially, like many other young men who joined the armed forces he was enthusiastic and patriotic, but the experience of war soon changed his outlook and he becomes more cynical:

> Tom ... moaned with him [Smith] about war; admitting that the flicker of patriotism that once irradiated his mind had been damped almost to extinction by the murderous issue of rivalry in patriotisms. And the whole thing was the outcome of political wangles. International treaties were the final scores in games of diplomatic cunning played for their own hands, and as much for personal as for national prestige, by politicians who hated each other like bulls and bears. ... They should try to survive if only to join in the coming protest. [8]

He reflects on his change of sentiment as the effects of the war begin to be felt:

> At half-past seven he was going out on patrol: no, not he: he had been

> murdered long ago. This fretting cursing wreck was not he. He was a young man filled with joyous life, one of God's Englishmen, captains of the earth, loving the glory that was England, responding to England's call with gladness … now God be thanked who matched us with this hour. He was that young fool; not this tired, scared, nervy, old cynic.[9]

Although the killing sickened him from the outset, he was cushioned from it when ground-strafing as it was remote and a pilot rarely saw the results:

> There was, however, about his particular method of murder a strangeness and unreality which relieved the horror of butchery. He pulled a wire and released a bomb. There was nothing dreadful about pulling a wire. … You got rid of the four bombs with alacrity (if they all dropped), very glad to lighten the aeroplane. Then with twice the life in the bus, you dived and zoomed and dived and zoomed, loosing off bursts at the wretched troops, keeping an anxious look-out for machine guns. … Again, you couldn't tell what sort of effect your shooting was having on a target of that sort; it must be doing damage, but the damage was remote and not a direct consequence of your actions. … It wasn't like going up to a man and sticking a bayonet into his neck or guts and giving it a twist; nothing like that: you pressed a lever. [10]

In combat, however, he endured mixed emotions

> God, it was exciting, this aerial combat; the flash of tracers, the cracking of guns; the dread of being hit, of hideous fiery death. … It stirred some primal lust of murder at the same time as his mind abhorred it. Poor devils, said pity: you have killed them, you are the strong cunning man, said unreason, the hero bathed in the blood of enemies. O God, what was he, man or beast? [11]

He did not have the inherent hatred of the enemy which most of the more successful Hun-getters had – they had no quarrel with each other; it was a lie and delusion that made them fight. Gould Lee was of similar mind:

> We don't hate each other. In fact, we probably hate strikers at home, stabbing us in the back, far more than the Huns we have

> to fight, who are risking their skins for their country just as we are – only they happen to have been born in Germany. [12]

His revulsion to all the killing and his increasing bitterness and anger towards the war is displayed again when he reflects on the death of his friend Seddon:

> He must not think of it: he would go mad. Or he must think: he died for England; who dies if England live? He must think: he died willingly that others might live; fighting for all he held dear. He must think that God had care of him, that he was a hero, that his death would help to bring lasting peace to the world … O curse those damned lies plastered over the brutish face of war. He must endure the truth he saw; the naked beastliness of this harpy; hating the system of lies and grab that bought it forth. There was yet one iron god that could make life noble: truth.[13]

The controversy over the leadership of the war ('Lions led by donkeys') still rages to this day and an extract from *Adjustment* illustrates where Victor's sympathies lie:

> Doubtless after years and years of application to cavalry drill and tactics and King's Regulations, they [the higher ranks] understood war; but it was always the last war, never the one they were fighting, which was so confoundedly different from what it ought to be that they never knew what to do next. Having a general rule that a war must be got on with, they were afraid to stand still. The armies might get together and ask each other what all the fighting was about. So attacks were made which captured an acre of useless ground, if they captured anything, at the cost of a thousand lives, often in conditions so bad that the wounded were drowned in mud. The effect of a successful attack was to make a salient which could only be defended with great difficulty, and usually had to be abandoned promptly to straighten the line. But loss of life only meant to professional soldiers that they were getting on with the war. Moreover, whereas the generals were only earning earldoms and baronies, the troops in the mud were certainly qualifying for the superior delights of heaven.

He expands on these views in *Winged Victory*:

> Let some of the bloody politicians and contractors and field marshals

> come and do a bit; the liason officers and brass hats whose lives were too valuable to be risked, blast their souls, with rooms at the War Office, or at Paris, or in châteaux miles away; the home-front and base-inhabiting nephews of ministers and millionaires, very remote and happy and patriotic, in khaki but out of the war. It was Tom, Dick, and Harry that would win the war with their blood .... [14]

On the political front, Victor leaned towards the left. He recognised the futility of war but he was not a pacifist. Although not a criticism of society as a whole, there is throughout the book a constant search for civilised values. He felt that the redistribution of wealth after the war would be essential if poverty was to be eradicated which he expanded upon in one of his unpublished papers.[15]

Victor was a thoughtful and sensitive person and his honest portrayal of the effect of continuous combat flying is the second main theme running through the book. His nerves first begin to be affected when the Squadron is detailed ground-strafing duties and the arrival of the fearless flight commander, Capt. Smith ('Beal') in March 1918, worsens the situation, which is compounded by stomach problems:

> But if he went sick it might be thought he had wind up. In a way it was true; he had got wind up. The thought of ground-strafing made him feel like a jelly that would not set. He lived in a state of utter funk ....[16]

In anticipation of the visit from the M.O. he muses:

> If he swung the lead a bit he might be invalided home. Not wind up; he would never be sent home in that disgrace. He would admit fear, but by God, he wasn't yellow. [17]

The stress of flying offensive patrols two or three times a day in machines which were often unreliable, inevitably begin to affect him to such an extent that Tom debates whether it would be better to escape from the strain and killing by landing behind the German lines and becoming a prisoner of war. This thought must have gone through many a pilot's mind but pride and the thought of letting down his fellow pilots soon extinguished this idea. It was the balance of fears that kept him going, the fear of his friends balancing fear of the enemy. In the end, Tom, like Victor, becomes utterly exhausted both mentally and physically, and is sent home to Blighty to recuperate.

Thrown together with total strangers, with little privacy, Victor took some time to adjust to a life very different from that which he was used to:

> I regret to say that just at present the other young men who inhabit this hut are painting their furniture blue with most vile smelling dope, for some mysterious reason, so I am rather disturbed in mind, especially as the blue is of a most displeasing tone.[18]

He soon settled down, however, appreciating the comradeship of his hut-mates:

> Tom felt that he was extraordinary lucky in his hut companions. He might so easily have had, in this chance association, incomprehensible colonials or boys straight from school with their usual poverty of ideas and plenitude of foul language: good fellows and all that, but better for a rag in the mess than arguments in the hut. [19]

When, one by one, these hut-mates with whom he could relate and who had become his friends are lost, he feels their deaths deeply. Seddon, the bank clerk who thought war was being fought in the interests of usury and funded by big business; Smith, newly married who longed for his wife; Allen, who was determined to be faithful to his fiancée, and finally Williamson, who became Tom's greatest friend and steadying influence. Like many other servicemen in wartime, he soon became conscious of the psychological danger of getting too close to his friends. After both Smith and Seddon are lost in quick succession he writes:

> He wouldn't have any more friends. He must be self-sufficient. Friends went, all of them, and he couldn't bear losing any more. [20]

After a few more months, however, he had learnt to detach himself from the death of his fellow pilots:

> The fifth man had vanished. No one minded that much; new youngsters came and vanished or killed themselves before anyone got to know them. Not one in ten settled down. [21]

Few fighter pilots survived for long on a front-line squadron – Victor writes that the average life of a pilot when he joined up was six weeks – but if one could survive the first three to four months the experience gained meant that the chances of survival were greatly increased. Eighty per cent of casualties were pilots who had done less that twenty jobs. During the seven months he spent in France first with No. 46 Squadron and later with No. 80 Squadron, twenty-eight pilots were killed, taken prisoner of war or were injured, the majority of these casualties occurring in the German offensive in March and the Allied attack in August.[22] Victor recognised the tragic loss of life amongst his fellow pilots as forty-three of the sixty-two pilots named in the novel become casualties.

With a pregnant wife at home and an unalloyed love of life, Victor was careful not to get into unnecessary scrapes although the unavoidable danger of ground-strafing was forever on his mind:

> He was more concerned about his own skin than that of such Germans as he happened to blow up or shoot up, and machine-gun fire from the ground was the very devil. [23]

It is interesting to note that research after the war indicated that, in general, married pilots were not as aggressive as single men and Victor had recognised this although he distinguished between those happily married and those less happy:

> Married men, thought Tom, really ought not to go to war until they had got tired of their wives, and then they ought, divorce laws being what they were. Those that were still happy were the most unenthusiastic, and those that weren't the most reckless, of warriors. [24]

Donald MacLaren, who obtained a copy of *Winged Victory* some years after it was published, remembered Victor as being somewhat 'dreamy' and an average pilot which seems to agree with Victor's own perception of himself, when describing Tom as only 'a slightly useful hack':

> Tom felt that he wasn't brilliant or ever likely to be brilliant, either as pilot or fighter. He was a careful hack. By mere survival and accumulation of experience he was becoming a slightly useful hack; he could give a mite of the experienced support that the real fighters needed. [25]

However Victor was a very competent pilot having survived both the 'March push' and the Allied offensive, and realistically he must have considered himself a good scout pilot:

> Of course he was no hero, but probably he was as good as most people: no, not as most people, as most pilots, and scout pilots at that. Most mere people hadn't the nerve to be pilots at all, and among those that had, scout pilots were supposed to be the pick. [26]

Not being a born fighter nor having the desire to become one, is reflected in Tom's worry that this will be recognised by his superiors and diagnosed as 'funk' and he is terribly concerned when he makes a flying error, that he will be thought incompetent. After his first crash in France his pride suffers:

> It was a failure, and it hurt his pride to fail ridiculously. He had taken on a job that officially assumed that he possessed all sorts of fine qualities of head and heart, and even if it was pure bluff, he hated his bluff to be seen through. Nothing hurts pride, he reflected, like being found out. [27]

His sensitivity to criticism is also revealed when he returns to the Squadron after another crash-landing due to an engine problem, and he is questioned by two of the flight commanders. He realises he had not done all he could to try to rectify the fault and he feels guilty:

> It was one thing to admit funk to oneself, or to confess it spontaneously to a friend, but it was damnable to be caught and indicted publicly. He hated being found out. [28]

Again, after making a forced landing on the aerodrome when his engine cut out in mist, he agonises as to how he could have avoided damaging the machine and his pride is hurt even though officially he was blameless:

> He had once again made a fool of himself in the sight of men; nothing was more irritating and depressing to him. He, an experienced pilot, an old hand. [29]

Victor loved flying and often went up for a 'joy ride' when he was not on duty:

> ... ordinary peaceful flying was a daily delight whose absence took

> flavour from the empty day. A half hour's flight every morning; a dash up to ten or twelve thousand feet, some foolery among the clouds if there were any, then some contour-chasing; that was the prescription to keep a man healthy and wise. So, although there were no jobs in the morning as the clouds were thick at two thousand feet, Tom went up for amusement ... he set off over the countryside at a height of ten feet and a speed of a hundred miles an hour, jumping over whatever got in his way, full of the joy and excitement and unique bliss of flying a rotary scout, fleeter than wind, lighter than gazelle, more powerful than tempest. [30]

The thrill of flying at low-level with the resulting sensation of speed, is always an attraction for pilots and Victor was no exception, describing the pleasures of contour-chasing:

> But contour-chasing was pure joy, charging across country at a hundred miles an hour, flashing past villages where nervous old women swooned as you roared by their bedroom windows, jumping trees and telegraph wires, scattering troops on the march, diving at brass-hats in their expensive cars; in fact being a great nuisance with complete immunity from reprisal. [31]

There was still a sense of awe and mystery surrounding flying, the newspapers calling pilots 'the knights errant of the air' and so they could get away with most stunts including the popular one of diving on high-ranking officers:

> Occasionally a brass hat would put in a complaint, but it was never possible to track the offending pilot, and as a rule it was all taken in good part, for there was still a certain glamour surrounding the R.F.C. and most people seemed to feel slightly honoured by its snook-cocking. To non-flying folk there was something marvellous about flying, and the aviators who came thundering about their ears were more wonderful than irritating. [32]

Professor M. S. Greicus in his booklet *Prose Writers of World War I* (Longman Group, 1973) writes that 'There is for Yeates, in flying, a suggestion that man's taking to the air, like his taking to war, has eternal qualities':

> It had become very familiar to Tom, this business of flying that once had been so tentative and unnatural ... The ground fled past and sank away

> in its immemorial manner. There was nothing strange about it; always the earth has behaved thus, if not actually, then potentially; what was actual at one point of time being part of the texture of all time, as if the all-pervasive human mind was already familiar with the aroma of all experience, of which the individual items were realizations in time of its possessions in eternity, and men seemed less to learn than to remember.[33]

Leighton Brewer, an American pilot who flew Spads with 13th Pursuit Squadron in 1918, wrote to Victor in October 1934 just after the American edition had been published.[34] He described *Winged Victory* as the most vivid and forceful account of flying during the war he had read. He wrote that the imagery of the descriptions of clouds, light and colour, together with the picture of the war-torn ground were especially effective. One such passage gives the reader a glimpse of the pleasures of flying in the evening sunlight:

> He went up, however, after tea for amusement, and wandered off towards the low sun. It was a delightfully calm unclouded evening and rather misty. Flying towards the sun was as if he were in the apse of an immense temple with walls of luminous gold, and the sun a present blinding-bright deity; such beauty and texture did the mind lend to mere molecules and vibrations, if such things were. [35]

His love of the English language and the descriptive power of his writing are evident in a number of fine paragraphs, which T. E. Lawrence referred to as 'purple' passages. These magnificent passages, one reviewer remarked, revealed that Victor was 'an artist in words' and one which deserves quoting in full is:

> Enormous red-copper clouds formed after every noon, resting on a dingy stratum of mist. The air was full of invisible precipices and rocks near the ground. The clouds towered higher than Camels flew; they were the authentic Himalayas of heavy summer, strange harvest of the sun-tilled air. The Fokkers showed up against their brazen sides, and the black smoke of Archie was not alien to their sultry fires.
>
> For millions of years had summer heat burdened the skies with this empty grandeur, nature's dream-world, only significant by its utter non-significance. At length human purpose had penetrated these

> eagle-baffling heights, the purpose of murder. Dominant, triumphant, intelligent murderousness had driven man to scale these airy precipices and rend grandeur's garment of silence with the terrible staccato voices of his machine guns and the idiot bark of exploding shells.The maniac clamour of war echoed through the blue halls of the winds; terror and brutality ranged the inviolable heavens; iron laughter shook the vault of sky and obscured the pathways of the stars.
>
> The contagion of man's evil vilified the clean high air; fear drove its invisible chariot among the clouds, leaving a spiritual miasma that choked the mind: fear, most anti-human of passions. It yellowed the sky's clarity and magnified the stridor of war into a mind-dinning yell of malice. There was a harsh rhythm of iron wheels in the stultified brain, echoing and clanging among metallic clouds; the sky had turned to brass.[36]

Williamson liked this passage, writing to Lawrence that he thought it was 'grand', but he felt Victor had to concentrate his thoughts on the climax of the story. He wrote on the manuscript before returning it to Victor, 'You see after this preparation of doom, the story has to be base, direct and arrow-straight to its climax of destruction. The above is a very fine passage; but it must not be let-down by any vacillations.' These colourful descriptions, some of which Williamson thought were 'Shakespearean', do set it apart from other war novels and one of the finest such passages, often quoted, also describes the delights of flying amongst the clouds:

> … satisfied that Y was not likely to fall to pieces, he dropped to the floor and contour-chased over its shining hillocks and among its celestial ravines. This was not the majesty of cumulus, with its immitigable towering heights and golden threatening; its soul of fire and shadow; pile on pile of magically suspended gleaming dream-stuff; glory of vision and splendour of reality; shapeless splendour of form; empty solidity; fantastic, mutable, illusory as life itself. This was the level-floating rain cloud, a layer only a few hundred feet thick, that makes the earth so dull a place when it eclipses the sky, and, concentrating all dullness there, leaves the region above it stainless, and very like conventional heaven. On those refulgent rocks should angels sit; like them insubstantial, glowing like them. Music should they make with golden wires, unheard; hymning the evident godhead of the sun, from whom the radiance

> flowed of those immaculable spaces: wings faintly shimmering with faint changing colour, and unbeholding eyes. In that passionless bright void joy abode, interfused among cold atoms of the air. Breath there was keen delight, all earthly grossness purged. [37]

Victor liked the sound of unusual and little-used classical words which prompts the reader to reach for a dictionary to glean their true meaning. As one reviewer aptly remarked 'what on earth, or even in the air, does the word thanatognomonic mean?' used to describe the smoke and flames left by an aeroplane going down (the word is derived from the Greek word 'thanatos' meaning death).[38] Williamson tried without success to dissuade Victor from using such idiosyncratic words and others such as 'vigesimation' (putting to death every 20th man), 'phantasmagoria' (a shifting scene), 'phenakistoscopic' (successive visual images), 'pullated' (hatched) and 'niagraed', which even defeats a dictionary search, remain.

Victor's love of literature is evidenced by the inclusion of quotations from, and references to, a number of classical works ranging from Shakespeare's *Sonnets* and Thomas Gray's *Elegy Written in a Country Churchyard* to lesser known books such as Jeremy Taylor's *Holy Dying*. As has been pointed out, his first suggested title, *This Tassel Gentle*, was taken from *Romeo and Juliet* and one of the alternative titles, *High Romance,* was taken from a Keats poem.

His conservative upbringing is revealed in his reluctance in the narrative to use expletives, even though they were common in the bawdy RAF mess. He wrote to Dunn:

> I believe ' …' and 'balls' just printable: but I flinched. I haven't Williamson's nerve.[39]

Victor had substituted 'testicles' and 'bollocky' in one of the songs[40] and had also, on Williamson's suggestion, included 'fucking' in one of the conversations[41] which he thought was appropriate. His publisher, however, disagreed and deleted these words and blanks appear in the published version.

Although Tom's flying experiences are largely based on Victor's own time on the Squadrons, other aspects of a more personal nature are quite different. Tom, unlike Victor, is a bachelor who had been in Spain when the war started and had served in the infantry before transferring to the RFC, whilst Victor had lived in London all his life and had joined the RFC straight from the OTC. Tom's sister with whom he stayed on leave was a war widow unlike Victor's sister, Augusta, who was living in the USA with her husband. Victor relates that Tom's mother had died from cancer early in the war, but both Victor's parents were still alive.

In many respects, Victor's personality seems to have been portrayed through Tom's friend Seddon who, like Victor, was married (although with two young children) and a bank clerk. The following passage succinctly summarises Victor's own character:

> But take Seddon, who had used to go daily to a bank in Lombard Street to add up other peoples money: gentle, sensitive, civilised, urban, married: with sympathies oblique to the war-lines of enmity now that propaganda and tiger-tail-lashings had taken the place of patriotic fervour, and young men no longer thanked God for matching them with that hour: it was impossible for Seddon to fight for the sake of fighting, to hate because he was told to hate, to have the heart to kill or be killed in cold blood: he must force himself to do what had to be done, to act contrary to intuition and spirit, and the struggle must be tearing his nerves to pieces. ... Why hadn't he gone into the A.S.C. like other married men? Pride, probably; he had felt himself fit to do what the best could do, and he was doing it.[42]

To write such a book with his health gradually deteriorating was a remarkable achievement and he must have realised that his days were numbered. His views on death therefore, portrayed through Tom's thoughts are poignantly relevant:

> He loathed death because it was the end of life, but he could hardly think that he feared it. Was it, after all, fear that troubled him, or was it love of life? ... According to most accounts life had a way of losing its sweetness ... but no, not for Tom Cundall; life could never lose its attractiveness for him while he was not in physical pain. ... He was supremely confident of ability to endure life with all its wear and tear and minute exacerbations. [43]

He reflects on dying later in the book when he again refers to his fondness of life:

> There was nothing to do but make up his mind to die with a good grace; if one must die, better do it as decorously as possible. It was nothing more than a falling asleep. No one was afraid of going to sleep. The only difficulty was that he was fond of life. Life was good.[44]

Whilst Victor's RAF personnel records show that his religion was Church of England, he is reputed to have indicated to the authorities when he enlisted that he was a Swedenborgian, a follower of a somewhat mystic sect formed by a Swede which had a Church in London.[45] Victor refers to this when writing that Tom had not attended a church service for some time, as he 'had met force with guile' by being a Swedenborgian which he describes as 'a creed very baffling to martinets.'[46] He had hoped that by this ruse he would escape the compulsory Church parades but unsurprisingly the authorities would have none of it and classified his religion as being 'C of E.'

He could not reconcile the established church's preaching of God with its endorsement of the war. How could the Padre who befriended him after he crashed talk about the love of God one-minute and then teach soldiers about gas and bombs a little later? He had therefore no time for organised religion but his strongly felt beliefs were based on a humanitarian view:

> But a good man is one in whom the bond of universal human sympathy does not fail. [47]

It is rather surprising, therefore, to read of Tom attending three church services even though he feels that the young padre would be better employed fighting the war. He is, however, careful to ensure that the other side of the argument is put forward through his friend Williamson, who counters that the padre is a decent fellow who honestly believes that his faith prevents him from fighting but wants to do what he can for the cause.

Also noteworthy is that after their daughter Rosalind was born in 1931, Victor decided that she should be baptised. He wanted Guy to have a career in the RAF and his friend Captain Dickinson advised him that it would be difficult for Guy to be granted a commission if he had not been christened. Victor accepted this advice and Guy was baptised at the same time as his younger sister, although he found this experience very embarrassing as he was by then nine years old. Guy did in fact follow his father's lead and joined the RAF in 1941. Victor alludes to his attitude towards baptism in *Family Life* after Julian's second child is born:

> Julian considered baptism to be a lot of nonsense, but as everyone else concerned seemed to think it desirable and proper, there was always the slight possibility that the child might later want to be received into the Church of England and find it embarrassing not to have been christened; there might conceivably be material occasions on which it would be a disability.

One of his favourite expletives was 'God's holy trousers' and he brings this phrase and a number of derivatives into his book in several places. 'God spare my belly and teeth' James, the Adjutant, retorts when Tom tells him he was mistaken for a spy. Tom, meanwhile, when trying to convince Williamson that he had been shot at declares ' I solemnly swear by God's holy trousers ....'

It has been demonstrated that Victor drew on his own experiences for most of Tom's flying exploits and that part of the book can be said to be autobiographical. He also purposely used the real names of some of the pilots (e.g. Capt. Thomson and 2/Lt. Smith) and left sufficient clues to enable a number of the other main characters to be identified (e.g. Capt. MacAndrews and Capt. Beal) whilst the descriptions of some of the other pilots are purely fictitious. Victor's own outlook on life can be gleaned from both Tom's and Seddon's characters and discussions. Writing about the war fifteen years after the event with all the difficulties he had suffered, it is understandable, as he himself admitted, that some of the views and conclusions expressed in the conversations are with the benefit of hindsight.

It soon becomes clear to the reader that *Winged Victory* was written from the heart and it cannot have been easy to have relived the strain and weariness of the seven month period covered by the book so vividly, especially as he was having lengthy spells in hospital and sanatoriums. This makes it all the more of an achievement as it contains no trace of self-pity and is actually quite humorous in places. It was in no small measure due to the support of his wife, and the love of his family, that he had the strength to continue writing when he was far from well, and that he managed to complete the novel in the short time that he did.

Notes

1 *VW*, Tribute p. 6.
2 Henry Williamson, Personal Tribute to V. M. Yeates in *John O'London's Weekly*, 26 January 1935.
3 Letter from Ben Ray Redman to Norah on hearing of Victor's death dated 29 January 1935.
4 Capt. W. E. Johns, *Biggles: The Camels are Coming*, John Hamilton 1932 – letter to H. Williamson quoted in Tribute, *WV*, p. 4.
5 *WV*, p. 231.
6 Ibid., Tribute p. 3.
7 Ibid., Tribute p. 6 – taken from the inscription which Victor wrote on the flyleaf in the copy of *WV* he presented to Henry Williamson.
8 Ibid., pp. 136/7.
9 Ibid., p. 355.
10 Ibid., p. 100.
11 Ibid., p. 252.
12 Arthur Gould Lee, *No Parachute*, p. 135.
13 *WV*, p. 336.
14 Ibid., p. 387.
15 Fragment of an essay entitled 'Professor of Modern History' held at HRHRC.
16 *WV*, p. 120.
17 Ibid., p. 128.
18 Letter to Florence Bard dated 3 March 1918.
19 *WV*, p. 168.
20 Ibid., p. 257.
21 Ibid., p. 438.

22 See Appendix C.
23 *WV*, p. 101.
24 Ibid., p. 104.
25 Ibid., p. 273.
26 Ibid., p. 191.
27 Ibid., p. 82.
28 Ibid., p. 119.
29 Ibid., p. 244.
30 Ibid., p. 213.
31 Ibid., p. 37/38.
32 Ibid., p. 38.
33 Ibid., p. 145
34 Leighton Brewer had just published in 1934 *Riders in the Sky*, Houghton Mifflin Co. Boston, which he described as a poetic narrative.
35 *WV*, p. 190.
36 Ibid., pp. 429/ 430.
37 Ibid., p. 35.
38 James Hilton in *The Daily Telegraph* 26 June 1934.
39 Cited in Stephen F. Clarke's Clearwater Books 'Spica' Catalogue 1986.
40 *WV*, p. 72. 'But rolling pins with — on
I've never seen before.'
and
'Never no more you bloody old 'ore,'
'Said — Bill the Sailor.'
41 Ibid., p. 376. 'This is what your — war does to a man.'
42 Ibid., p. 143.
43 Ibid., p. 123.
44 Ibid., p. 169.
45 H. Cecil, *The Flower of Battle*, p. 47.
46 *WV*, p. 130.
47 Ibid., p. 306.

CHAPTER ELEVEN

VICTOR'S LEGACY

Jonathan Cape took the entire front page of *The Spectator* on 22 June 1934 to advertise seven of their new books, and one of these was *Winged Victory* which was described as the story of the friendship of young pilots on the Western Front – this was two days before the publication date. The first reviews, eagerly awaited, appeared in *The Daily Telegraph* and *The Times Literary Supplement* on 26 June, just two days after the book was published. James Hilton in *The Daily Telegraph* wrote that the 'lucky coincidence' of a good flier who is also a good writer had happened and, like many later reviewers, praised the descriptive quality of the writing, particularly the flying scenes which depicted what it really felt and looked like, something earlier writers had failed to do.

The late twenties had seen a war-book 'boom' and by 1934 the general public were somewhat weary of reading about the Great War. James Hilton recognised this trend when concluding his review by remarking that it might have rivalled Erich Remarque's *All Quiet on the Western Front* (1929) if published earlier, but now its appeal would be probably to a more discerning readership, a prophecy which proved to be correct.

The reviewer in *The Times Literary Supplement* was also encouraging describing it as:

> ... a long, bitter, faithful and truthful book, in its uncompromising courage the best intimate account of the War in the air which has yet appeared.

The reviews which appeared in the other weeklies were favourable.

H. M. Tomlinson in *The Spectator* stated that this was one of the real books on the War and the book critic in *The Illustrated London News* called it 'a mighty book' and hoped everyone would read it.[1]

The critic in *The Times* of 10 July wrote that:

> It is doubtful whether anything which is still worth saying about the War in the air as it seemed to a pilot in 1918 is left unsaid by this very remarkable book. … His descriptions of air fighting are written with the descriptive power of a pilot who is also something of a poet. … This is a late War book; it is one of the very best.

Most of the newspapers reviewed the book, some reviews were fairly comprehensive, others short – *The Daily Herald* and *The Daily Mail,* for example, covered the book in just one paragraph. In August, *The Observer* included it in its 'Choice of the Year Books' describing it as 'a personal account of service with the Air Force during the War, a vivid and remarkable pendant of time.' Barrington Gates in *The New Statesman and Nation* enthusiastically described it as 'a superb history' and he was not alone when he commented that he could not get his [Cundall's] voice out of his head. Gregory Dunn in Cape's summer edition of their in-house magazine *Now and Then*, wrote:

> … probably no previous writer has shown so completely as Mr Yeates the excitement of air combat, the comradeship of an Air Squadron, and the devastation and disgusting waste of men and material by war. His descriptions of flying, rising at times almost to poetry, are surely unsurpassable….

Dunn had approached it as a novel, but soon realised that Tom Cundall was the author himself and it was an unsparing piece of autobiography. In summing up, he expressed the view that it was 'an indictment of war, a commentary on the human spirit, a textbook on men and Air Tactics.' Victor was pleased with this review, but Williamson was not so impressed as he felt it was on the whole uncomplimentary, and in a fit of pique asked Victor who Dunn was.

The only adverse critical review appeared in *The Daily Express* in which James Agate wrote disparagingly:

> Apart from the aeronautics, I doubt whether the author has enough to say to make another very long war-book worthwhile.

He did however preface this by saying he was probably a bad critic as:

> My grandfather would have nothing to do with a railway train. My father would not get into a motor car. I have no use whatever for the airplane.

A review of the book which appeared in the *Army Navy and Air Force Gazette*, although generally positive, was critical of the author's apparent sneer towards the crews of the Army co-operation two-seaters. Victor was upset by this accusation, as his criticism was confined to the RE8 two-seater machines and not their crews whom he admired:

> To go on active service in such an ark was an occupation for heroes, although the people who flew them did not appear to think themselves so heroic as unfortunate.[2]

He wrote to the editor for an explanation and had the reply that he understood the reference was towards the end of the book but could not be precise, as the reviewer did not now have the volume with him. He invited Victor to write an occasional article for the *Gazette,* however, and suggested the issue could be clarified in one of these contributions by giving the Army co-operation crews the credit which he knew Victor felt they deserved. Amongst his surviving papers are pencilled notes, which appear to be the draft of a proposed article in response to this suggestion, in which he compares favourably the crews of the two-seater army observation machines with the single-seater scout pilots, although no record of it having been published has been found:

> If one thinks of the four flying aces of the Empire pack who won fame in the first war in the air, one probably thinks of Ball, McCudden, Bishop and Mannock. They were not indeed aces during their lives or, in the case of Bishop, during his active service. It was not a war-time term but a later importation from the French corresponding to the American film star and having the

same tendency to be used indiscriminately. The newspapers could not find anything more picturesque and apt than such phrases as intrepid birdman.

But the remarkable thing is that all four were pilots of SE single-seater fighters, that remarkable success of the Royal Aircraft Factory, which perhaps more than any other factor helped to regain air supremacy in 1917 and retain it during 1918.

And if one considers the aces who were not so widely famous, Trollope, MacLaren, Barker, Brown and the rest, one notices that they are Camel pilots, Sopwith's greatest success in single-seater fighters. But it is to be remarked that Camels spent much more of their time than did SEs ground-strafing, the most dangerous of all flying warfare, but a form which did not add to the fighter's bag of Huns; and fame was attained solely by running up a big score.

It is no disparagement to the fame of these terrific warriors to point out that they had opportunities which others did not have, for all military glory is dependent on opportunity and it is only just to the memory of these others that we should remember that fame and glory were the reward of Hun-getting only. The pilots and observers of two-seaters were not eligible. They had routine jobs to do; 'art-obs' (spotting for artillery), photographing, bombing, reconnaissance and sometimes a little ground-strafing, a particularly deadly occupation in a heavy machine. They also had the special duty job of dropping and picking up spies. The picking up was altogether nerve shattering. The pilot would have to go twenty or thirty miles into Hunland (with top protection of SEs) and visit perhaps seven pin-points to look for a signal such as a hand-torch flashed. If he got his signal he had to land at that point, wait to pick up his man and take off again before interruption. It is difficult to imagine that this could be done successfully, because of the daylight publicity; but it was, again and again.

Another thoroughly uncomfortable job was that of the photographing machine following a bombing raid, to take immediate pictures of the damage. This unfortunate was the object of the enormous hate aroused and he had a large camera in

> the back seat instead of an observer, so was very defenceless against attack by 'scouts'.
>
> These jobs were done by Bristol Fighters and DH4s and 9s which were good machines. It is hardly possible to say as much of RE8s; at any rate I have never heard a flying man praise them. They were slow and stolid but dangerous to inexperienced pilots. Somehow in flight they looked strangely like butterflies. In these unloved machines [crews] went to and fro over the lines trailing an aerial in the thankless task of spotting for batteries which seemed not to receive or to misunderstand most of the messages.

As we have seen, to achieve his object of showing how the stress of flying continuous combat missions affected the pilots, Victor considered it was necessary to chronicle the day-to-day life of the Squadron. The critic in the *Glasgow Herald* felt that this became wearisome and boring after a while and it should not have been necessary to describe every routine flight, casualty and binge to achieve this aim which could have been suggested more artistically. Although there is, perhaps, some justification in this criticism, the book would have lost much of its appeal and authenticity if it had been edited more severely, even though the later abridged paperback editions proved popular.

Although he had refused to write it himself, it is surprising that the blurb on the dust-jacket said nothing about the author, not even a reference to the fact that he had served in the RFC/RAF. Indeed one of the reviewers in America commented that although the book did not say so, it was quite obvious that the author had himself been a wartime pilot. A brief description of the author would have been sent to the newspapers with a review copy of the book but only in *The Daily Express* do we find a biographical note. This referred to him being a pilot during the war, who afterwards lost all his money through taking up commercial flying in Spain (which was not strictly true as the venture collapsed before it began) and that he did much of his writing in hospital.

It appears that Williamson sent Victor a copy of the letter he had received at the end of May from T. E. Lawrence in which he (Lawrence) commented most favourably on a proof copy of *Winged Victory* which he had been reading. Victor queried with his publisher whether a quote from Lawrence in any advertisement would help sales. Cape replied that although Lawrence would willingly pass an opinion on a book, he did not like it to be used for publicity and he (Cape) did not wish to trouble him again having used him in the past. In any event, he had doubts as to the current effectiveness of Lawrence's endorsements as a number of books had been so publicised in recent years which he felt lessened their impact from a sales point of view. Through Williamson's efforts, however, extracts from Lawrence's letter were in fact used for publicity and were included in an advertisement in *The Observer* as early as December. The following quote was also included on the dust-jacket of the Second Impression which came out in November, and a similar quotation appeared on many of the subsequent reprints:

> How fortunate the R.A.F. has been to collar for itself one of the most distinguished histories of the war! And how creditable that it deserves it. ... Admirable, wholly admirable. An imperishable pleasure.

The Imperial War Museum in London after receiving good reports, wrote to Victor asking whether a copy could be donated to their library, and he arranged for Cape to send a copy to the librarian. The Ypres League also noticed the book and Victor was invited to write an article for their Journal.

The American public as early as April had received advance notice of the forthcoming book from Frank Swinnerton, the London correspondent of the *Chicago Tribune*. He reported he had been told 'by someone who should know' that a book soon to be published in America called *A Test to Destruction* was the finest novel of the war in the air ever written, its author being V. M. Yeates who had been described to him as a poet. The informant was obviously Henry Williamson, who was still referring to Victor as a poet and who was also using his own suggested title for the book. The book was

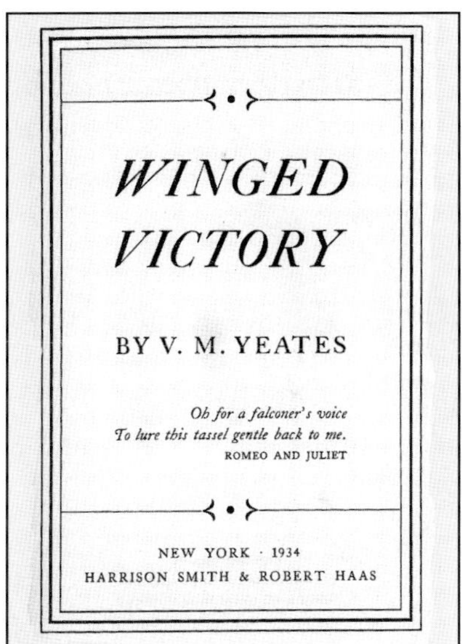
WINGED VICTORY

BY V. M. YEATES

Oh for a falconer's voice
To lure this tassel gentle back to me.
ROMEO AND JULIET

NEW YORK · 1934
HARRISON SMITH & ROBERT HAAS

THE STRIKING COVER OF THE U.S.A. EDITION, AND THE TITLE PAGE WITH THE QUOTATION FROM *ROMEO AND JULIET*

launched in New York on 1 October and was priced at $2.50.

The title page of this edition differed from the English one as the quotation from *Romeo and Juliet* 'Oh for a falconer's voice To lure this tassel gentle back to me.' was included – the quotation was slightly incorrect as it should have read 'Oh for a falc'ner's voice, To lure this tassel-gentle back again!' This alludes to Victor's original preferred title *This Tassel Gentle* and although it is unclear whether the quotation was added on his suggestion, it is more likely to have been on Williamson's recommendation in view of the mis-quote – Williamson had already referred to Victor as 'The Tassel Gentle' in the inscription in the copy of *The Gold Falcon* which he had presented to him. The dust-jacket of the US edition was also more colourful than the plain blue and white English one.

The American reviews were all encouraging, one of the most complimentary being that in *The Saturday Review of Literature* which was written by Ben Ray Redman, who had himself been a scout pilot during the war with No. 79 Squadron flying Sopwith Dolphins. He enthused:

> If any historian, in any future generation, wishes to know what it meant to be a fighting pilot on active service with the Royal Flying Corps during 1918, he need only to read *Winged Victory*. Here is the whole story set down minutely, faithfully, brilliantly and movingly ....

Victor liked this review and wrote to Ben Redman to thank him. He replied that he hoped he had done something to help sales and went on to say that Clayton Knight, the artist whose sketch had appeared with the review, had written apologising for the editor who had used a drawing depicting a SE5 rather than a Camel. He quoted from Knight's letter:

> It is an amazingly thorough job of writing and, as you say, the first of its kind. I am recommending it to anyone who wish to know what it was all about but I wonder how many will truly appreciate it who were not knocking around the air over France during the war. Especially such parts as where he describes 'my guts turned to jelly.' I was exhausted for days when I read it.

Unfortunately Victor did not live to read Ben Redman's letter as it was written at the end of December.

The reviewer in *New York Herald Tribune* thought it stood alone as the most complete interpretation in fiction of air warfare of the Great War whilst *The New York Times* felt that it deserved 'high rank' in war fiction.

Cape arranged for the book to be marketed in Canada through Thomas Nelson & Sons and *The Winnipeg Free Press* picked it out, the critic writing that to read *Winged Victory* was to live again in those exciting times.

Although Cape felt that it would make its way gradually, not being a type of book that heavy advertising would result in it becoming a best seller, sales initially were quite promising. In the first week to the end of June, 336 copies were sold of which 46 were in Canada and by 9 August Jonathan Cape was commenting that sales were going reasonably well with over 600 copies sold. He did, however, express a cautionary note by remarking that many novels fade away after about two months, but he hoped that *Winged Victory* would be different. Notwithstanding this note of caution, a second impression was ordered which was printed in November. Cape also mentioned that he had just received a letter from T. E. Lawrence who said how much he liked the book and was doing all he could to encourage people to read it – Lawrence was of the view that 3/4000 copies would be sold which, unfortunately, would be insufficient for Victor to realise his dream of taking his family abroad to a warmer climate.

In America, sales were not as good as had been expected, with 559 copies sold by 15 November although Harrison Smith hoped this situation would improve once Redman's review in *The Saturday Review of Literature* had had time to take effect. As the book was never reprinted in America, however, it can be assumed that sales did not improve and the copyright was not renewed when it eventually expired in 1962, notwithstanding the success in the United Kingdom of the 1961 reprint.

Williamson had suggested to Victor that as soon as he had finished correcting the proofs, he should begin writing another book, perhaps a true to life novel on family life. Victor agreed, realising that due to his debilitating illness, writing was the only way he could earn a living, and hoping that if *Winged Victory* became a success it would help to sell a second book.

As he had not worked for over eighteen months the family was increasingly finding it hard to make ends meet, and it was only by generous contributions from Norah's family that they managed to keep afloat. Victor, fortunately, had a little income each month from commission on sales as a number of loyal customers continued to send orders for timber and building supplies through him. Realistically, he acknowledged that in time, as he wrote to Norah, 'all business will fade away' and he tried, therefore, to press on with the new book, generally known as *Family Life*, as quickly as his health allowed. Although he was soon writing 500 words per day he found it very difficult, bemoaning to Williamson that he was feeling 'sterile as sulphuric acid.'

He described the book as 'a slapstick comedy of family life' and

THE SIX STONE STEPS TO THE ENTRANCE OF 22 WEMYSS ROAD, REFERRED TO IN *FAMILY LIFE*

although it was unfinished when he died, he had written some 55,000 words. It recounts the problems of his main character, Julian, and his wife bringing up a young family of three in difficult circumstances and their fraught relationship with his parents and sisters. His mother was possessive with a tendency toward hysterics whilst his father was a nonentity, and he becomes estranged from one of his two sisters. Money was scarce with nothing to spare for extra food, clothes or holidays, although their status necessitated them employing a housekeeper – a situation close to Victor's own position after the war. Both Julian and his wife had been employed by a bank before the war but Julian, like Victor, did not return to his former profession when he left the services but became an incorporated accountant. They lived in the two upper floors of a rented property which is described as having six stone steps leading to the front door – this will have been based on the period when Victor was living in Wemyss Road, Blackheath, where one also had to climb six steps to the entrance.

Much of the book, however, revolves around the trials and tribulations of Julian's long-standing friend, Major Kelsey, and his attempt to find a wife, and the exploits of a man-about-town Gordon Webster, whom Major Kelsey despises and who has no difficulty in attracting the opposite sex. As already mentioned, Major Kelsey is based on Victor's friend, Captain Dickinson who committed suicide in 1931 after killing his ailing sister with whom he lived.

Williamson, conscious of the fact that the family was in straitened circumstances and Victor's health was worsening, tried to help. He endeavoured to get a number of newspapers interested in *The Croydon Front 1917*, the article Victor had written describing his training days at Croydon. Unfortunately he had no success although *The Daily Mail* did accept one article, probably *The Croydon Front 1917*, and Victor received a cheque for five guineas from the newspaper although they were uncertain whether they would use it. (I have been unable to find such an article in the paper at this time). Williamson also attempted, unsuccessfully, to use his influence to interest the newspaper in serialising *Winged Victory*.

In September he encouraged Victor to apply for a grant from The Royal Literary Fund which aided impoverished writers, but Victor found himself unmotivated to do this (probably through pride) and kept postponing his application. However it appears that he eventually submitted an application as the Fund made a useful grant of £50 the following month. Williamson also sent a cheque for £25 which he said was a refund of the amount he had received from the Fund when he was beginning his writing career, and rather than returning it to the Fund, he was sending it to him. Victor initially refused the gift and sent it back but Williamson immediately returned it and this time he relented and it was accepted.

Henry Williamson was of the opinion that *Winged Victory* would make a good play, 'a tense drama', and he wrote to Victor asking for permission to adapt it and suggested that the royalties be divided equally. He asked Victor to sign a letter signifying his agreement and although no evidence has come to light as to whether this offer was accepted, there are grounds to believe that Victor did have some input into the proposal, and Williamson continued to pursue this idea after Victor's death.[3] In addition, he explored the possibility of turning the book into a film and he sent a summary of the novel to a film production company for consideration, but unfortunately neither of these approaches were successful.[4]

Regrettably, Cape's note of caution that sales often dropped off after the first few months proved correct, Victor writing to Norah in November:

> The weather is nice & the Saturday Review, but alas sales aren't. One waits & waits ....waits.

Williamson, somewhat extravagantly, had all along encouraged Victor with his writing, promising the book would be very successful and he would have been conscious of the fact that his prediction was not being realised. He tried to revive interest by sending a copy to John Masefield, the Poet Laureate, and told him something of Victor's plight. He also forwarded a copy to Lord Trenchard who was then not only the Chief of Police but also the Chairman of the RAF Benevolent Fund. Saddened by the book, Lord Trenchard invited Victor to meet him on 9 November and Victor managed to keep the appointment at New Scotland Yard even though by this time he was very ill. Whilst he was in central London, he also took the opportunity to have a portrait photograph taken which shows him looking frail and drawn.

In late November his doctor, concerned with his worsening health and with the assistance of the London Council, arranged for him to be moved away from the polluted air of the London suburb to the south coast, where it was hoped the fresh sea air would help his condition. He was sent to the Fairlight Sanatorium in Ore, near Hastings where he shared a room with three other patients.[5] He took some time to settle down finding it almost impossible to write, and he initially found the Matron difficult, but after an altercation matters improved. The Sanatorium's doctor ordered a month's bed rest and he was soon able to resume writing *Family Life* in a more peaceful atmosphere as his room-mates were now spending most of the day in the lounge. The inclement winter weather in early December, however, did nothing to assist his progress:

> What a day! The rain is a solid grey mass here. One can only see 200 yards. …. The windows simply must be shut today or the room would be flooded: not very suitable for a sanatorium.

He hated the enforced separations from his wife and children and he wrote to Norah regularly whilst he was in the sanatoriums. As one would expect, these letters included the latest news on his health and his concern for his family, suggesting Norah should see the doctor when she mentioned she had a cough, and that his daughter, Joy

Studio portrait, November 1934

should matriculate before getting married. In spite of the often dismal surroundings and the times when he was feeling unwell, he retained his sense of humour – for example he closed one letter by:

> Sparrows & thrushes hop: starlings walk. I wonder why? And what a hurry starlings are in! They look like business men.

Again, this is how he described the difficulties in getting a bath:

> Now I am at 'stage 4', and can have a bath 'when I like.' But in the morning the doctor does a round, & one must be in bed. In the afternoon I get up, and it would be too much of a strain to have a bath right after. After tea, an hour after, temperatures are taken, so I can't have a bath just before temps. After temperatures, there is a 'rest hour' till supper. I can't have one just after supper, and if I wait long after supper, it is too late to have a bath.

With his children in mind, his later letters from Fairlight often ended with a humorous sketch depicting a scene from a pantomime. He always used his pet name for Norah addressing his letters 'My dear Pussycat' or 'My dearest Pet', and he signed them 'Vic' as he was known to his family and friends.

By 13 December he was writing that he was feeling better and the next day, conscious of the help the book had received from the quotes of T. E. Lawrence, he wrote to Gregory Dunn:

> I am here following the dim scent of health ... I don't know that any thanks for his help ever reached T. E. from me. If you are seeing him would you mind saying how I am beholden to him? Cape may have thanked him for me, but I don't know.[6]

This was probably the last letter he wrote. His sudden, tragic death therefore the following day at 7.30am on Saturday 15 December when he finally succumbed to pulmonary tuberculosis, came as a great shock to everyone, and especially to Norah and the family – he was just thirty-seven years old.

Norah immediately wrote to Henry Williamson to tell him the sad news, but before the letter had time to reach him he had left for Brighton to visit friends, accompanied by Ann Thomas who was both his secretary and the mother of his fifteen month old daughter, Rosemary. On the Monday afternoon Williamson travelled to Fairlight with the intention of discussing with Victor his idea of turning *Winged Victory* into a play, only to be met by the Matron with the tragic news that he had died the previous Saturday. In *The Genius of Friendship*, an elegy for T. E. Lawrence, Williamson states incorrectly that he arrived at the Sanatorium on the Saturday, shortly after Victor had died, and no doubt this was done deliberately to heighten the effect.[7]

On the following day he called to see Norah at 569 Sidcup Road only to find she was out, but met her 12-year-old son Guy whom he tried to comfort. He called again on the Wednesday and, not unnaturally, found Norah grief-stricken, but her emotions seem to have irritated him as he left after a short while. He remembered the family at Christmas, however, sending a cheque for £5 as a present for the children.

Williamson wrote a short obituary for *The Times* which appeared on 24 December and he also sent a letter to the *Saturday Review of Literature* informing its readers of Victor's sudden death. He wrote a long Personal Tribute for *John O'London's Weekly* which was included in the issue published on 26 January 1935. This article upset Norah as she felt Williamson had put too much emphasis on Victor's illness and she would have preferred it to have been more of a celebration of his life. Williamson was hurt by this criticism of his writing and replied in a sense of pique that he had not mentioned Victor's home life which from the impression he had gained, had been less than perfect. Norah never forgot this barbed comment which was totally unfair and it soured their friendship thereafter. She had always been somewhat wary of Williamson, as on previous occasions when he had visited them he was usually accompanied by an attractive young secretary whom she suspected was also his girlfriend, and she had sympathy for his long suffering wife, Loetitia, who was left at home to look after their young children. Nevertheless she allowed a slightly shorter version of the Tribute to be included in the later editions of *Winged Victory* – unusually some copies of the second impression dated November 1934 (before Victor's death) also included the Tribute, which indicates that these must have been bound in late December or January 1935.

Notwithstanding these misgivings, she agreed to hand over to Williamson the manuscripts of *Adjustment* and also the unfinished 55,000-word novel *Family Life* which Victor had been writing when he died. She also gave him the rights to adapt *Winged Victory* into a play or film, but asked him to remember Victor's conviction that it should be all his own work and to re-write as little as possible. She quite rightly realised that Williamson had the family's interest at heart and importantly, he had the contacts to promote Victor's literary work. He also asked whether the letters he had written to Victor during the previous eighteen months could be returned to him. When her daughter Joy handed these to him he was annoyed to find that the envelopes had been destroyed, saying this would lessen their value. In later years, as he indicated to the former No. 46 Squadron pilot, Gerald Hudson in a letter written in 1964, he had explored the possibility of publishing the correspondence between them but it appears that Norah raised objections and the project was quashed:

> I prepared a book on VMY – his marvellous letters etc. – & mine to him – while he was writing *Winged Victory* but alas, the action of another – I'd waited since 1934 to put it out – forbade.

On hearing that Victor had succumbed to his illness, Williamson must have immediately written to T. E. Lawrence as he (Lawrence) was writing on 31 December to G. Wren Howard, Jonathan Cape's partner, that it was fortunate Victor had managed to complete *Winged Victory* before his death. It was a very good book, he recommended it to everyone and every RAF mess had a copy.[8] Lawrence was also continuing to praise *Winged Victory*, describing it as the best air-book yet to David Garnett and he wrote to Nancy Astor that it was one of the best English books of 1934. In his reply to Williamson, no doubt because he had seen a number of Victor's letters, he wrote that he felt a personal loss even though they had never met and hoped he did not leave a family in difficulties.[9]

Williamson sent Lawrence a copy of the Tribute which he had written for *John O'London's Weekly*, who replied that he read it with 'a sense of shame' and that sales of the book would have helped Victor ultimately. He again expressed concern about his wife and children who were part of the tragedy and asked whether any help could be found for them. He also suggested that the Tribute should be included in one of Williamson's forthcoming books – Williamson accepted this suggestion and it appears in *Goodbye West Country* which was published in September 1937. This book also contains a reproduction of the charcoal portrait of Victor when he was eighteen together with the photograph taken in November 1934 which had appeared in the Tribute in *John O'London's Weekly*, the only photograph of Victor to have been published.

In addition to his own writing, Williamson was not only engaged in converting *Winged Victory* into a play, but by May 1935 he was also revising the 'fragment' of the novel *Family Life*. He amended about one fifth of the manuscript and although he tried to keep to the spirit of the book, he was worried that Norah would not trust him to change it sympathetically. He hoped that Faber would agree to publish the unfinished book, sandwiched between a preface which he would write and an epilogue based on his Tribute. He had written to Lawrence on 13 February 1935 describing *Family Life* as a portrayal of Victor's own life told 'with such a lovely light touch', and on Saturday 11 May he wrote to Lawrence again asking whether he could call and stay with him at his cottage, Clouds Hill, near Bovington Camp on the following Tuesday, 14 May. The purpose of this meeting has been the subject of much discussion and speculation over the years as in his contribution to *T. E. Lawrence by His Friends* (1937), Williamson had written that he dreamed of an Anglo-German friendship and he felt that Lawrence and Hitler must meet and 'I wrote thus to him.' Later in *Genius of Friendship – T. E. Lawrence* (1941) he indicated that he wanted to ask Lawrence to address a meeting of ex-servicemen in the Albert Hall to encourage pacification in Europe in an attempt to avoid further conflicts. Both of these pretensions, however, are entirely false and figments of Williamson's imagination. The letter actually referred to *Family Life* and indicated that he had been making alterations 'mostly toning down savageries', as Victor's portrayal of his family, particularly his mother and sisters, was too terrible and if Lawrence would care to see the typescript, he would bring it with him.[10] This comment has resulted in at least two writers mistakenly referring to *Family Life* as an autobiography, which is far from the case, although it is clear that Victor used his own experiences as the basis for the story.[11] Lawrence received the letter on the Monday morning and realising that he would have to reply immediately, rode down to the village post office at Bovington on his Brough Superior motorcycle to send a telegram confirming lunch the following day. On his way back to his cottage he swerved to avoid two young cyclists, lost control and crashed into a hedge, sustaining severe injuries from which he failed to recover. He died in the hospital at Bovington Army Camp six days later on 19 May.

Over the years there have been numerous biographies written about T. E. Lawrence, and interest in his life and character continue to intrigue. Because his death is linked to the sending of the telegram to Williamson, most biographers refer to the proposed meeting when Victor's book was to be discussed. Many of these writers, however, have mistakenly stated that the book to be discussed was *Winged Victory*, and this was perpetuated in the catalogue for the T. E. Lawrence exhibition at the National Portrait Gallery in 1988. In Lawrence's authorised biography published the following year, however, Jeremy Wilson rectified this mistaken belief by correctly describing that an unpublished work by V. M. Yeates, the author of *Winged Victory*, was to be the subject of discussion at the proposed meeting.[12] This Lawrence/Williamson/Yeates connection has ensured that *Winged Victory* has been introduced to the many Lawrence devotees as well as those interested in aviation and the war and has helped the book's popularity in recent years.

Williamson had now lost two of his friends within a space of six months and he often referred to this in his later writings. He joined them together when his *Salar the Salmon* was published in September 1935, with the following dedication:

To
T. E. LAWRENCE
of
Seven Pillars of Wisdom
and
V. M. YEATES
of
Winged Victory

He also referred to them in the introduction which he wrote for *The Unreturning Spring*, an account of the life of James Farrar, a Second World War fighter pilot, taken from his letters which Williamson edited and which was published in 1950:

> I have known several men of genius, first among whom I count the man known to the world as Lawrence of Arabia. Another constantly in one's mind – that is, one's life – is V. M. Yeates, who wrote that great and lonely book *Winged Victory*, a story, unembellished, of two friends in the Royal Flying Corps in the First World War, a book which, in a very small way, it was my privilege and, in a sense, duty, to help produce.[13]

Norah was left penniless, but appreciated that to be able to receive future royalties she would have to obtain Letters of Administration to Victor's estate as, surprisingly, he had died intestate. These were issued on 18 January 1935 and showed his assets valued at just £3.7.6 (£3.37).

Despite the family's grief, she realised that, with four children to support and a home to run including mortgage repayments of £40 a year, she had to take urgent steps to try to obtain some financial assistance especially for the educational needs of the children. As Victor had not received a war pension, notwithstanding his fatal illness had been brought on by the strain of flying in the war, Norah was not entitled to a war widow's pension and she wrote to the Prime Minister, Ramsay MacDonald, explaining her hardship and appealing for some assistance. His office passed on this letter to the Royal Literary Fund who replied that she might be entitled to a Royal

Bounty Grant, but the outcome is not known. She applied to the Fund herself, however, which helped by awarding her a Dependants Grant of £100, £40 of which was received in February 1935 with payments of £30 due in each of the following two years.

On hearing of Victor's death, Lord Trenchard wrote expressing concern at her 'bad circumstances' and strongly recommended that she should write to the Royal Air Force Benevolent Fund and promised to write to the Secretary himself, as Chairman of the Fund, no doubt endorsing the application. The Fund made an immediate grant of £5 and agreed to make a weekly contribution of £1 a week towards living expenses. The Professional Classes Aid Council which provided some needy cash for clothes for the younger children, also paid a similar weekly maintenance grant and the Officers Association made a further contribution.

Although these charitable gifts were most welcome, they were insufficient to maintain the family's long term needs and Norah was forced to look for ways of earning a living. This would be difficult, as she still had to care for her youngest child Rosalind, who was then four years old. The royalty payments by this time amounted to very little, sales in the first twelve months having reached approximately one thousand copies. Cape also had an arrangement with Williamson that he would receive 5% commission on sales, presumably as an introductory fee, but it appears he generously passed this commission on to Norah which would have been of some help. Although the commission receipts on sales of building materials continued, these sums were unreliable and would soon cease. She decided to try to supplement her income by buying ladies lingerie from a wholesale warehouse in East London and selling it by simply walking around the area, knocking on doors. This was exhausting work, but she bravely persevered and gradually built up a small business which assisted the family's finances at this critical time.

Williamson was impressed with Norah's industry, writing to Lawrence that she was 'OK not KO' and describing her in *Goodbye West Country* as 'a grand person'. As Faber had declined the invitation to publish *Family Life*, he now approached Jonathan Cape who, unfortunately, was also of the opinion that Yeates was not known sufficiently well as a writer to justify publishing an unfinished book which, on its own merit, did not warrant publication. Royalties from such a book would be minimal and he felt that Williamson would be better engaged in seeking to help Norah financially by getting a few people who had known Victor to make a cash donation and Capes would be willing to contribute twenty guineas to such a fund.

Her eldest daughter, Mary, who was known during her childhood as Molly, was 17 years of age, and she left school and obtained a job as a secretary which enabled her to contribute to the family's meagre income. With the help of a grant from the London County Council, Joy was able to continue her education at the City of London College, leaving school when she was seventeen and was employed locally. By this time Mary was working at United Dairies so both daughters were now able to contribute towards the household expenses, but unfortunately, this resulted in the charitable maintenance grants being reduced. Guy continued his education at a local school.

Early in 1935 the magazine publisher, George Newnes Ltd, felt that there was by then a large enough market for a monthly magazine devoted solely to aviation and they decided to publish *Air Stories* which was advertised as 'Britain's only monthly air thrills magazine.' They had obtained approval to publish extracts from *Winged Victory* and when the magazine was launched in May 1935 at a price of seven pence, it contained the first excerpt under the title 'Cundall of the Camels.' It explained that it was taken from a new book by V. M. Yeates 'which has been widely acclaimed as the finest novel of the Great War in the Air that has ever been written.' Vivid charcoal sketches of air combat in typical magazine fashion accompanied the extracts which were between ten and thirteen pages in length. The first extract was well received, the second issue announcing that 'No feature in the first number of *Air Stories* proved more popular than this remarkable record of a Camel squadron pilot of the RFC on the Western Front.' However only one further extract was printed and this in the third issue in July, but nevertheless Norah would have received some welcome income from the serialisation.

CUNDALL OF THE CAMELS

By V. M. YEATES

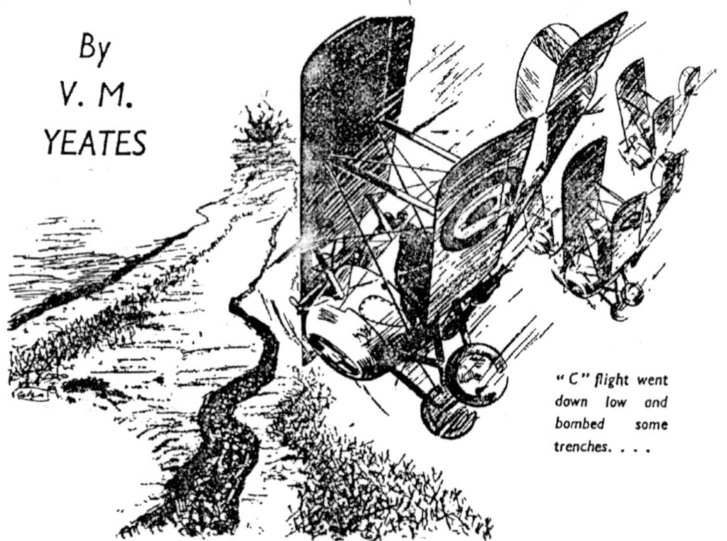

"C" flight went down low and bombed some trenches. . . .

"AIR STORIES" is privileged to have secured the right to publish "Winged Victory," a new book by V. M. Yeates, which has been widely acclaimed as the finest novel of the Great War in the Air that has ever been written.

We present in this number the first of a series of extracts, each one complete in itself, from this remarkable record of a Camel pilot on the Western Front. Never have the sensations of war-time flying been more vividly conveyed than in these brilliant descriptions of training experiences, dog-fights, patrols, ground "strafes" and the hectic life of the mess, in which the very spirit of the old R.F.C. lives again.

Here is a veritable epic of War in the Air—reminiscences that will roll back the years for all who fought and flew, and amaze those who know only the safety and peaceful purpose of present-day flying.

Camels are . . . . Camels

"DER-DER" shouted the klaxon in its blaring gurgle, and again "der-DER." It was time for "A" flight to prepare to go up. The klaxon was the major's pet. If he was in the office a little before the time at which a flight was due to go up he morsed "A," "B," or "C" with a switch-key controlling the klaxon, a powerful instrument attached to a tree in front of the mess. If he was not in the office, the adjutant was supposed to sound it. If nobody was there and the horn was not sounded, the flight went up just the same. Its chief effect was to make people with ragged nerves curse at it.

Apart from his klaxon the major did not bother them unduly. He was a shy, ineffective man who made efforts to be convivial on binge nights and did not care for flying Camels. The only flying he did was going up to see if the weather was dud, and his average flying time was about ten minutes a week.

Flying Camels was not everyone's

67

A NEW MONTHLY MAGAZINE *AIR STORIES* FEATURED EXTRACTS FROM *WINGED VICTORY* IN ITS FIRST THREE ISSUES. THIS IS FROM THE FIRST ISSUE, MAY 1935.

Even though sales of *Winged Victory* were disappointing, it continued to attract the attention of the more discerning readers who were interested in the war years. One such person was Sir Eugen Millington-Drake, the Minister to Uruguay, who was building up a collection of selected books on the Great War. A chosen book was specially bound and then sent to the author with a request that he sign the book for the collection. Being unaware of Victor's death, he wrote to him in August 1935 with a copy of *Winged Victory* in the special binding and Norah, being helpful, pasted Victor's signature taken from one of his papers onto the half title page. In 1938 the collection was donated to Eton College and the volume is now part of the College's library.

Although Norah stoically continued with her lingerie business, she obviously found it very difficult, and so looked around for more congenial and lucrative employment. In May 1938 she obtained a job as a tracer at the Office of Works in London, forcing her to send Rosalind, who was then seven years old, to a boarding school run by a charity. After the outbreak of the Second World War the Office evacuated staff out of London to Southport in Lancashire, and after some heart searching she decided to move. To escape the London bombing her two elder daughters, Mary and Joy had been evacuated to Newbury two days before the war started, as the parents of Mary's boyfriend (he also worked at United Dairies) had invited them to stay at their small-holding in a village just outside the town. Shortly afterwards, Mary obtained a job on the railways, initially at Reading but later at Cirencester when she became an inspector and also a Trade Union member. She spoke fluent French and was invited to assist the BBC in broadcasting to occupied France, travelling to London to record the programmes from Bush House.[14] Guy, at his mother's insistence, moved with her to Southport and obtained a job in the Office of Works Accounts Department, but in June 1941 he left to follow in his father's footsteps and joined the RAF although poor eyesight precluded him from training as a pilot.

Towards the end of the war, the Office of Works moved their offices back to London. This enabled Norah to return to her home in Sidcup

Road and she continued to work for the Ministry of Works, as it was then called, until she retired at the age of sixty when she qualified for a pension. She looked after her parents until their deaths in 1945 and Guy stayed with her for a year when he was discharged from the RAF in August 1946. As she became older, she decided it would be an advantage to be nearer to one of her children and in 1959 she purchased an apartment in Selhurst Road, SE25. Joy was the nearest, living in Mitcham with her four children, and so Norah was able to make frequent visits to her daughter and grandchildren.

With the outbreak of the Second World War, many new pilots were required and the instructors on the training units concentrated, quite naturally, on flying techniques rather than flying in combat situations. As a result, pilots were keen to find out what air fighting was really like and they soon heard about *Winged Victory* which became in great demand. Air Vice-Marshal J. E. ('Johnnie') Johnson recalled:

> Someone told us that an excellent novel, published at ten shillings after the First War, was well worth reading because it contained all the lessons of air fighting. So we sent a pilot to London to search the second-hand bookstalls and get half a dozen copies. The booksellers, it turned out, knew what we were after, but the book was out of print and recent demand had pushed up the price to three pounds! [15]

The pilot came away empty handed and AVM Johnson did not read the book until after the war had ended.[16]

In 1961, acting on the suggestion of the Library Association who had evidence of a demand for the book, Cape agreed to a new hardback reprint which was published on 28 October priced at twenty-five shillings (£1.25). It contained not only the Tribute by Henry Williamson which appeared in some of the second impression editions of the 1934 reprint, but also a new Preface which he wrote to up-date this edition. It included on the inside rear flap of an attractive newly designed dust-jacket by R. G. Williamson, a reproduction of the charcoal portrait which Victor had originally suggested might be used as the frontispiece in 1934.

Williamson had not forgotten Victor after twenty-seven years and was still keen to do all he could to publicise the book. With this new edition available, he arranged for his friend, the well-known journalist and broadcaster Kenneth Allsop, to write an article on its rebirth for the *Daily Mail* which chose it as its 'Book of the Month' for October 1961. The article appeared on 21 October and included an interview with Williamson on the background to how the book came to be written. The article was entitled 'Wingless Victor flies again ...' and Allsop, who himself flew in the RAF in the Second World War, related that he became aware of the book in 1941, when it was in the library at Cranwell, and at that time pilots were paying £5 for the scarce copies which were to be found. Williamson commented that he had been surprised to learn that it was to be republished and although he had included a character named 'Cundall' in some of his novels as 'buoy-markers of a submerged masterpiece' it had, perhaps, 'made its own way to the surface.' He had first introduced a character called 'Tom Cundall', a fellow bagman during the last term at school, in his novel *Young Phillip Maddison* (1953) which has already been referred to, and he appeared again in his subsequent novel, *How Dear is Life* (1954) playing for the 'Old Boys' football team. In *A Fox Under My Cloak* (1955) Cundall is about to be commissioned into the Royal West Kent Regiment but later appears as a pilot in the RFC. He is also included in Williamson's next novel *The Golden Virgin* (1957) in which he is credited with shooting down the German airship L31.[17]

At Williamson's suggestion, the newspaper article was followed up by an interview with Kenneth Allsop on the popular BBC television programme 'Tonight' which was broadcast on 27 October.

The resurgence of interest in the Great War during the sixties resulted in a much greater demand for the book compared with when it was first published and by 21 November, less than a month after the new edition appeared, G. Wren Howard a director of Jonathan Cape Ltd, reported to Norah that its demand had almost embarrassed them, having completely sold out with 3578 copies sold and with orders for a further 541 copies outstanding. Capes had to rush though a second reprint which was available in late November. This was also soon sold out and a third reprint was issued the following year in 1962.

The popularity of the book prompted Wren Howard to enquire about Victor's first attempt at a novel, *Adjustment*, the typescript of which had been loaned to Williamson and who had been reluctant to release it when Norah had asked for its return. Wren Howard thought it would be quite wrong for Williamson to tamper with it as this could detract from its value. It was not until 1962 that Williamson eventually returned the manuscript but when Capes read it they concluded, as Jonathan Cape himself had done in 1934, that it was not at all marketable.

The well-deserved success of *Winged Victory* was noticed by the literary committee of The Reprint Society who wished to publish an abridged version as they felt that this would enhance the book. Wren Howard, knowing Norah's concern that Victor's work should only be amended if absolutely necessary, tried to reassure her by saying that everyone with whom he had discussed it with, agreed that the book would be improved if it was shortened. He was sure the editor, who was a great admirer of the book, would do it sympathetically. This new version, which was condensed from the original 456 pages to 305 pages, omitted much of the technical descriptions of the aircraft and deleted or shortened many of the political and economic debates between Tom and his hut-mates. It was published in 1963 for the members of the World Book Club, priced at eighteen shillings (90p), the price being justified as it was a deluxe volume and quarto bound in leather with a silver RFC badge embossed on the front board. It is unique as it is the only edition which includes the charcoal portrait of the author as a frontispiece. The royalties of 10% were divided equally between Norah and Cape.

Following the success of Cape's reprint, the publisher World Distributors (Manchester) Ltd produced the first paperback edition in 1964 under their Consul Books label at a cost of three shillings and sixpence (18p). It stated, incorrectly, that it was 'complete and unabridged' but it was in fact the revised shortened version published the year before by the Reprint Society and ran to 315 pages. Unfortunately the cover did not depict a Sopwith Camel but an SE5.

This paperback edition also proved successful and was reprinted by Consul Books with a slightly re-arranged cover two years later in 1966, when the price had risen to five shillings (25p).

In 1969 the well-known publisher Sphere Books contacted Jonathan Cape Ltd. with a view to bringing out another paperback edition and this was published later in the year at a price of six shillings (30p). Again, this was the abridged version (although the book does not state that this is the case) which would have been done partly to keep the cost down, and followed the earlier trend in depicting an SE5 on the cover. In the first twelve months it sold 2800 copies.

Cape must have noticed the continued demand for the book as they reissued their hardback edition in 1972 although the price had increased to £2.95. The design of the dust-jacket was identical to the 1961 edition, but the blurb was updated and consisted of quotations from the detailed review which H. E. Bates had written for the *Sunday Times* when it was reprinted in 1961. The other difference was that the small reproduction of the charcoal portrait was omitted from the inside flap.

Another publisher, Mayflower Books, approached Cape in 1974 as they wished to publish for the first time the full unabridged version in paperback and this appeared later the same year at a price of sixty pence. The cover this time depicted the correct aircraft, a Sopwith Camel, and shows it attacking a German machine. This edition sold well and it was reprinted the following year although the price had increased to seventy-five pence.

The London publishers, Buchan & Enright in the early 1980s began publishing a number of outstanding military books, and included *Winged Victory* in their 'Echoes of War' series. Although in large paperback form, it was an attractive reprint, the cover being a detail taken from an original watercolour of a Sopwith F.1 Camel entitled 'The Blind Spot' by N. G. Arnold, which is held by the Imperial War Museum. This was the unabridged version which sold at £5.95 and was available from August 1985. So popular was this edition that it was reprinted in 1990 (£6.95) and again in 1993 (£7.95) going out of print as recently as 2000. This was noticed by the specialist publisher, Grub Street, who in April 2004 brought out a new paperback edition at £9.99. This is the unabridged version, although it is unfortunate that the cover does not depict a Sopwith Camel, but reproduces the painting of an SE5 which appeared on the Consul paperback reprints published in the 1960s.

When *Winged Victory* was first published in 1934, the general public had grown weary of reading about the Great War after the glut of war books which appeared in the late 1920s, hence its disappointing sales. Nevertheless it was highly praised by former pilots who recognised its authenticity. Similarly there was demand for the book from aircrew in the Second World War, but it was not until its reprint in 1961 that it was more widely read when it came to be regarded as the classic account of aerial warfare in the First World War. Being fiction, this is at first sight somewhat surprising, but as has been shown, Victor relied heavily on his own experiences in his writing and its accuracy has been recognised by many later writers on the War. It has often been quoted as an authoritative source, one of the latest examples being *The Great War in the Air* published by the prestigious Smithsonian Institute in the USA. This includes passages from the book to back up the author's statements regarding the short life expectancy of Camel pilots engaged on ground-attack duties, and that Canadian pilots were largely to be thanked for the British air supremacy in early 1918.[18]

Denis Winter used it intensively when writing *The First of the Few* in which he quotes a number of extracts and in *Swifter than Eagles* (1964), a biography of Sir John Salmond, John Laffin acknowledges that, although fiction, it is one of the great classics of air fighting and refers to it when stating that most pilots in March 1918 had a feeling that death was inevitable. A former WWI pilot and well-known aviation writer, Arch Whitehouse, also wrote that among those books which gave him much pleasure and knowledge was 'the outstanding novel of Camel squadron life, *Winged Victory* by V. M. Yeates, which provides the most authentic delineation of war flying that has come to my attention.'[19]

Extracts are still being included in air anthologies seventy years after the book was published. In *Men in the Air*, advertised as the best flight stories of all time and published in USA in 1990 and reprinted in 1995, the editor includes in the World War One section under the title 'A Most Remarkable Escape' one of the more popular extracts, namely the description of the patrol in which Capt Beal is killed when Tom manages to survive although badly shot up. As recently as 2002, Tor Books in the USA were intending to include a long extract describing the events of 21 March 1918 when Tom is shot down and is befriended by the Padre of the Army Corps School in their forthcoming anthology *Flights of Fiction.*

More recently, a film producer has expressed an interest in acquiring the motion picture rights, so Williamson's original idea may yet come to fruition.

Victor was also remembered in 1997 by the makers of a WWI flight simulation computer game *Flying Corps Gold* in which the Camel pilot featured is named V. M. Yeates.

oooooOooooo

Norah died on 23 September 1982 at the age of 90. Despite her long life, she had experienced only sixteen years of marriage, the latter years being extremely worrying with four young children to support whilst Victor's health was steadily declining and money very short. After his death, before she obtained a permanent job which resulted in the heartrending decision of moving from the area, she had courageously gone about earning some money selling clothing 'on the knocker' which was both exhausting and unsociable. She was very proud of her husband's book and derived much pleasure from seeing its deserved recognition and popularity in later years when it was reprinted in 1961, her only regret being that Victor had not lived to see its success.

Through lack of funds, Norah had been unable to erect a headstone above his grave when he died, but in 1997, the centenary of his birth, Joy, Guy and Rosalind, their three surviving children arranged for this to be rectified. At a dedication ceremony held at Hastings Cemetery on 28 September 1997, at which two of the children took part, the

THE HEADSTONE IN HASTINGS CEMETERY WAS DEDICATED ON 28 SEPTEMBER 1997.
GUY YEATES IS PICTURED READING HIS TRIBUTE TO VICTOR AT THE CEREMONY

new headstone was unveiled and extracts from *Winged Victory* were read and flowers planted around the stone. It was most appropriate that not only a number of Victor's grandchildren were present but also some of his great-grandchildren, as in one of his letters to Williamson he had predicted:

> Generation will say to generation; Read *Winged Victory*. My great grandchildren will be known.

It was fitting that Norah should also be remembered for her fortitude and the simple inscription reads:

VICTOR MASLIN YEATES
30.9.1897 – 15.12.1934
AUTHOR OF WINGED VICTORY

AND IN MEMORY OF
HIS COURAGEOUS WIDOW
NORAH
WHO DIED 23.9.1982

Ever since it was first published in 1934, *Winged Victory* has been acknowledged as the classic account of air warfare in the Great War, evidenced by the fact that it has remained in print for the past forty years. This is proof, if proof is needed, of the reputation and esteem it has gained over those years when many other well-known war books have not been reprinted. It is a fitting memorial not only to Victor, but also to the courage of all his fellow pilots who flew without the protection of parachutes, in flimsy, often unreliable aircraft, in the cold atmosphere of up to 20,000 feet. T. E. Lawrence's prediction has been proved correct when he wrote to Henry Williamson shortly after Victor's death:

> … I'm sure it will go to some thousands in the end. The big seller makes its bang and drops dead; the slowly growing sale lasts for years and brings in as much, eventually. I cannot see *Winged Victory* dying short.[20]

Notes

1 H. M. Tomlinson, who was too old to enlist, had been the war correspondent of *The Daily News* and his well-known novel *All Our Yesterdays* was published in 1930 (Heinemann) which covered the period from the start of the Boer War to the Armistice in 1918.

2 *WV*, p. 49.

3 In a letter to T. E. Lawrence dated 10 December 1934 Williamson refers to Victor's annotations of his rough scheme for a play – see *T. E. Lawrence Correspondence with Henry Williamson*, page 169.

4 A summary of the novel was sent to R. Humphreys Screen Services Ltd. on 18 November 1934 – see *Henry Williamson, Tarka and the Last Romantic*, p. 177.

5 Fairlight Sanatorium is now a Home specialising in the care of people with learning difficulties and is known as Barrington House.

6 Stephen F. Clarke, quoted in Clearwater Books 'Spica' catalogue 1986.

7 Henry Williamson, *The Genius of Friendship – T. E. Lawrence*, p. 71.

8 *The Letters of T. E. Lawrence*, edited by David Garnett, Jonathan Cape 1938, p. 840.

9 In view of his enthusiasm for the book, it is surprising that a copy of *Winged Victory* was not in Lawrence's library when he died. It is assumed that it had been passed on to someone else to read.

10 Williamson's original letter dated 10 May 1935 was not found amongst Lawrence's papers after his death which heightened the mystery. Its content however, appears in *T. E. Lawrence Correspondence with Henry Williamson* p. 177. Although Victor only had one sister, Augusta, Williamson in his letter refers to his 'sisters', as in *Family Life* the main character Julian had two sisters.

11 Phillip Knightley and Colin Simpson, *The Secret Lives of Lawrence of Arabia*, Thomas Nelson & Sons Ltd 1969 p. 270. The authors indicated that Williamson had written to T. E. Lawrence to get his advice about the unfinished autobiography of V. M. Yeates, the author of *Winged Victory*.

12 Jeremy Wilson, *Lawrence of Arabia*, Heinemann 1989, p. 934.

13 James Farrar, (H. Williamson Editor), *The Unreturning Spring*, Williams & Norgate, 1950, p. 9.

14 Mary, using her married name of Mary Wolfard, recalled her wartime experiences under the title 'The Railway Inspector' for an anthology of personal reminiscences of the Second World War entitled *Don't you know there's a War On? The People's Voice 1939-45* which was edited by Jonathan Croall and published in 1989 by Hutchinson.

15 Air Vice-Marshal J. E. (Johnnie) Johnson, *Full Circle*, Pan Books 1968, p. 143. AVM Johnson was the top-scoring Allied fighter ace of World War II with 38 victories.

16 Letter to the author from AVM J. E. Johnson, December 1997.

17 The Zeppelin L31 was commanded by Heinrich Mathy, the famous German airship captain, and was shot down in flames over Potters Bar on 1 October 1916 by 2/Lt. W. J. Tempest (No. 39 Squadron RFC).

18 John H. Morrow, *The Great War in the Air*, Smithsonian Institution Press 1993, pp. 314 & 316.

19 Arch Whitehouse, *The Years of the Sky Kings*, Macdonald 1960, p. xiii.

20 Extract of letter quoted in *Genius of Friendship – T.E.Lawrence*, p. 72.

APPENDICES

APPENDIX A

A DELETED CHAPTER

This is the text of the original Chapter XVIII of Phase One of *Winged Victory* which was omitted from the published version after discussions with Jonathan Cape as it was felt that it repeated some of the debates which appeared in Chapter VII.

'Personally' said Tom, 'I think it's been a damned depressing sort of day. I've been feeling blue and yellow all through. If I hadn't had a few drinks I should be sitting beating my breast and moaning.'

The four of them were sitting around their tortoise stove idly companionable before turning in for the night. The usual racket was going on: FEs setting out on their bombing expeditions; heavy howitzers roaring; German shells bursting a mile or two in front; Archie barking; distant bombs exploding; yells and howls from the mess where a few people in various degrees of drunkenness were having a rough house.

'Personally' said Williamson, 'I haven't noticed anything particularly depressing .....'

'You wouldn't.'

'In fact, as there has only been one job it's been better than most.'

'The atmosphere's been queer. I expect it's spring coming' Seddon remarked.

'In the spring a brighter iris changes on the burnished dove, doesn't it Bill?' Williamson had a liking for Tennyson, which appeared to Tom unnatural and horrible. 'In the spring a brighter war paint decorates the flying Hun.'

'Oh I know you don't like Tennyson, Tom .....'

'Well, hell, who would? Isn't he largely responsible for this 'ere war?'

'I shouldn't have thought so.'

'This week's theory of the war. Come on Tom, tell us how Tennyson started the big war.'

'Certainly, Mr Seddon. But you've only got to look at his portrait to see it. Solemn, pompous, long-haired, sham. He threw away his soul to become soulful – and a lord. And wasn't it that finishing coat of sham and solemn soulfulness and snobbery that disguised from everyone what contemporary civilisation was based on, naked imperialism and grab? Art should be some sort of interpretation of life; T and Co were plasterers, painters, and decorators. Mind the Germans started it. Beethoven suddenly came over all soulful. Gaiety and humanity informed the greatest art of all time, that of Mozart; and then came the crash. I'm not trying to run down Beethoven. His soulfulness never got very far away from the tradition of gaiety, and the combination resulted in musical miracles. But gaiety died away, and the new art led straight to the romantic suet puddings of Brahms, that master of depressing intervals, and to the foggy metaphysics and catarrhal erotica of Wagner ..... '

'Brahms, didn't he write Hungarian dances?'

'Yes, but they're a very small part of his work. I mean the symphonies and piano concertos and most of the songs. Of course, he's not all pudding. And Wagner, of course, when he forgets his world philosophy for a bit is one of the biggest miracle men imaginable. His purely musical ideas are ... I don't know what they are, but they're the real thing. And he wrote Meistersinger. And yet he went in like no one else for weird and solemn soul theories. It's that dreadful be-whiskered solemnity, and moral earnestness that's the trouble. It spread from Germany to England, growing more and more hairy. Look at Carlyle; a splendid fellow, but hopelessly earnest, embogged, and soul-bothered. Victoria requested Mr Sullivan to compose oratorio. Tennyson took up the tone and shammed with great moral earnestness. Kipling wrote his recessional hymn, that artificial tulip of national hypocrisy.'

'Just a moment Tom. I suppose you like Bach and Handel with all their piety?' asked Williamson.

'I do.'

'If you don't mind me saying so, I think you are temperamentally orthodox but for some reason in revolt. But you can't help being offended by Protestantism. If you live long enough you will cool down into a Roman Catholic.'

'Look here, you can't treat Carlyle like that. I leave Tennyson to Bill to defend if he wants to but Carlyle was a great protester against the conditions around him.'

'True, but how ineffectively he protested; and the only substitute he offered was a sort of return to mediævalism. All that Carlyle succeeded in doing was to create an atmosphere of heavy German solemnity that helped to obfuscate the mental atmosphere and pseudo-religious soul-strife (which) always flourishes in mental fogs. It all led to the last supreme misbirth, the national soul. As soon as nations have souls they have to be virtuous and as they can't be that, they are hypocrites. It becomes treason to think they can do anything base; but of course they do, and the baseness of other nations is as easily discernible to a patriot as the perfect virtue of his own. Every nation becomes symbolised as a virtuous and noble virgin amid vile ravishers. Hatreds abound and when somebody influential wants a war, the peoples of nations with souls, now that nations have souls, being full of hatred fairly leap to it. War has become pure murder in a big way. Formerly they used to have comparatively jolly little wars fought by professional armies that were recognized to be the blackguard element of the nations concerned and they were compensated for the risk of suffering and death by opportunities of loot and rape. But now, by God, entire nations murder each other and the wish of real patriots is that the whole enemy population should be exterminated; haven't you heard them? Slavery being immoral, they must kill.'

'You're right, Tom; by jove you're right. But why blame Tennyson and Brahms? It's the financiers and traders .....'

'Oh yes, Seddon, I know that; but don't you see that those friends of yours flourish most in an atmosphere of solemnity? When it's the fashion to be preoccupied with your own and your neighbour's souls and whiskers and over-souls and righteousness according to Wilberforce or Mrs Ward and to stuff yourself with patent virtues, then sweating, slum building, usury and grab and imperialism flourish; the men doing these things have only to go regularly to church with large families and prayer books, and grow whiskers of a holy shape, and they are Good Men, and there's an end of the matter.'

'The only comfort I can get out of all this' said Williamson, 'is that I gather you blame the Germans for starting this – umm – fog of holiness originally, so that they have done something to deserve being shot at.'

'That's right' said Tom. 'If I hadn't heard the Eroica I simply couldn't go on with the war.'

'Good' Williamson went on. 'It's nice to know someone who knows why he's fighting. I suppose you wouldn't consider the invasion of Belgium as a reason?'

'Well, I don't think so. It's difficult. Weren't Belgium and Holland jig-sawed together out of sundry old dukedoms by Metternich or someone to be a strong buffer state together? But as the Dutch were a bit overbearing, being a nation of heroes, the Flemings and Walloons insisted on separate government, and they got it because Palmerston backed them up, it being an axiom of British foreign policy that Antwerp must be in very friendly hands. And to make Belgium alone strong enough as a buffer state, the diplomats got together under Palmerston's terrible eye and in eighteen thirty something floated the treaty which the Huns are reported to have recently called a scrap of paper. But if you set up a buffer state, you must expect to have it buffed, and the theory is that the prospect of having to buff a small state first will put an aggressor off, as his real prey will probably have time to get ready for him and he will arrive at the frontier already a trifle puffed or buffed. That is exactly what happened in our little war. Belgium was heroic, and France was, for the time, saved. I suppose our treaty obligation was to send an army to Belgium; what we are doing is to send our entire fit male population all over the earth. Personally, I think that is out of proportion to our interest in Belgium.'

'Exactly. Well put Tom. Only you're wrong about our treaty obligation. There's nothing about armed intervention. The war is entirely sentimental. But we are in fact fighting to save our foreign investments, and as we personally haven't any, we're fighting to prevent British and other financiers being badly hit by German industrialists.'

'Oh go on' said Williamson.

'Bill, that is exactly true' Seddon insisted.

'But that's not the only thing we're fighting for' Tom remarked. 'We're fighting for the British ideal of freedom. You know what that is; being fined instead of put in quod, and having a home that is a castle while you can keep the bailiffs out and the landlord quiet.'

'This is all very sparkling' said Williamson, 'but let's look at the reality for a moment. Although we may not know it, we are fighting for policemen.'

'If you want to be convincing in the basic reality line, you must offer us something more convincing than policemen. You must derive war from some fundamental trait of human nature in the mass; infantilism, I should think would do. There is no protoplasmic craving for policemen in human nature, and if there were .....'

'Oh shut up Tom. What I mean is that civilisation is a way of living where everybody agrees to disarm and to have policemen to make them behave according to law. The shock of this war will force us to agree to an international police force to keep us all in order.'

'By jove, I think you're right there.' For the first time Smith's richer northern speech embellished the talk. 'We'll never dare have another bust up like this.'

'The idea's fine, but .....'

'Precisely. As Seddon so vigorously puts it; but if we're discussing reality, we'd better admit at once that the only international policemanizing that will be done when we have won this war, will be the policing of Germany and such of her associates as seem worth while bothering about; that is, have any blood left to be sucked. Can't you imagine the rush for spoils? You can safely bet there's all sorts of secret agreements about who's to have what. I dare say that's why we're still fighting and didn't make peace in 1916. The lion's skin has been already cut up in theory and now we've simply to kill the lion or perish in the attempt.'

'True. And you want to remember that this war is run on money. God knows how much money has been created by financiers for fighting; and the more money there is, the greater the power of its creators. With Germanic resistance crushed, these blood-suckers will have a clear field. The only sort of international police that seems to me possible is a policing by a dominant international financial gang, a sort of semi-private armed force to protect the gang's interests. Creditors must have power over debtors. In time it would lead to world-wide peace. They would keep their English slaves in order with Chinese garrisons; their French slaves with Negroes; the German slaves with Mongols and so on.'

'Good God, man, no one could stand that.'

'You can get used to anything. And what could you do? A mob can't fight machine guns. But that's only a dream, not a prophecy. Though wasn't something like that done in the later Roman empire, Tom?'

'I think foreign garrisons were used.'

'I expect you will find that debtor nations will cling to nationalism, and financial internationalism will only get hold of creditor nations. The debtors may yet save the world; and as the great debtor after this little war will no doubt be Germany, we can only hope that somehow she will save us from ourselves and our money.'

'This is getting absolutely fantastic' said Williamson, 'And you were talking just now about the resistance of Germany being smashed.'

'I know; but you can't keep sixty million stalwart people smashed for long at a time, unless there's internal degeneracy, and I think Germany's too new for that .....'

'But it might split up into its constituent states' Tom interrupted.

'True. I think that might be disastrous for everyone.'

'You're getting more pro German every minute.'

'Order, order' cried Tom. 'One must follow one's argument whithersoever it leads.'

'I'm not pro German, I'm pro English; but it has occurred to me that even Germans may have their uses. Suppose they are constitutionally fitted to withstand the enslaving movements of international finance.'

'If there are any.' Williamson qualified.

'There certainly are some. Take a creditor nation. The people are kept in order by the import trade which produces sufficient unemployment for the purpose; a creditor nation can afford an excess of imports. At the same time, profits are made by the export trade – industry is not run for the nation. The people as a whole have no hold over it. They are helpless. In debtor nations, it is pure enslavement by investment. They have to work on the border of starvation to pay interest, and the more they pay the more they have to pay, since most of the interest is at once re-invested. Now do you think that the action of finance is enslaving?'

'I can't argue with you. You appear to know something about it. I admit I don't.'

'That's the trouble. No one does know anything about it, but it goes on. It's a technical subject. Anyhow, if Germany is likely to resist, then Germany may be very useful to humanity.'

'Wait a minute' said Tom. 'Hasn't Russia rather taken the lead in anti-finance with this wonderful revolution that has put us so badly in the cart? Isn't it something to do with international communism and isn't communism the real alternative to finance?'

'Heavens, have I got to answer that?'

'Go on' said Williamson, 'you're not timid.'

'Thank you, Bill. Well then, I don't suppose the Russian Revolution will last 1ong or do anything in particular. What did the French revolution achieve?'

'It established the metric system, the guillotine, and Baroness Orczy.'

'And the Russian will do even less .....'

'Here, you ask a physicist if the c g s system [centimetre-gram-second] isn't pretty good for a revolution. And you shouldn't underrate the usefulness of the guillotine, while the Scarlet Pimpernel has given as much pleasure as Terror gave pain. What about communism; all for each and each for all?'

'I think it's too untried to be an immediate solution. Besides, it doesn't seem to fit human nature. We have a sense of property and we must compete to some extent.'

'Very well then. Property and competition in non-essentials such as earrings and snooker. Now where's the objection?'

'I don't know.'

'Of course there's an objection. Some people wash and some don't. Some spit and ... you know what I mean. How can you lump them all together in a commune?'

'Quite right, Bill. But you've only got to educate all the children of the nation together in boarding schools, and those difficulties would vanish.'

'You've reached an impasse, Tom. You can't do that till you've got communism, and you can't have communism till you do that. Next idea please.'

'Gosh, I am demolished. Then we get back to where we were. Property, finance, nationalism, competition, war. Perhaps it's best not to finish this war, as we shall only have to start another, and it's sure to be worse.'

'I'm disappointed with you chaps. I thought I was going to learn something the way you were talking, and now you say you're back where you started, and no wiser in spite of all the fine talk.'

'All arguments lead back to where they started, but sometimes they go a long way round. But as a matter of fact we started with Tennyson; no wonder if we haven't been far after such a poor beginning.'

Williamson shook his head 'You're just obtuse about Tennyson and I shan't argue about the colour of [a] flower with a blind man.'

'But where have we been? Does it all really mean anything, what we've been saying? Do we get at reality through words? We say the war is due to this and that; but the war is millions and millions of tiny events, and every event is the outcome of every other event that has ever happened. The more we define, arrange, simplify, the further we get from reality; and a word is an almost infinite simplification. I believe it took humanity about a million years to invent the first word. And when we use them in complicated strings, it is complication of simplification and the result is about as much like reality as ...'

'As what?'

'A barometer is like a fine day.'

'And when we use them philosophically, it is like standing on our heads and trying to kick the man.'

'Talking about reality, don't you find life out here very unreal? I don't know whether it's flying or fighting or the queer life as a whole, but nothing seems quite real.'

'Yes, I feel very much like that, Seddon.' replied Tom. 'I look at myself in the glass sometimes to see who I am.'

'I shouldn't put it as strongly as that' said Williamson, 'but I think I know what you mean. It seems like acting in a play.'

'Yesterday I would have said that everything out here was very real, but after my first job over the lines to-day I'm not so sure. They say some Fokkers attacked us, but I didn't see any. I thought 1 heard someone shooting, but as I couldn't see anything I thought I was mistaken. And then they say we chased a two-seater. I didn't see any two-seater. I didn't know where we were or what we were doing. If I have any more jobs like that one I'll say I'm no good in the air and go to the infantry. The only thing I did see was you going away with a dud engine.'

'You were lucky your first job wasn't ground-strafing. And as there's a day's rest from bombing to-morrow you'll have another upstairs job.'

'Day's rest! I bet they find us a nice little job of going after balloons or an escort twenty miles over to help the holiday spirit. Why the devil won't it go really dud for a few days? All the waiting about, waiting for the next job, waiting for the klaxon, waiting for the war to end, waiting to be killed, waiting for leave, waiting for dark, waiting, waiting, waiting .....'

'Yes, it's worse than scrapping, When I'm up and at it I don't think I feel so bad as when I'm sitting about with nothing to do but worry about myself. I expect most people aren't bothered much about being killed, but they're bothered a lot by bothering about it.'

'For goodness sake cut out this morbid stuff,' exclaimed Williamson.

'I'm beginning to think Tom's right about its being a damned depressing sort of day. If you two must be morbid, don't go infecting Smith and me.'

'Bill, you must be in a bad way if you can't stand a spot of gloom. When I was out this afternoon I saw a thing I've never seen before and don't particularly want to see again. Somebody came diving out of a cloud in flames. He was well alight, blazing like hell; must have come down a few thousand feet I should think. It was weird to have a thing like that appear suddenly from nowhere. It made me think. Tomorrow, or next week or next month, or today, I should be doing something like that. An explosive bullet or even a tracer would do it. There would be a spurt of flame. Say I was at ten thousand feet, what on earth could I do? Desperately try to side slip down, I suppose. What a hope! When it got too hot I should blow my brains out with my automatic. Say I was at five hundred feet. Might manage to side slip to the ground alive, and crash and burst the petrol tank and be burnt to a cinder. I hate to think of flames taking off my eyelashes in mid air.'

'Then for God's sake don't. I'll turn in and read a little Tennyson to cheer me up. And I hope you'll feel better in the morning.'

APPENDIX B

No. 46 SQUADRON OFFICERS ROSTER 19 FEBRUARY 1918

Maj. R. H. S. Mealing (C.O.)
Capt. R. R. L. Thom (Recording Officer)
Lt. F. H. Astle (Armament Officer)
2/Lt. E. D. Leishman (Equipment Officer)
Capt. D. W. Forshaw (Flt. Comdr.)
Capt. G. E. Thomson (Flt. Comdr.)
Capt. C. J. Marchant (Flt. Comdr.)
2/Lt. P. W. S. Bulman MC
2/Lt. H. P. Blakely
2/Lt. D. R. MacLaren
2/Lt. G. D. Falkenberg (POW 12/3/18)
2/Lt. J. W. Muir (KIA 12/3/18)
2/Lt. H. N. C. Robinson
2/Lt. R. H. Edelston (POW 23/3/18)
2/Lt. G. A. Lambourn
2/Lt. C. Marsden (WIA 28/3/18)
Lt. H. G. W. Debenham
Lt. G. D. Jenkins (WIC 27/3/18)
2/Lt. T. L. Johnson (WIA 11/3/18)
2/Lt. R. K. McConnell
Lt. A. G. Vlasto
2/Lt. A. L. T. Taylor (POW 16/3/18)
2/Lt. M. M. Freehill
2/Lt. J. R. Nicholson
2/Lt. V. M. Yeates

APPENDIX C

SQUADRON CASUALTIES 6 FEBRUARY – 31 AUGUST 1918

NO. 46 SQUADRON 6 FEBRUARY to 8 AUGUST 1918

11 March	2/Lt. T. L. Johnson	Camel B5441	Seriously injured
	Engine failure, crash landed.		
12 March	2/Lt. J. W. Muir	Camel B9157	Killed
	Last seen at 07.00hr diving on troops near Moeuvres. Aged 19 from Galashiels, Selkirk.		
12 March	2/Lt. G. D. Falkenberg	Camel B9317	Prisoner of war
	Shot down 07.00hr whilst strafing troops at Moeuvres. Repatriated 18/12/18.		
16 March	2/Lt. A. L. T. Taylor	Camel B5442	Prisoner of war
	Shot down at 08.45hr over Lagnicourt. Repatriated 14/12/18.		
21 March	2/Lt. G. E. F. Elliot	Camel C1641	Wounded
	Left Bapaume advance landing ground at 18.00hr – failed to return.		
23 March	2/Lt. R. H. Edelston	Camel C1564	Prisoner of war
	Shot down at 14.00hr SE of St Leger by Ltn. Paul Bäumer of Jasta 2. Repatriated 23/12/18.		
24 March	Lt. J. D. Currie	Camel C1554	Prisoner of war
	Left on patrol 15.00hr – last seen near Sailly Saillisel. Repatriated 14/12/18.		
24 March	Lt. W. J. Shorter	Camel B9195	Killed
	Killed when he climbed too steeply taking off, stalled and spun into ground. Aged 20 from Harborne, Birmingham.		

27 March 2/Lt. R. E. Lindsay Camel C1637 Wounded
Crashed away from aerodrome.

27 March Lt. G. D. Jenkins Camel B7311 Wounded
Crashed whilst low flying near Albert pm.

27 March 2/Lt. F. C. Bailey Camel D6459 Died of wounds
Dived too steeply and spun into ground.
Aged 21 from Ash, Kent.

28 March 2/Lt. C. Marsden Camel C1649 Wounded
Shot down Albatros at 10.00hr over Boiry-Notre-Dame but elevator controls shot away during combat. Crashed 150yds behind British lines. Pilot burnt aircraft after regaining consciousness.

6 April Capt. S. P. Smith Camel D6491 Killed
Shot down by Manfred von Richthofen (76th Victory) at 15.30hr near Lamotte/Villers-Bretonneux.
Aged 22 from Aldershot, Hants.

29 April` 2/Lt. E. J. Smith Camel C1617 Killed
Shot down in flames at 11.20hr just inside British lines.
Aged 26 from Bradford, Yorkshire.

2 May Lt. L. C. Hickey Camel C1685 Killed
Last seen at 17.00hr just prior to combat with 6 enemy scouts near Estaires.
Aged 18 from London.

3 May 2/Lt. R. L. G. Skinner Camel B7357 Killed
Shot down at 13.00hr at Estaires/NW of Don by Ltn. P. Billik (14th victory) of Jasta 52.
Aged 20 from Callander, Perthshire.

15 May Lt. H. L. M. Dodson Camel C1643 Injured
Slightly injured when overran aerodrome and dropped into sunken road.

30 May Lt. G. R. Priestly Camel D6601 Seriously injured
Ran into crops when taking off for OP.

19 July 2/Lt. H. L. Cross Camel D6681 Prisoner of war
Last seen at 17.45hr diving at ground target.
Repatriated 13/12/18.

20 July	Lt. A. J. Cyr	Camel B9273	Prisoner of war
	Left on a bombing mission at 08.00hr. Last seen at 10.00hr 9000ft W of Armentières. Shot down by Untoff Marat Schumm (5th Victory) Jasta 52. Repatriated 13/12/18.		

NO. 80 SQUADRON 9 AUGUST TO 31 AUGUST 1918

9 August	Lt. J. R. Orr	Camel D9429	Killed
	Left at 18.30hr and shot down by Machine-gun fire from ground. Crashed near Etinehem. Aged 26 from Downpatrick, County Down.		
9 August	Lt. C. S. L. Coulson	Camel	Wounded
	Hit by rifle fire from ground.		
10 August	2/Lt. L. K. Baker	Camel	Wounded
	Wounded by machine-gun fire from ground.		
15 August	2/Lt. G. Smith	Camel F5956	Killed
	Collided in mid-air with AW FK8 and crashed in flames. Aged 19 from Barnsley, Yorkshire.		
22 August	Lt. H. W. Phear	Camel E5177	Wounded
	Left at 07.30hr on OP and hit by Machine-gun fire from ground near Bray-sur-Somme. Returned to aerodrome.		
22 August	2/Lt. A. L. Tupman	Camel F1969	Killed
	Left at 06.45hr and shot down N of Bray-sur-Somme by Ltn. Ernst Udet (59th victory) of Jasta 4. Aged 19 from Walmer, Kent.		
25 August	Lt. A. W. Chadwick	Camel F6184	Wounded
	Hit by machine-gun fire from ground.		
30 August	2/Lt. V. G. Brindley	Camel F6151	Killed
	Left 08.00hr and hit by machine gun fire near Warloy-Baillon. Made forced landing and crashed. Aged 27 from Johannesburg, South Africa.		

APPENDIX D

AIRCRAFT FLOWN BY V. M. YEATES

WHILST TRAINING

No. 4 TS, Ruislip (*16 June to 1 August 1917*)
Maurice Farman Shorthorn – B1983, 5885, A6839, A6851 (first solo flight 26/6/17), B1992 (crashed 27/6/17), B1969, A7064

No. 65 Squadron, Wye (*8 August to 24 August 1917*)
Avro 504J – B3160

No. 40 TS, Croydon (*24 August 1917 to 6 February 1918*)
Avro 504A/J – B915, B965, B3141, B3146, B3185 (first Avro solo 5/9/17), B3231, B3232
Sopwith Pup – A6228 (first flight in Pup 17/12/17), B5252 (crashed 21/1/18), B6094
Sopwith Camel – B6322 (first flight in Camel 13/1/18?), B7318

IN FRANCE

No. 46 Squadron (*12 February to 9 August 1918*)
Sopwith Camel – B9157, B5442, B9195, B5247, B9197 (forced landing 21/3/18), B9271 (crashed on landing 29/4/18), B5409 C1572 (shot down 25/3/18), C1617 (crash on landing 28/3/18), C1685, C1637 (forced landing 3/5/18, crashed at aerodrome 11/5/18), C1659 (forced landing 9/5/18)
D6407, D6424, D6585 (forced landing 30/5/18), D6603, D6671, D9405

No. 80 Squadron (*9 August to 31 August 1918*)
Sopwith Camel – D9433, F6184

APPENDIX E

V. M. YEATES' COMBAT RECORD

(all Camel victories with No. 46 Squadron)

1918

Date	Aircraft / Time / Altitude	Location	Result
3 May	**C1637** 13.00hr 14000ft Shared with Capt. D. R. MacLaren (B9153)	NW of Don	Two-seater crashed
6 May	**C1637** 18.00hr 10000ft Shared with Capt. D. R. MacLaren (D6418), Capt. C. J. Marchant (B9211), 2/Lt. J. H. Smith (B9299)	St Venant	DFW in flames
15 May	**D6585** 12.50hr 11000ft	Armentières	Pfalz
20 May	**D6585** Shared with Capt. D. R. MacLaren (D6418)		Balloon in flames
22 May	**D6585** 09.20hr 7000ft Shared with Lt. A. G. Vlasto (B2522), Lt. J. A. R. Coté (C1675), Lt. N. Bruce (D6424)	W of Estaires	LVG in flames
3 August	**D9405** 18.35hr 5000ft	E of Lens	FokkerD.VII crashed

INDEX